Engendering Revolution

Women, Unpaid Labor, and Maternalism in Bolivarian Venezuela

RACHEL ELFENBEIN

University of Texas Press Austin

Requests for permission to reproduce material from this work should be sent to:
Permissions
University of Texas Press
P.O. Box 7819
Austin, TX 78713–7819
utpress.utexas.edu/rp-form

⊗ The paper used in this book meets the minimum requirements of
ANSI/NISO Z39.48–1992 (R1997) (Permanence of Paper).

Library of Congress Cataloging-in-Publication Data
Names: Elfenbein, Rachel, author.
Title: Engendering revolution : women, unpaid labor, and maternalism in Bolivarian
    Venezuela / Rachel Elfenbein.
Description: First edition. | Austin : University of Texas Press, 2019. | Includes
    bibliographical references and index.
Identifiers: LCCN 2019000652 | ISBN 978-1-4773-1913-0 (cloth : alk. paper) | ISBN 978-1-
    4773-1914-7 (pbk. : alk. paper) | ISBN 978-1-4773-1915-4 (library e-book) | ISBN 978-
    1-4773-1916-1 (nonlibrary e-book)
Subjects: LCSH: Poor women—Venezuela—Social conditions. | Poor women—
    Venezuela. | Women—Political activity—Venezuela. | Unpaid labor—
    Venezuela. | Feminism—Venezuela—History. | Venezuela—Social
    conditions—1999– | Venezuela—Politics and government—1999–
Classification: LCC HQ1582 . E54 2019 | DDC 305.48/4420987—dc23
LC record available at https://lccn.loc.gov/2019000652

doi:10.7560/319130

*For my mother, Christine Bastl, who raised and cared for me,
and for my Alma, whose life and presence have taught me so deeply
about the work of mothering*

Contents

Tables and Images

Tables

Images

Acknowledgments

The first seeds of my idea for this book began to germinate far from Venezuelan shores, during my time living and working in South Africa. There, I witnessed how poor and working-class women's unpaid labor was vital to household and community survival in the face of structural unemployment, the HIV/AIDS pandemic, and neoliberal state restructuring. I became interested in institutional mechanisms to recognize such work and socially protect the workers who carry it out as a means to mitigate their vulnerability to poverty, gender violence, and disease. These experiences triggered my curiosity in Venezuela and the implications of Article 88 in that country's new constitution for poor women's welfare and power. Such experiences were also personal. Perhaps no one has taught me more about the value and intensity of such work than the women of the Lukhele and Khumalo families in Nhlazatshe, Mpumalanga, South Africa. Through the years, they have opened their homes to me, fed me, cared for me, and treated me as family. Siyabonga kakhulu, mndeni wami.

I am grateful to my PhD supervisory committee—Hannah Wittman, Elisabeth Jay Friedman, Alison Ayers, and Jane Pulkingham—whose strong and committed guidance was integral to helping these seeds bear fruit. Hannah, thank you for seeing potential in these seeds, for your energy, and for supporting me through the thick and thin of my PhD process. Elisabeth, I feel I have found a feminist big sister in you, and your wisdom and constant encouragement have been indispensable to this book and my growth as a feminist scholar. Alison, thank you for your radical energy and ideas and your compassion. Jane, thank you for making valuable contributions to my ideas and my writing.

The mentorship of several other professors from Simon Fraser University (SFU) contributed greatly to developing this project, including Adrienne

Burk, Eric Hershberg, and Nicole Berry. And I am grateful to Maxine Molyneux and Kathleen Millar for their comprehensive comments on my dissertation.

Funding from the Fulbright US Student Program, the SFU Dean of Graduate Studies, and the SFU Department of Sociology and Anthropology supported my dissertation research and was instrumental to undertaking my fieldwork in Venezuela.

Estoy agradecida a todxs que participaron en mi investigación en Venezuela y a todxs que la facilitaron. Gracias por invitarme a conocer sus mundos, sus experiencias, y sus conocimientos. Estoy especialmente agradecida a Gioconda Espina y Juana Delgado, quienes compartieron su sabiduría conmigo y ayudaron a facilitar mi investigación en Caracas. También estoy especialmente agradecida a Mónica Berrios, quien me abrió las puertas de las instituciones estadales regionales de las mujeres e igualdad de género y me proveyó un hogar institucional en el estado Falcón. Gracias a todxs lxs que fueron empleadxs de la Secretaría para el Desarrollo e Igualdad de Género, el Instituto Regional de la Mujer, y la oficina regional falconiana del Ministerio del Poder Popular para la Mujer e Igualdad de Género durante mi investigación, por compartir sus experiencias laborales conmigo. Gracias a Gabriel Páez por apoyarme tanto en mi búsqueda para documentos en los archivos de la Asamblea Nacional. En particular, estoy agradecida a Eneida Castillo, Georalberth Oliver Castillo, Luis Bautista, Masaya Llavaneras Blanco, Elba Medina, e Inocencia Orellana, cuyo apoyo durante mi estadía en Venezuela fue tanto personal como profesional.

Much of what grew into this book was written back on South African shores. I am extremely grateful to the former staff of Industrial Health Resource Group, and especially to Nicholas Henwood, Richard Jordi, and Ashraf Ryklief. Thank you, comrades, for providing me with a vital workhome to return to. Your passion, dedication, and commitment to participatory bottom-up development (in addition to your wonderful senses of humor) inspired me and helped me to keep my bearings as I navigated my place in and out of the academic world.

I am also grateful to the Teaching Support Staff Union at SFU, and to Karen Dean, for providing me with a community and space to engage in praxis while on campus at SFU.

Special thanks to Kerry Webb at the University of Texas Press for advocating for the publication of this book. Thanks too to the editorial team at University of Texas Press, who helped to shepherd this book through to publication. And I am grateful to the anonymous reviewers whose comments have helped me to enrich it.

The multiple forms of support of close friends has animated and grounded me throughout the many stages of bringing this book to life. Jesse Peterson and Joanna Flagler, the love from both of you through these many years has buoyed me. Thanks to Agnieszka Doll, Anita Fellman, Melodie Kline, Itrath Syed, Cathy Walker, Ed Steinhart, Christina Bielek, and Efe Peker for your friendship in Vancouver. And during different stages in the United States, Amy Fox, Liz Henderson, and Jared Abbott, your support has meant so much to me. I am very grateful to Potiphar Nkhoma, Femke Brandt, and Hanna Richter, for the friendships that we have cultivated from and beyond South Africa. Margie Struthers and Dan Pretorius, you have given me a vital sense of home in South Africa. Gracias a Ed Pompeian y Rachael Boothroyd-Rojas por ser mis panas en Venezuela y a Lila Aizenberg por su apoyo desde Argentina.

I am eternally grateful to my mother, Christine Bastl, who taught me from an early age how to care for others and to challenge gender boundaries. Mom, the countless ways you have supported me has enabled me to learn, grow, and undertake this project. To my siblings—Randy Elfenbein, Elizabeth Elfenbein, Michael Elfenbein, Carolee Marano, and Debbie Preg—thank you for the sense of belonging you have provided me over the years.

To my partner, Nathaniel Mahlberg, your steady presence, love, and support (and all your unpaid editing!) enabled me to plug ahead and bring this project to fruition. I am blessed with your fundamental belief in me and my work, and with the gift that we share of our Alma Violet. I am grateful to all the women who have cared for Alma, especially to the grandmothers, whether by relation (Linda Mahlberg and Christine Bastl) or by surrogacy (Cyndi Asmus and Sherry Norman), so I could tend to the final stages of bringing this book to life. And Alma, thank you for the daily light, lessons in love and care, and inspiration you have provided me since the day you were born.

Glossary of Abbreviations and Terms

acta compromiso   Commitment agreement

AD (Acción Democrática)   Democratic Action, the social democratic party under *Puntofijismo*

Amor Mayor   Bolivarian government mission providing pensions for poor elderly adults

ANC (Asamblea Nacional Constituyente)   National Constituent Assembly

Araña Feminista   The Feminist Spider, a national network of socialist feminist activists and organizations

BanMujer   Woman's Development Bank

barrio   Popular-sector neighborhood. Some *barrios* are quite large, with hundreds of thousands of people.

Barrio Adentro   Bolivarian government mission providing free, community-based primary health attention

BCV (Banco Central de Venezuela)   Venezuelan Central Bank

Caracazo   The popular uprising on February 27 and 28, 1989, in reaction to the introduction of a structural adjustment package, which was met with brutal state repression

CCT   Conditional Cash Transfer

CFP (Círculos Femeninos Populares)   Popular Women's Circles

Chavista   The range of political forces aligned with Hugo Chávez from 1998 to 2013

Chavismo   The movement encompassing a range of forces in state and society aligned with Chávez from 1998 to 2013

Communal Council   Legalized territorially based local communal government

CONAMU (Consejo Nacional de la Mujer)   National Woman's Council

CONG (Coordinadora de Organizaciones No-Gubermentales de Mujeres)   Coordinating Committee of Women's Nongovernmental Organizations

COPEI (Comité Independiente Electoral)   Independent Electoral Committee, the Christian Democratic Party under *Puntofijismo*

CPFMJ (Comisión Permanente de Familia, Mujer, y Juventud)   National Assembly Permanent Commission on Family, Woman, and Youth

Economic Associative Unit   Bolivarian government term for de facto organizations of two or more people administering a common economic project

EFOSIG (Escuela de Formación Socialista para la Igualdad de Género)   School of Socialist Formation for Gender Equality

Falconiana   A woman from Falcón state

FEVA (Federación Venezolana de Abogadas)   Venezuelan Federation of Women Lawyers

Frente de Mujeres   Women's Front

gobierneras   Women perceived as servile and obedient to the government

Grupo Ese   Group organizing for women's and LGBTTI rights in 2007 constitutional reform referendum

Hijos de Venezuela   Conditional cash transfer program providing per child cash allowances to extremely poor households

IFI   International financial institution

INaMujer   National Woman's Institute

IVSS (Instituto Venezolano de Servicios Sociales)   Venezuelan Institute of Social Services

IWD   International Women's Day

LGBTTI   Lesbian, gay, bisexual, transgender, transsexual, and intersex

LOSSS (Ley Orgánica del Sistema de Seguridad Social)   Organic Social Security System Law

LSS (Ley de Servicios Sociales)   Law of Social Services

MBR-200 (Movimiento Bolivariano Revolucionario-200)   Bolivarian Revolutionary Movement-200

Mercal   Bolivarian government mission distributing and selling low-cost basic food products

Mi Casa Bien Equipada   Bolivarian government mission providing low-interest credit from a state bank to purchase discounted household appliances

MinMujer   Ministry for Woman's Popular Power and Gender Equality

missions   Set of Bolivarian government social and economic programs targeting the popular sectors

MVR (Movimiento de la V República)   Fifth Republic Movement

NGO   Nongovernmental organization

oficialista   Official

palanca   lever, a term colloquially referring to someone with leverage or influence with state authorities

Patriotic Pole   Electoral bloc coalition of actors, organizations, parties in support of Chávez

patrullera   (Female) patrol officer in the PSUV

PDVSA (Petróleos de Venezuela)   Venezuelan state oil company

Popular Sectors   People from the poor and working classes

PSUV (Partido Socialista Unido de Venezuela)   United Socialist Party of Venezuela

PT   Pink Tide, a political term referring to new Latin American leftist governments in the twenty-first century

Puntofijismo   Regime of governance from 1958 to 1998 premised on power sharing between AD and COPEI

Puntos de Encuentro (Encounter Points)   Local groups of popular women organized by INaMujer

Red Todas Juntas   All (Women) Together Network

Ribas Mission   Bolivarian government mission providing free secondary education to adults

sector   A smaller territorial unit within a *barrio*, such as the immediate neighborhood of several hundred people

Engendering Revolution

The Unpaid Labor and Suffering of the Women Undergirding the Bolivarian Revolution

The Dialectical Relations between Popular Women and the Bolivarian State

Approximately six months before the 2012 Venezuelan presidential election, state gender institution[1] authorities convened several hundred poor and working-class mothers from across the rural state of Falcón to celebrate the sixth anniversary of Madres del Barrio Mission. Established by President Hugo Chávez's decree, Madres del Barrio—"Mothers of the *Barrio*" (*barrio* is the Venezuelan term for a popular-sector,[2] or poor and working-class, neighborhood)—was a discretionary conditional cash transfer program targeting poor homemakers with social assistance, political activities, and microcredit. Chávez's decree stated that Madres del Barrio fulfilled Article 88, the first constitutional article in the world to recognize housework's value for society and specifically entitle homemakers to social security.

On this celebration day, the Madres del Barrio, mostly dressed in Bolivarian government-issued T-shirts and tracksuits, entered a university auditorium in Coro, Falcón's capital, to a slideshow of revolutionary images and figures, such as Simón Bolívar and Che Guevara. These images included a photograph of Chávez embracing a weeping Madre del Barrio and a slide proclaiming to the *madres* in relation to the upcoming election: "With You, Everything; Without You, Nothing!!!"

The celebration began with live music performed by state gender institution authorities, followed by a male municipal Madres del Barrio authority, who emceed and titled the event as "Women in Revolution." He and the other state authority speakers invoked the *madres* present as activists in centuries-long struggles for women's rights and colonial independence. Yet they chose not to discuss Madres del Barrio Mission and the progress

Figure I.1. Madres del Barrio Mission sixth anniversary celebration, Coro, Falcón, 2012 (photo by author)

that it had made in poor homemakers' lives in the years since its inception. Rather, they used their time onstage on the mission's anniversary to call on the *madres* to campaign for Chávez's reelection.

The male state coordinator of the mission, in particular, employed a revolutionary maternalist discourse to beckon the Madres del Barrio to campaign for Chávez. He began his speech by recognizing the centrality of the Madres del Barrio and their labor to Venezuela's Bolivarian revolution, noting that the women present "were making the homeland day by day" through their participation in businesses, employment, political struggles, and communal councils, in addition to their housework. He attributed the *madres'* centrality to the revolution to Chávez's leadership of it, because Chávez had given these women "the opportunity to participate and be protagonists in this process in all spheres of society" from which they were previously excluded. Their particular struggle for social inclusion and visibility, this coordinator asserted, constituted part of the broader revolutionary struggle. He declared the greatest mission that lay before the Madres del Barrio then was to reelect Chávez on October 7. He described that mission and the *madres'* role in it:

Now, we are moved by a great mission—the October 7th Mission—to consolidate our commander Hugo Rafael Chávez Frías in the presidency . . .

and therein lies the great importance of women's participation in this Venezuelan process. . . . It's you who are the protagonists, it's you who vote . . . it's you who suffer, it's you who cry, it's you who pray for the commander's health . . . so that this revolution carries forward. It's important then that you, with this patriotic commitment, do not faint . . . and we continue together until victory. Remember that the women in Venezuela have the majority electoral vote: they are the ones who are more involved in voting. We need 12 million votes to give a resounding victory. . . . And it's you who sustain this revolution. Because of this, it has been said that this revolution has a woman's face.

After a number of state authorities spoke similarly about the Madres del Barrio's crucial revolutionary and electoral roles, they gave the *madres* the stage to speak and perform music and dance. For the remainder of the celebration, the *madres'* voices about the political process—in which they were held by these state authorities to be central protagonists—were contained to chanting, singing, and shouting for Chávez's health and reelection.

*   *   *

Six years before this celebration in Falcón, when Chávez publicly announced that he would establish Madres del Barrio Mission, organized popular-sector women from Miranda state, the Red Popular de los Altos Mirandinos, wrote an open letter to Chávez sharply critical of the possibility that this new state oil-funded program would actually benefit poor homemakers. In this letter, they expressed that they believed the mission would be a vehicle for state authorities to create a "new form of exploitation" of popular women:

We women homemakers home-workers,[3] the great majority . . . 70–80 percent of the participants in the whole country, have come along transforming into community leaders and defenders of this revolution, of this participatory democracy. We are those that are carrying out the actual work that carries this revolution forward. We work ad honorem and we suffer the contempt of the state bureaucracy that takes advantage of us, using our work to project itself politically, give itself credibility, appropriate the few resources that have been obtained after many struggles, and hope to administer them and even direct them. . . . We have not expelled the elite and their caste of corrupt politicians and their regime of terror to enable a new generation of thieves to settle in so that it can take advantage of our revolutionary work. (Red Popular de los Altos Mirandinos, 2006)

The Red Popular de los Altos Mirandinos (the Red) noted that their critique was based on their experiences of being "obligated to beg for what is ours by constitutional right." They cited multiple instances of participatory community organizing in which they generated proposals and trained community members for projects to uplift their communities, only to have Bolivarian state authorities make them wait in uncertainty for public resources promised to help them carry out such projects. Such "exploitat[ive]" actions by the government, according to the Red, threatened to undermine participatory democracy, and with it the revolution. Among the Red's multiple proposals to Chávez for Madres del Barrio Mission to operate differently and transparently and for recognition of women's struggles, they proposed that "revolutionary social work" be recognized as "productive work that should be remunerated. As women who, as our president has said well, are the foundation of the revolution, it is not just that we have to depend on charity from our comrades or family members for performing our revolutionary labor" (Red Popular de los Altos Mirandinos, 2006).

*   *   *

Both these snapshots of Madres del Barrio Mission highlight the fundamental role of popular women, their unpaid labor, and their suffering in building, defending, and sustaining Venezuela's Bolivarian revolution during Chávez's presidency. Although both frame popular women as vital revolutionary subjects, these two snapshots conflict in their conceptions of why popular women suffered within the revolution and the state–society relations that produced such suffering. In the first snapshot, the state coordinator draws on and resignifies the hegemonic gender role of women as altruistic mothers and represents them as caring so much that they suffered for their president. In the second snapshot, organized women note that state actors and institutions attempted to seize popular women's unpaid labor for their own ends, which in turn produced popular women's suffering. In short, the first snapshot frames popular women as suffering *for*, or in service of, the Bolivarian state, whereas the second quote frames popular women as suffering *because of*, or at the hands of, the Bolivarian state.

Placed in juxtaposition, these two snapshots reflect a crucial tension within the Bolivarian revolution under Chávez's tenure and form the main focus of this book: the dialectical relations between popular-sector women and the Bolivarian state based on the role of popular women's unpaid labor in the revolutionary process. I argue that the Bolivarian revolution cannot be understood without a comprehension of the gendered nature of state–society relations, and particularly the gendered division of labor upon which it was based. Emerging in response to the social, political, and economic failures of the neoliberal model, Venezuela's revolution aimed to restructure state–society relations through expanding popular participation and inclusion. At the beginning of the twenty-first century, the Bolivarian revolution stood at the forefront of a larger inspirational yet controversial movement of attempts to construct post-neoliberal social contracts in Latin America, a region rife with entrenched gender, class, and racial inequalities. This book sheds light on gendered implications of attempts to institute post-neoliberalism and popular power. I do so by examining Venezuela's decision to become the first country in the world to constitutionally recognize housework's socio-economic value and entitle homemakers to social security, and by assessing the outcomes of this recognition for popular women's labor and power.

Venezuela's Bolivarian revolution presents a unique case for understanding how state recognition of the role of popular women's unpaid labor in national development affects their power. During Chávez's presidency, the revolution created new opportunities for popular women's organizing, articulations with the state, recognition of their unpaid labor, and social and economic assistance. As popular women and women workers and leaders within the state frequently noted, the Bolivarian process rendered them "visible" as "the face" of the revolution. Yet, such visibility also rendered popular women's unpaid labor and organizing vulnerable to state appropriation. Through its institutions, policies, and discourses, the Bolivarian state reproduced the hegemonic maternal gender role for popular women, while resignifying it in service of the revolution. The state expected them to be both mobilized and contained for what it saw as the revolution's broader interests, as with the first snapshot of Madres del Barrio in Falcón. I show that popular women performed much of the unpaid social and political labor necessary to build and sustain the revolution—even as many of them remained socially, economically, and politically vulnerable.

States, Societies, and the Invisible Labor of Poor and Working-Class Women

Since the 1960s, a wide range of feminist scholars, activists, and policy-makers have drawn attention to how socially naturalized conceptions of unpaid reproductive labor render it invisible. That is, commonsense understandings of the unpaid work that maintains and reproduces people day by day and generation by generation make it appear as if it just naturally happens. Such understandings obscure not only the fact that it *is* labor but also the unequal power relations that shape how this labor is performed and who performs it. Feminist thought has highlighted the detrimental implications of rendering this work invisible for women—the people who are primarily responsible for it because of the dominant maternal gender role assigned to them. At the same time, feminism has brought to light the beneficial implications of this invisibility of women's unpaid labor for capitalism. Women's unpaid labor not only ensures household reproduction; it also subsidizes capitalist profitability by providing a constant supply of labor without charge. The invisibility of their unpaid labor makes it appear as if it incurs no cost (Bennholdt-Thomsen and Mies 1999; Mies 1986, 1988, 28; von Werlhof 1988). Yet being unpaid and unrecognized for this work leaves many women dependent on breadwinners, often without social protection, and vulnerable to poverty, exploitative relations, and violence.

Women's invisible unpaid labor has been foundational to neoliberal capitalism in particular. Under neoliberalism, which champions market fundamentalism, states' roles in economies have generally been transformed from buffering market forces through public investment and welfare to promoting market expansion and distribution of resources. As "financial security has replaced social security as a policy goal" (Hershberg and Rosen 2006, 7), states have been restructured to enable privatization, trade liberalization, economic deregulation, and the dominance of capitalist property relations (Dagnino 2007). Neoliberal capitalism has therefore redrawn divides between the public and private spheres of societies by conceptualizing the (private) marketplace as the domain of true freedom and the (public) welfare state as a barrier to market expansion, profitability, (Postero 2007), and human rights. While neoliberalism deregulates and promotes markets, it simultaneously regulates and disciplines peoples by advancing ideologies of individual and family self-sufficiency, wherein each individual and family should be responsible for themselves and expect nothing from their society (Hershberg and Rosen 2006, 10). Many states, in turn, have retreated from reproductive duties by eroding their public sectors and cutting back and privatizing their welfare services. Middle- and upper-class people have been able to turn to the market to access essential goods and services, yet welfare state contraction has offset many reproductive burdens onto poor and working-class families and communities. The neoliberal social and economic policies that states employ are often underpinned by naturalized assumptions about the gendered division of labor in the private sphere (Kabeer 2007; Luxton 2006), because deeply entrenched gender-role expectations charge women with responsibility for families' and communities' reproduction. That is, such policies often implicitly rely on common-sense presumptions about the availability and inexhaustibility of women's unpaid and/or poorly paid labor to absorb the costs of neoliberal state and economic restructuring (Mackintosh and Tibandebage 2006, cited in Hassim and Razavi 2006; Lind 2005).

Indeed, numerous studies have shown how neoliberal restructuring of states and societies in the Global South (Antrobus 1993; Feldman 1992; Jayaweera 1994; Mblinyi 1993; Moser 1993) and the Global North (Bezanson 2006; O'Connor, 1993; Pascall and Lewis 2004; Vosko 2006) have exacerbated poor and working-class women's invisibility and socioeconomic vulnerability. These studies have explained how poor and working-class women have developed new survival strategies to fill in the gaps generated by public-sector cutbacks. For example, in 2001 the Ghanaian government, under pressure from international financial institutions (IFIs), commercialized water services and increased water tariffs by 95 percent, rendering clean drinking water inaccessible to many poor and working-class families. Women and girl children then assumed the everyday burden of collecting water—often from polluted sources—for household consumption (Kwengwere 2007). Termed "the invisible adjustment," such new survival strategies by women have included intensifying their unpaid and paid labor (as in the example above), decreasing household expenditure, spreading out the resources that they do control, sacrificing their own needs, and engaging in community welfare service provision. Even as this invisible adjustment by poor and working-class women has tended to leave them in the lowest-paid and most flexible, informal, unorganized, and unprotected working conditions, it has made neoliberal policies possible (Momsen 1991). The invisible work of poor and working-class women thus has enabled state retreat from social reproduction.

In Latin America in particular, the 1970s oil crisis and global economic crisis followed by the 1980s debt crisis precipitated the neoliberal restructuring of the region. These damaging economic developments pushed regional governments to redirect national surpluses away from popular-sector welfare needs toward debt reservicing to IFIs. To stabilize their economies, Latin American governments employed structural adjustment programs, which Washington, DC–based IFIs and US government institutions imposed upon them as part of the "Washington Consensus" on free-market-led development. These neoliberal policies reduced and privatized many social programs, such as public health, water, and education; reduced trade and investment barriers; weakened labor regulations; and, in turn, generated a generalized social reproduction crisis for the popular sectors (Robinson 2004).

Many popular-sector women in Latin America responded to these socioeconomic crises in the 1980s and 1990s by organizing collectively within their neighborhoods in communal kitchens, childcare cooperatives, and piecework production (Barrig 1994; Jelin 1990a, 1996; Lind 2005; Moser 1993; Safa 1990). Maternal gender roles, Amy Lind notes, were central to such popular-sector survival strategies: "it was . . . grassroots women who 'mothered' the [neoliberal] crisis, both individually and collectively" (Lind 2005, 94). That is, the traditional role of motherhood was materially and symbolically mobilized to meet family and community survival needs during crises precipitated by neoliberal policies (95). The collectivization of popular women's work often helped to mitigate household vulnerabilities, and also provided popular women with spaces to develop skills and senses of solidarity around their shared gender identity and experiences (Cubitt and Greenslade 1997; Jacquette 1994; Jelin 1990a; Safa 1990; Stephen 1997). Yet, this form of organizing often did not develop into shifting burdens of popular women's reproductive labor to men and/or the state. Rather, it often intensified their labor and reinforced the gendered division of labor (Barrig 1994), as many popular women took on a "triple burden" of unpaid housework, paid labor, and community organizing (Craske 2003; Jacquette 1994).

Indeed, recognizing the utility and success of popular women's "volunteer" labor in compensating for the socioeconomic crises set off by neoliberal policies, Latin American states and IFIs began to appropriate their community organizing initiatives. Such institutions co-opted rising popular democratic demands by depoliticizing their autonomous initiatives into mechanisms to implement neoliberal state goals (Dagnino 2007). For example, Latin American states and IFIs increasingly contracted popular women's organizations to provide social services, such as day care, thereby further privatizing welfare and poverty-alleviation strategies (Barrig 1994; Craske 2003; Lind 2005; Molyneux 2001). Rather than treating such "voluntary" organizing initiatives as temporary measures to mitigate neoliberal crises (Barrig 1994), Latin American states "institutionalized [popular] women's struggles for survival" (Lind 2005), establishing them as permanent features of national development strategies (Barrig 1994; Lind 2005). As Maxine Molyneux (2001) concludes, popular women's unpaid labor "became central to the success of [Latin American] post-adjustment poverty alleviation strategies in a curious alliance between communitarianism and neoliberalism" (148). This institutional reliance on popular women made their roles in community development more visible (Lind 2005), but it did not transform the ways popular women's labor was valued. Their "voluntary" participation in such "poverty-alleviation strategies" tended not to lift them out of poverty. Rather, such participation tended to intensify their workloads and re-produce the gendered division of labor and gender inequalities (Barrig 1994; Craske 2003; Lind 2005), because it did not challenge the structural deter-minants of popular women's poverty, vulnerability, and marginalization.

Many contemporary states—especially in their neoliberal formations—operate under implicit assumptions of the gendered division of labor and poor and working-class women's capacity to ensure social reproduction where states retreat from the public sphere. However, in its attempts to con-struct a post-neoliberal social contract, the Bolivarian state, during Chávez's tenure, explicitly recognized poor and working-class women's roles in en-suring household and community reproduction and expanded the public sphere and mechanisms for popular political participation.

At the beginning of the twenty-first century, Venezuela stood at the forefront of both popular resistance to neoliberalism and institutional artic-ulations of such resistance through the election of "Pink Tide"[4] (PT) gov-ernments in Latin America. Taking advantage of a crisis of Venezuela's es-tablished political system, which was exacerbated by neoliberalism, Chávez rose to presidential power at the end of the 1990s by promising to depart from the Washington Consensus and instead privilege social justice, pop-ular participation, and national sovereignty through refounding Venezue-la's political system. Venezuela's 1999 National Constituent Assembly and 1999 Constitution initiated the drive to institutionalize anti-neoliberalism in Latin America through constitutional reform processes (Lind 2012b, 546) attempting to reshape social contracts between states and societies. The Chávez regime radicalized as it consolidated, ushering in the "Bolivarian revolution" and increasingly articulating and fulfilling leftist demands from the movements supporting it. The regime went on to claim its central goal to be twenty-first-century socialism—a form of socialism that would recog-nize and promote popular participation and direct democracy, and institute a new production model for Venezuela—and began to develop a juridical-institutional framework to support the construction of this socialist vision. Bolivarian Venezuela's left turn helped expand the political terrain for other governments and movements in the region (Hershberg and Rosen 2006, 15) to legitimately pursue left turns, inspiring some regimes to embrace twenty-first-century socialism as part of the larger regional shift away from the neoliberal Washington Consensus.

Leftist and left-leaning candidates and political parties came to national power in the majority of Latin America[5] at the beginning of the twenty-first century by recognizing popular and social movement demands to redress inequalities exacerbated by neoliberalism. Supported by a regional com-

modity boom and responding to the technocratic ways elite-controlled regimes had imposed neoliberalism on the popular sectors, some PT regimes,
such as Venezuela's, tended to combine populist governance with their new
socialist aspirations (Beasley-Murray, Cameron, and Hershberg 2009).

Populism refers to a political phenomenon (Weyland 2001)—a mode
of competing for, gaining, and exercising political power.[6] What makes a
political phenomenon populist, then, is what Ernesto Laclau (1977, 2005)
describes as the linking up of a range of unfulfilled "popular-democratic
demands" against a dominant political system and ideology. Such popular-
democratic demands emerge from subjects excluded by the dominant power
bloc and mobilized against it. These demands can arise and cohere with
each other when a dominant political-institutional system undergoes crisis and can no longer maintain its hegemony and its ability to absorb and
neutralize such demands (Laclau 1977). Populist state leaders aim to articulate the will of the people directly by recognizing popular demands and cri-
tiquing dominant power blocs (Beasley-Murray, Cameron, and Hershberg
2009). To do so, they tend to bypass bureaucracy and previously established
institutions of interest mediation, such as political parties and legislatures.

Through representing and uniting a range of popular-democratic demands, populism is also a mode of linkage between political leaders and
subjects. Populist leaders lead because, as empty signifiers, they share features common to the various links on chains of popular-democratic demands, and the links on these chains, in turn, identify with them (Laclau
2005). Populism, therefore, is not necessarily an antidemocratic, despotic
mode of gaining and exercising political power (Laclau 2005). Rather, in
incorporating previously excluded subjects, such as popular-sector women,
and challenging entrenched, rigid institutions in their favor, it can be a
deeply democratic phenomenon (Kampwirth 2010). Further, populism can
be a mutual and interactive relation between the "people" and the leader
that represents them, and it is fundamentally about the dynamic relation
between the two.

Across the globe, populist movements and governments of both the Left
and the Right have risen in response to neoliberal capitalism's and established political systems' combined failure to bring about broad-based security and prosperity. Twenty-first-century Latin American populisms, however, have hewn to the left, professing broader-based social, political, and
economic inclusion. Unlike contemporary right-wing populist governments,
Latin American populist PT governments have sought to include and represent groups historically excluded from liberal democratic institutions,
such as the popular sectors, women, and indigenous peoples, and they have

tended to use rights-based approaches to reshape state–society relations and address inequalities (Friedman and Tabbush 2018). Indeed, some of these governments, such as Venezuela's, employed feminist discourse in their governance frameworks (Lind 2012b).

Pink Tide governments varied in how they addressed inequalities, but they generally sought to reverse (some) neoliberal policies and reintroduce states' progressive interventionist roles in markets and societies. Redressing economic inequality through increasing public spending, (re)nationalizing public services and industries, and expanding social policies became central to PT governance (Friedman and Tabbush 2018). Even as PT governments asserted their national sovereignty and independence from the Washington Consensus and US imperialism, they largely relied on a sustained primary commodity boom, and extractivist industries in particular, to finance their pro-poor policies. Their ongoing reliance on extractivist-funded redistribution did not structurally transform their economies, leaving to question whether their progressive redistributive policies could be maintained.

These developments have prompted debate about whether countries governed by the Pink Tide had entered a "post-neoliberal" period. Despite some PT governments', like Venezuela's, aspirational claims to socialism, post-neoliberalism in Latin America should not be confused with anticapitalism, because socialism did not take over as the dominant production and distribution model in any of these countries (Lind 2012b, 541). Nor does post-neoliberalism signify the end of neoliberalism (Fernandes 2010, 24). Rather, post-neoliberalism implies that neoliberal policies have not ceased but have "lost their quasi-hegemonic position" (Lind 2012b, 541). Did the PT's rise to power signal neoliberalism's retreat from dominance in Latin America?

Analysts do not agree whether Pink Tide governments ushered in a "post-neoliberal" order for Latin America,[7] yet they all see post-neoliberalism as containing some degree of continuity with neoliberalism. That is, none note the disappearance of neoliberalism from countries governed by the PT altogether. These countries remained positioned in the global economy as primary commodity exporters, continued to work with multinational corporations, and did not undergo major transformations in property ownership.

At the same time, analysts widely acknowledge that Venezuela's Bolivarian government under Chávez represented the left end of the PT spectrum and went the furthest in challenging neoliberalism and expanding state control of the economy. Venezuela cut off its relationships with IFIs and renationalized and restructured the oil industry to promote nonmarket forms of essential goods and services distribution and alternative modes of production (Fernandes 2010; Leiva 2008; Meltzer 2009). Judy Meltzer

(2009, 103), for example, contends that the Bolivarian government supported a form of participatory democracy that went beyond more market-oriented versions of community development being fostered elsewhere in Latin America. The Bolivarian government, according to Meltzer, "repoliticized problems of poverty and inequality" (103) by prioritizing free public welfare services and promoting a republican form of active citizenship among the popular sectors, including opportunities for participatory management and oversight (99).

Yet debates over the Venezuelan and Pink Tide governments' continuities and breaks with neoliberalism have largely left gender relations unexamined, even though social reproduction, through expanded social policies, has been essential to their development frameworks (Lind 2012b, 549). Most analyses of PT governments' post-neoliberal aspects focus on class dimensions of their poverty-relief efforts, while neglecting such policies' gendered dimensions and how they have both relied on and affected gender power relations. A range of scholars analyzing the Bolivarian process have noted that popular women were central to the revolution's grassroots programs and politics (Espina and Rakowski 2010; Motta 2012; Spronk and Webber 2011; Valencia 2015; Vargas Arenas 2007). Yet explanations of popular women's centrality to the Bolivarian revolution and the implications of these gendered foundations for post-neoliberalism have largely been left out. Given that gender subordination is a widespread and deeply entrenched form of social disempowerment and is constitutive of neoliberalism, how PT governments addressed gender relations is a fundamental gauge of their promotion of social justice and their post-neoliberal turns. Indeed, as Lind (2012a, 260) contends, centering policies, politics, and struggles around social reproduction in analyses of Latin American PT governance can "cause us to rethink conventional typologies of left versus right and neoliberal versus postneoliberal."

This book therefore examines Bolivarian Venezuela during Chávez's presidency (1999–2013) through the lens of social reproduction. Though carrying on with Bolivarianism, Venezuela during Nicolás Maduro's presidency (2013 to the time of this writing) has experienced a long-term political and economic crisis that has severely undermined the state's capacity to redress poverty and inequalities. Focusing on gender relations under Chávez's tenure (rather than Maduro's) better illustrates the post-neoliberal extent of the Bolivarian revolution.

Within Bolivarian Venezuela during Chávez's presidency, restructuring the relations of reproduction rather than production relations, in tandem with fomenting popular participation in the public sphere, became key to reshaping state–society relations and pursuing post-neoliberalism. The development, diversification, and expansion of the forces of production were central to the socialist ideals but not the practices of the revolution. Rather, extracting the nation's oil to fund welfare service expansion in the popular sectors was fundamental to the revolution's development and continuation. The Bolivarian state relied on popular-sector organization for both expanded and decentralized public service delivery, and for political legitimacy.

Because of the hegemonic maternal gender role of women's primary responsibility for household and community reproduction, popular women and their labor were central to the Bolivarian state's organizing logic and public-sector expansion during Chávez's tenure. Their gendered responsibilities were reconfigured to undergird the state's social, economic, and political policies. From President Chávez on down, state authorities, such as the Madres del Barrio coordinator cited above, publicly recognized that the Bolivarian revolution had "a woman's face," as they were aware that women were driving popular-sector organization and mobilization in support of the government.

State recognition of women's unpaid labor is a foundational ideal to the Bolivarian state and post-neoliberal social contract. Venezuelan national visibility of women's unpaid labor began in 1999 when the country decided in Article 88 of its new constitution to recognize housework as "an economic activity that creates added value and produces social welfare and wealth" and to entitle homemakers to social security in accordance with the law.[8] Article 88, the new constitution in which it was embedded, and the 1999 National Constituent Assembly that drafted them formed part of the larger Bolivarian state transformation project that arose in response to multiple crises Venezuela faced under neoliberalism.

Yet the Venezuelan republic's refounding, the Bolivarian government's anti-neoliberal and later socialist and feminist stances, and the revolution's progression did not necessarily signal a defining rupture with old state institutions, policies, and social and political practices. Within the Bolivarian process, bottom-up participatory organizing and top-down state–society relations and radical and reformist currents coexisted in tension with each other. This book examines how popular women and their unpaid labor were central to such contestations within the revolution during Chávez's presidency, and how they underpinned the Bolivarian state. And it asks these questions: How did popular women and their unpaid labor support "post-neoliberal" national development? Did Bolivarian Venezuela's institutional reliance on popular women's unpaid labor differ from neoliberal governments' "institutionalization of women's struggles for survival"? What consequences did Bolivarian state–society relations have for the gendered division of labor, gender roles, and gender justice in Venezuela? What does the role of popular women's unpaid labor in the Bolivarian revolution reveal about the gendered nature of the revolution and "post-neoliberal" political projects more broadly?

A Feminist Cultural Materialist Lens to Examine Post-Neoliberal State Transformation

To examine the role of popular-sector women's unpaid labor in Bolivarian state transformation and the broader revolution, I use a feminist cultural materialist lens. This framework explores the integration of ideas and material reality from a feminist perspective. That is, this lens views gender as multivalent, because gender relations, the gendered division of labor, and gender subordination cut across interconnected spheres of politics, economy, and culture.

Even as it draws from the Marxist tradition, feminist cultural materialism goes beyond classical Marxism's focus on political economy to incorporate insights from socialist feminist and subaltern studies on the intersections of culture with politics and economy in a society. This lens sees both gender and the state as at once material and ideological, because both fashion economies, divisions of labor, and subjects' identities and imaginations. It allows for a nuanced analysis of the co-construction of gender relations and the state; that is, how gender roles and gendered divisions of labor shape states and how states shapes gender roles and gendered divisions of labor.

To assess the post-neoliberal claims and gendered implications of the Bolivarian revolution, I draw from Nancy Fraser's (2009) theorization of gender justice as occurring in three interconnected dimensions: recognition (cultural), redistribution (economic), and representation (political). Fraser contends that under capitalism, the gendered division of labor is a crucial point where "three interpenetrating orders of gender subordination" of women intersect: "(mal)distribution," (non) or "(mis)recognition," and (non) or "(mis)-representation" (104). In other words, the gendered division of labor under capitalism broadly relegates the bulk of responsibility for unpaid care work to women; devalues unpaid and paid work performed largely by women; renders women inferior to men in private and family life; marginalizes women in political life and enables men to dominate the political system; and bases welfare and [formal] labor market regimes on a [gender-normative and heteronormative] male breadwinner model (104). How a state intervenes in the gendered division of labor, recognizes the women performing unpaid labor, distributes resources to them, and enables their representation in political processes therefore shows its commitment to overcoming gender subordination and achieving gender justice.

In a post-neoliberal society, states would question the commodification of essential goods and services and take concrete policy measures toward decommodifying them (Macdonald and Ruckert 2009) through progressive redistribution. Decommodification occurs when essential services, such as health care and water, are rendered as rights and people do not have to depend on money and market participation to access them (Esping-Andersen 1990). Given that capitalism and neoliberalism in particular rely on the gendered division of labor, a post-neoliberal society would also need to recognize labor that has not been commodified and has largely been performed by women because of their gender roles. Fraser (2009) suggests that such a society would then need to address the intersections of redistribution, recognition, and representation by valuing care work, spreading out responsibility for care work among everyone, and by cultivating a "participatory democracy . . . that uses politics to tame markets and to steer society in the interest of justice" (116).

Because it shapes the gendered division of labor, the state plays a key role in gender (in)justice. The state is involved in both the mode of production and social reproduction—the range of activities, relationships, and identities involved in the maintenance and reproduction of people from one day to the next and from one generation to the next (Cameron 2006; Ferguson 1999; Luxton 2006; Power 2004). It intervenes in productive and reproductive labor processes and mediates between them because the relationship between productive and reproductive labor is dialectical under capitalism. A primary contradiction exists between the imperative for capital accumulation and reinvestment, on the one hand, and the need to uphold the standard of living of the population, continually supply labor, and consume goods and services, on the other hand (Armstrong and Armstrong 1983; Cameron 2006; Picchio 1992). Social reproduction therefore is not merely natural, functional, and harmonious. Rather, conflicts and compromises around state allocation of resources to social reproduction arise, and such conflicts are central to understanding relationships among social classes (Cameron 2006) and the character of a state.

Because maternal gender roles charge women with primary responsibility for reproduction, the state's involvement in reproduction means that it is a gendered institution (Conell 2001; Hassim 2006). That is, "the formal and informal rules that make" up the state "are both based on, and reproduce, gender relations" (Friedman 2000b, 35). In mediating the relationship between production and social reproduction, the state "shapes[s] and stabilizes[s] a particular system of class relationships and, within it, a gender order, . . . a set of social relations characterized" by a gendered division of labor and a gender discourse supporting that division (Cameron 2006, 46–47). How the state shapes a gender order has crucial gender implications for its subjects because it can enhance and/or constrain the life chances and opportunities of different members of society according to their specific positioning within the gendered division of labor. Gender, gender relations, and the gendered division of labor therefore are not peripheral to but indeed constitutive of the state. For this reason, understanding the state necessarily entails understanding the gender order that it rests on and shapes.[9]

Social reproduction is a dynamic process that varies across time and space and is open to change. Just as a particular state—which is based on particular configurations of gender relations—undergoes transformation, so too can the gender order within that state. State transformation can alter the ways that the state does or does not recognize the gendered division of labor, does or does not distribute wealth to women performing reproductive labor, and does or does not enable their representation, inclusion, and participation in political processes. State transformation therefore has crucial implications for popular women, their status, and their power. How state transformation both draws on and affects the gender order speaks to the nature of the state and its commitment to gender and class justice.

The state, in its everyday actions and its larger transformations, is also a normative institution, drawing on and shaping ideologies and identities within its territory. Through its discourses and practices, the state plays a moral regulatory role, helping to fashion the moral orders of its subjects and their gender roles, in particular. Gender identities rooted in motherhood and family ideologies, in turn, have helped historically to uphold the gendered division of labor—and the modern state.

In modern Latin America, women's identity and work have been historically, politically, and culturally constructed as rooted in the heterosexual family and household. Women have been charged with household tasks historically viewed as part of the private sphere of reproduction and the family; men have been associated with tasks interpreted as part of the public sphere of society and politics (Jelin 1990b, 2). Latin American states have shaped and reproduced this distinction between women's positioning within the private sphere of the home and men's positioning within the public sphere of social and political life. For example, historically states in the region have framed welfare regimes around a male breadwinner model, in which full social rights have been accorded on the basis of permanent, full-time employment. Women who have performed solely unpaid household labor, performed part-time paid labor, and/or worked in the informal sector therefore have not had access to certain social rights, such as public pensions, or may have been able to claim them only derivatively, through their relationships with men. Because the majority of working-class women in Latin America have historically congregated in low-paid and informal sectors of employment, their access to social protection has often been through their status as men's dependents (Molyneux 2006, 46). The welfare state thus has operated as an "interpretive system that gives meaning to particular notions of social positioning" (Hassim and Razavi 2006, 21), because it has privileged (typically) male wage workers over (typically) female unpaid and/or informal-sector workers and entrenched the public–private divide.

Although states have promoted motherhood and gender-normative and heteronormative family ideologies throughout modern Latin American history, women across social classes and ethnicities in the region have used their traditional roles as mothers to challenge the public–private divide (Molyneux 2001).[10] The politicization of motherhood has often been associated with the promotion of the ideal national subject (Molyneux 2001; Radcliffe and Westwood 1993), to which political parties and regimes throughout the region have appealed (Craske 1999) in their nationalist projects. At the same time, women themselves have invoked and politicized motherhood to oppose and resist state abuses (Radcliffe and Westwood 1993) during authoritarian periods, and to expand their realm of work to neighborhood issues and to protest structural adjustment programs under neoliberalism. Through such instances of autonomous organizing, women have resignified their roles as mothers (Molyneux 2001). States, therefore, do not simply determine maternal and family ideologies—motherhood and "the family [are] deeply and consistently contested terrain in Latin America" (Radcliffe and Westwood 1993, 12). Precisely because motherhood is a normative identity, it provides a culturally acceptable starting point from which women can organize (Craske 1999). Giving them "room to maneuver in the public sphere" (Jacquette 1994, 228), motherhood has allowed women to use their identities strategically for social and political change. Latin American women's organizing through politicizing their motherhood illustrates that gender identities "are not simple unities but deeply contradictory phenomena, in which the contradictions can be exploited for counter-hegemonic gains" (Radcliffe and Westwood 1993, 26). These examples of women's politicization of their maternal identities also show that motherhood is not an essential identity, but is constantly negotiated, and its meaning is open to change and transformation.

The state shapes its subjects' identities and gender identities, in particular, and, at the same time, subjects of the state in turn shape the state through their representations of it (Gupta 1995, 2005). Akhil Gupta (2005) explains: "States, like nations, are imagined through representations and through signifying practices; such representations are not incidental to institutions but are *constitutive* of them" (28). States are constituted in ongoing processes at multiple geographic levels through discourses that represent states and give them meaning to the subjects that inhabit them and are interpellated[11] by them. This discursive focus shows that the state is incessantly produced and state–society relations are under constant negotiation (Secor 2007). Attention to different subjects' interactions at multiple levels across the state's territory can illuminate how a state's meaning is contested (Gupta 1995, 377). The state, then, is a contested territory in which power relations, such as gender power relations, play out, are reproduced, and/or are reconfigured and resignified through discourses, institutions, and practices.

The Magical Revolutionary Bolivarian State

Venezuela's Bolivarian process during Chávez's tenure, in its reaction against neoliberal globalization, reasserted the primacy of the nation-state's sovereignty in the political decisions made within its territory.[12] The nation-state's material and discursive role in shaping its subjects was central. Indeed, the name given to this process connotes carrying forward the colonial independence movement led by Simón Bolívar. The Bolivarian state and many of its subjects represented this process as a revolutionary stage in the long, historical struggle for Venezuelan national sovereignty and independence. Particularly important to this revolutionary independence narrative is the twenty-first-century Bolivarian state's intervention in the extractive industries and redistribution of oil revenue to popular subjects. Renationalization of the oil industry enabled the Bolivarian state to generate massive public revenue and enhance its international bargaining power so that it could increasingly exercise its autonomy from the Washington Consensus, undertake pro-poor statist policies (Levitsky and Roberts 2011a, 409), and stoke the national imagination of rapid, revolutionary transformation.

Using his theorization of the modern Venezuelan petrostate as a "magical state," the Venezuelan anthropologist Fernando Coronil (1997) notes both the historical continuities and ruptures that make up the Bolivarian state. Prior to Chávez's presidency, Coronil characterized the modern Venezuelan state as a "magnanimous sorcerer"[13] that induced collective fantasies through sowing the nation's oil wealth. Coronil wrote of the magical state's construction as the "deification" of the state that occurred when it combined its power over the political sphere and the nation's oil and transformed Venezuela from a peripheral agricultural country to a modern oil nation in the twentieth century. "By condensing within itself the multiple powers dispersed throughout the nation's two bodies, the state appeared as a single agent endowed with the magical power to remake the nation" (4). He contended that the Venezuelan state exercised this "monopoly dramaturgically, securing compliance through the spectacular display of its imperious presence . . . the Venezuelan state ha[d] been constituted as a unifying force by producing fantasies of collective integration into centralized political institutions" (4). The state was able to generate such fantasies by promising to rapidly transform the nation's oil wealth into massive development projects that would bring modernity and progress to Venezuela. It could create this illusion in part because its abundant revenues, which came from oil rather than taxation of its own citizens, enabled it "to embody powers that seem[ed] to come from itself" (2).

In Venezuela's transformation to an oil nation, the figure of the president became central. The president took on the appearance of a magician, who, in the context of limited institutional capacities, harnessed the state's power to manage the nation's oil wealth and pull modernity and development out of his magician's hat (Coronil 1997, 83; n.d.). For if the state was to realize these magical powers, it required masterful and charismatic leadership. At the same time, the Venezuelan people would have to believe in the president's illusory capacities for his magical powers to become real, for him to be able to seduce and enchant them (Coronil 1997; n.d.). For charisma "suggests not just a one way, top down flow, but a dynamic interaction: a mutual construction. Charisma entails a charismatic community that confers charisma to the leader. Similarly, the notion of magic suggests trickery, but also the real power of unseen forces" (Coronil n.d., 5). The "magical state" therefore is not just performed and enacted by state leaders, but it also enraptures the subjects that bring it into power. "It casts its spell over audience and performers alike. As a 'magnanimous sorcerer,' the state seizes its subjects by inducing a condition or state of being receptive to its illusions—a magical state" (Coronil 1997, 5).

Under Chávez's presidency, the Bolivarian state, Coronil (n.d.) asserts, became "perhaps the most magical of all" (5). For Chávez was not just using the state's powers to control the nation's oil wealth and modernize and "develop" the country. He was also transforming Venezuela's meaning through his representations of the state and the nation from its subaltern subjects' standpoints. Embodying the Bolivarian state's magnanimous sorcerer powers, Chávez facilitated the shifting of fantasies from those of collective integration of the whole nation to those of collective integration of the majority—the popular sectors. These are fantasies that reflect crucial realities that both preceded Chávez's presidency and enabled Chávez to come to power. That is, that *Puntofijismo*—the previous regime, the pacted democracy[14] enacted by the nation's political and economic elite—fundamentally excluded large portions of the popular sectors, and the social, political, and economic exclusions it engendered were exacerbated under neoliberalism. During Chávez's presidency, then, collective fantasies underwent a radical inversion:

> What comes out of the Magician's Hat is now different: . . . A radicalization of the narrative of History itself . . . it is not just more "development," or more modernity, but a different kind of development and modernity. If other presidents . . . would bring progress to Venezuela out of a hat, Chávez claims to bring a different Venezuela out of a hat. This change . . . requires an overproduction of words—a framing to explain particular changes within a general scheme. (Coronil, n.d., 8–9)

Discourse, according to Coronil, was both prefigurative and central to the Bolivarian state's magical revolutionary transformation into a state that placed the subaltern at its center. He states:

> It is not just that words are produced as part of the revolution, but that words produce the revolution. . . . In the case of Venezuela the revolution is verbal before it is social. It is anticipatory—the narrative of revolution prefigures or perhaps even replaces revolutionary transformations. In the context of limited historical transformation, the production of a new history requires a verbal framing which make [*sic*] them meaningful as radical events by being placed within a narrative of a revolutionary history. (Coronil, n.d., 15)

Some analysts, such as Cristobal Valencia (2015, 187–188), contest this characterization of Bolivarian Venezuela as a magical state, arguing that the popular sectors were "establishing their own authority over resources" through everyday grassroots democratic participation, yet Coronil's theorization does not deny the historical ruptures and insurgent social movements, forms of organization, and political practices that occurred with the Bolivarian process. Rather, it highlights the central role that the imaginary—the magical radical narrative—played in not just conceptualizing but also shaping the national popular revolution. It is to assert that discourse in large part constituted the Bolivarian revolution during Chávez's presidency. Coronil explains:

> It is not that there are no changes, but that changes, however limited or grand, cannot match what is expected of them, the historical work they seek to produce: the transformation of Venezuelan society and people. To do this, they have to be . . . placed as part of a historical break: from the production of lettuce in farms in the heart of Caracas to joint oil ventures with transnational capital in the oil industry, Chávez has to present events as revolutionary, inscribe them within a larger narrative, lift them out of ordinary context and present them as part of epic. (Coronil, n.d., 16)

The narrative about such events, which often were practices inherited from the past or similar to those occurring in nonrevolutionary regimes in Latin America, helped to make the Bolivarian process extraordinary, to mark its historical rupture and radical transcendence. And though Chávez's "nominalism . . . [did] not mean there . . . [was] no distinction between words and world" (Coronil, n.d., 22), the magical state that his revolutionary narrative induced merged words "with world, confusing the boundaries between representations and the real" (22). The Bolivarian revolution, then, in large part was what Chávez and the Venezuelan people, acting together, aspired it to become. The charismatic relationship between the leader and the people carried on from Venezuela's past engagements with modernity was resignified and amplified. They were now interpellated as revolutionary actors conjoined not just in national development but also in a moral process radically resignifying notions of democracy, virtue, justice, inclusion, and the commons.

The discourse of developing a participatory, protagonistic, popular democracy was fundamental to crafting a narrative of Venezuela's revolutionary transformations and its historic break from its *Puntofijista* past as a liberal democracy controlled by elites and marked by multiple exclusions of the popular sectors.[15] Indeed, the concept of participatory democracy is foundational to the Bolivarian state-making process. The 1999 Constitution both enshrined participatory democracy for "the common good" and presented it as part of the epic process of sovereign Venezuelan state-building that began with the colonial independence movement of Simón Bolívar and had yet to be fully realized. The Constitution asserted that the state's sovereignty derived from the Venezuelan people, who were recognized as at once differentiated and, together, the source of political power—the constituent power that created state institutions and resided over them. It stated that "sovereignty resides untransferable in the people, who exercise it directly" through participatory democratic mechanisms and "indirectly" through the vote (Constitución de la República Bolivariana de Venezuela 1999). The 1999 Constitution also granted the Venezuelan people the right to participate in government and revoke government mandates. As it framed the people as sovereign subjects who both gave the Bolivarian state its form and had the power to take it away, the Constitution presented them as central protagonists in state-making and governing processes. Thus, the foundational document to the Bolivarian state framed it as a state that arose from and acted through the exercise of popular power, a state that acted jointly with the popular sectors.

Popular Women, Unpaid Labor, Maternalism, and the Making of the Bolivarian Revolution

Engendering Revolution shows how the Bolivarian state conjured fantasies of popular women's rapid collective integration into the magical revolutionary remaking of Venezuela. In its reshaping of state–society relations and reframing of the state's narrative from its subaltern subjects' standpoints, the Chávez regime particularly interpellated popular women as central protagonists in the Bolivarian revolution. Unlike the *Puntofijista* regime wherein the state largely marginalized popular women and their gender interests[16] and often impeded their mobilization, the Bolivarian regime made popular women, their gender interests, and their political organization visible. The 1999 Constitution employed gender-sensitive language by recognizing female subjects (the structure of the Spanish language genders all subjects), in addition to recognizing unpaid housework's socioeconomic value and enshrining homemakers' right to social security. The gender-sensitive language that ran throughout the Constitution framed the way Bolivarian state actors identified the people they represented because they were conscious of publicly recognizing the existence of both male and female subjects and ensuring that female subjects were acknowledged in official state texts. In public events with popular women, state gender institution authorities often cited Article 88 as evidence of the Bolivarian state's revolutionary

Figure I.2. Women's meeting with President Chávez, Caracas, 2012 (*source*: Agencia Venezolana de Noticias)

character. Chávez and state and party authorities consistently employed a revolutionary maternalist discourse to beckon popular women to participate socially and politically in the revolution. Such discourse both honored and reinforced women's maternal altruism (Espina and Rakowski 2010), while resignifying popular mothers as revolutionary subjects who articulated popular power through their social and political work. And since making his socialist turn after several terms in power, Chávez turned his discourse even further leftward by declaring: "There is no socialism without feminism."

The Bolivarian state's inclusion of women under Chávez's tenure was not merely discursive, as it also extended to positions of power and institutions. Many more women were appointed to positions of public power in state ministries and in the courts (García and Valdivieso 2009),[17] even as the number of women elected to positions of power remained low, especially at regional and national levels and higher up the state apparatus (Aguirre, Bethencourt, and Testa 2009). And women constituted the majority of members of community councils and other forms of state-sanctioned community-based popular organizations.[18]

As a Bolivarian state banner that formed the backdrop to the stage at a 2012 Chávez presidential campaign event proclaimed: "Without the combative woman, the REVOLUTION does not exist!"[19] This was a state populated by leaders who knew that popular women and their labor and organization by and large sustained it. In other words, they knew that there was no Bolivarian state without popular women's participation.

This gendered political opening in the Bolivarian process, combined with the process's radical populism and central notion of popular power, generated new opportunities for women's organizing. Organized women, inside and outside of the state, worked together to demand that the state create and maintain state women's and gender equality institutions, including the maintenance and expansion of the State Woman's Institute (INaMujer) and the establishment of the Woman's Development Bank (BanMujer), the Ministry for Woman's Issues, which later became the Ministry for Woman's Popular Power and Gender Equality (MinMujer), the National Public Defender of Women, and district attorneys for violence against women. Various new (semi)autonomous[20] and state-directed popular women's organizations and new articulations between state institutions and popular women's organizations also emerged in the Bolivarian process. Women's rights activists within and outside the state also successfully organized for a new and more expansive law on violence against women during Chávez's presidency. And feminist organizations used Chávez's feminist and socialist turns to legitimate their demands for broader popular cultural and social change for gender equality.

Since the ratification of the 1999 Constitution, women's movement leaders and organizations also struggled to expand the legal concept of work and labor-based social protection, using both Article 88 and the organizational footholds they gained within the state to legitimate these demands. They strategically developed articulations between activists and organizations within and outside the state to wage these struggles.

In turn (but not necessarily because of those struggles), the Bolivarian state redistributed the nation's oil wealth to institute a number of new public programs, which recognized popular women's unpaid reproductive labor and, in some instances, lightened their reproductive burdens and/or socialized them. These public programs (outlined in table 1.1) include Madres del Barrio, Mi Casa Bien Equipada, Simoncitos, Bolivarian Schools, Technical Water Tables, Amor Mayor, Hijos de Venezuela, Barrio Adentro, Mercal, and popular cafeterias.[21] Yet, by the end of Chávez's presidency, Madres del Barrio, Mi Casa Bien Equipada, Simoncitos, Bolivarian Schools, Amor Mayor, Hijos de Venezuela, and popular cafeterias were not universally

Table I.1. Bolivarian state programs recognizing and/or alleviating popular women's reproductive burdens

Name	Focus of program
Madres del Barrio Mission	Conditional cash transfer program targeting poor homemakers, which the state claimed was in accordance with Article 88
Mi Casa Bien Equipada Mission	Low-interest credit from a state bank to purchase discounted household appliances
Simoncitos	Free public early education centers for children up to six years of age
Bolivarian Schools	Free full-day public schools providing free meals and health services to students
Technical Water Tables	Community-based organizations documenting water service problems, proposing solutions to them, and working with the state to implement such solutions
Amor Mayor Great Mission	Pensions for poor elderly adults
Hijos de Venezuela Great Mission	Conditional cash transfer program providing per child cash allowances to extremely poor households
Barrio Adentro Mission	Free community-based primary health attention
Mercal Mission	Distribution and sale of low-cost basic food products
Popular Cafeterias	Preparation and provision of free meals in popular-sector communities

available *within* the popular sectors.[22] However, for the most part, these new public welfare programs relied on popular women's unpaid or poorly paid labor and their community organization for their rollout. In other words, popular women's unpaid labor and organization undergirded the Bolivarian state's new oil-financed welfare programs within popular-sector communities. Together, oil and popular women's unpaid labor helped to re-fashion state–society relations.

The Bolivarian state promoted and in some cases directed popular women's organization in these public programs and other social, political, and economic programs supporting the revolution. It did so by drawing on deeply entrenched and unquestioned gender ideologies, which assumed that popular women were available to support the government and their labor was elastic and could be intensified. In addition to encouraging popular women to extend their care work to their communities, the Bolivarian state instituted a number of new programs to foment their participation in production, such as BanMujer, Madres del Barrio cooperatives, and Feminist Brigades of Socialist Production. Such programs provided interest-free or low-interest microcredit to women's collective enterprises and were designed to fit into the broader national revolutionary project of supplanting capitalism and dependence on the extractive industry with a new socialist production model promoting endogenous development. Yet they generally did not address the burden of popular women's unpaid care work. Rather, the Bolivarian state maintained its revolutionary maternalist approach to popular women, invoking their maternal roles in their households and communities, resignifying them in service of the revolution, and relying on and deepening the gendered division of labor. The ways in which the Bolivarian state promoted their labor and organization in the revolution's name generated tensions between them and the state.

I focus on popular women as a social group within Bolivarian Venezuela, but their experiences of the gendered division of labor and their gender interests were not uniform.[23] Venezuela is a multiracial and multiethnic society marked by racial and ethnic cleavages produced by legacies of European colonialism, slavery, and domination by the Global North. These cleavages intersect with class differences: the wealthy and the elite are disproportionately white, whereas the popular sectors are disproportionately *mestizo*, black, and indigenous. These cleavages also affect women differently according to their positioning within these hierarchies. The gender order in Venezuela therefore is racialized: *mestiza*, black, and indigenous Venezuelan women's experiences of oppression are compounded because of the intersection of their gender with their race, ethnicity, and class.

At the same time, the gendered division of labor and gender inequalities existed across racial and ethnic divides in Bolivarian Venezuela. The Bolivarian state relied on the gendered division of labor and particularly invoked popular women as revolutionary subjects. Yet popular women disproportionately experienced economic precarity and lack of labor-based social protection *because* of the gendered division of labor. Their experiences of unpaid labor and their gender interests during Chávez's tenure were not unified. Yet focusing on the intersection of gender and class relations in this multiracial and multiethnic society is essential for understanding the gender order promoted by and shaping the Bolivarian state.[24]

An Extended Case Study from the Standpoints of Popular-Sector Women

Engendering Revolution is a story as much about disarticulations as it is about articulations between Venezuelan society and the Bolivarian state and between women in these spheres. It tells a story of relations between popular-sector women and a popular revolutionary process by shedding light on how the revolution during Chávez's presidency both advanced and sidelined their gender interests. It is also a story of articulations and disarticulations between women's struggles for rights and the implementation of these rights, as it traces victories and forestalled initiatives in women's organizing for rights to recognition and social protection of their unpaid labor from *Puntofijismo* through Bolivarianism. *Engendering Revolution* tells how women's organization and disorganization around their gender interests shaped state–society relations in the revolution.

This case study brings together stories of multiple women, of the popular sectors and middle and governing classes across various forms of organization, and their relationships to the Bolivarian state from 1999 to 2012. Weaving these stories together into a narrative about the gendered nature of the Bolivarian revolution, I use extended case study methodology (Burawoy 1998) that locates the everyday world of popular women, their work within their households and communities, and their social and political participation in the wider context of Venezuela. This methodological approach studies "the everyday world from the standpoint of its structuration, that is by regarding it as simultaneously shaped by and shaping an external field of forces" (15). It is concerned not only with how broader processes promoted or constrained popular women's power but also with how popular women's everyday work and forms of organizing shaped state policies and practices. By focusing on the interconnections and tensions between multiple levels of social and political life, the extended case study method captures the unevenness of Bolivarian state reach and transformation. It illuminates how such unevenness constituted the Bolivarian state-making process.

Engendering Revolution weaves together participant observation and interviews with document, archival, and media analysis. I used these research methods across geographic spaces in Venezuela with a variety of sources at various levels (politicians, policies, archives, policymakers, workers, leaders, and bureaucrats) of the state (local, regional, and national) and sources at household and community levels, such as popular-sector women and their organizations. In Caracas, Venezuela's capital, I conducted document and archival analysis and in-depth interviews on women's rights organizing processes before and during the 1999 National Constituent Assembly (Asamblea Nacional Constituyente, or ANC) that generated the 1999 Constitution, and post-ANC legislative and policy processes related to Article 88 of the constitution. I conducted my field research, focusing on relations between popular women and the Bolivarian state, in Falcón state and several urban centers of Venezuela. This involved participant observation of feminist and women's rights organizing events, Falcón state gender institutions, and events that Falcón and national state gender institutions held with popular women; in-depth interviews with popular women organized and not organized by the state, state gender institution workers and authorities, and feminist activists; and document and media analysis. I engaged all interview participants in a postinterview participant-validation process in which I gave each of them a summary of their interview and the opportunity to review, discuss, and analyze the summary. I made confidential the identities of all the popular-sector women and state gender institution workers whose voices and experiences I have included in this book, and I have given all of them pseudonyms. I then combined data from these various sources and the interactions between them to illuminate how popular women's experiences of unpaid labor, organization, and power were structured in Bolivarian Venezuela.

In approaching popular women's lived experiences, their representations of them through our interview processes, and my observations of them as a researcher, I drew from Dorothy Smith's feminist "everyday world as problematic" methodology (1987, 1999), which focuses on uncovering women's experiences from their standpoints as a means to understand societal organization.[25] In the Bolivarian Venezuelan context, I began from popular women's experiences and then extended to their intersections with broader societal processes to explain how they were differentially incorporated into the Bolivarian process, how the Bolivarian state shaped their unpaid labor, and how they in turn shaped the Bolivarian state.

Using reflexive scientific methodology means "embrac[ing] not detachment but engagement as the road to knowledge" (Burawoy 1998, 5). That is to say, because the research process *is* social, the research product cannot be separated from the process and the researcher cannot be separated from the research design. Each field research encounter is unique: context and power effects always shape the research site and outcomes. At the same time, the researcher's intervention in a social order helps to reveal how that order is structured (Burawoy 1998).[26]

Thus, as a white academic woman researcher from the Global North, I do not aim to reduce the effects of my power, but to understand how my research intervention in Bolivarian Venezuela, and the pressure I exerted upon it by attempting to know it, reveals how that world was structured. Inquiries about the Bolivarian process were highly charged, especially when they came from me, a US American, given the history of problematic engagements between the United States and Bolivarian governments, historical US interference in the Bolivarian process, and the fact that the Bolivarian process was at least discursively defined as a nationalist, anti-imperialist, anti-neoliberal project. Context and power effects were highly interactive in Bolivarian Venezuela.

Context and power effects shape what we can know about the social world and how we can know it, and they can limit our ability to know the social world we study. No matter what our intentions may be as social researchers, unequal power relations "are nevertheless always there to render our knowledge partial" (Burawoy 1998, 23). Our social positions, therefore, both open up and limit possibilities of understanding the social relations we aim to study.

Indeed, this book illustrates how all knowledge is partial. This basic epistemic truism is especially salient for understanding what was known and what was not known in politically polarized Bolivarian Venezuela in which dividing lines had set and festered between *los esqualidos*[27] and *los rojos rojitos*[28] and where popular frustrations with top-down state and party initiatives and the slowness of state service delivery had surfaced and resurfaced. This was all the more so in the Venezuela of 2011 and 2012, twelve to thirteen years into Hugo Chávez's presidency, when he was afflicted with a publicly unnamed cancer in a presidential election year. It was into this context that I set out to construct knowledge about how constitutional rights to recognition of housework's socioeconomic value and homemakers' social security affected popular homemakers' power and state policies and practices. This charged and complex field of power relations was confusing and hard to navigate at times. Access to information was politically mediated and often dependent on political appointments, relations, and connections; where some Bolivarian government representatives would open access to data and programs, others would close them down. As political polarization became entrenched and the Bolivarian government radicalized, a "*Chavista*[29] siege-mentality" set in (Wilpert 2007), generally rendering information about government programs more difficult to obtain during the latter years of Chávez's presidency. State actors blocked me from accessing information about some of the poorest women's experiences with the Bolivarian state, women for whom exclusion and invisibility had been common experiences and who had mostly been forgotten throughout history. I discuss this methodological difficulty in accessing information about popular women's engagement with the state throughout this book, not because of standard representativity and validity issues, but precisely because it sheds light on the central issues that this book addresses: how popular women were incorporated into the Bolivarian revolution and their power and control in this process. This methodological issue reveals how lack of access to information about popular women and government programs incorporating them was constitutive of the Bolivarian state and public sphere.

Engendering Revolution is a text produced from the information I was able to gather and the experiences I was able to observe and weave together in that politically charged conjuncture within the Bolivarian process. Yet, it is a text that is haunted by what I do not know, what the research participants with whom I engaged did not know, what they would not share with me, and documents missing from the public sphere.

This absence of knowledge about the Bolivarian process does not only produce a vacuum. It is also productive. Part of what made the Bolivarian state magical under Chávez's presidency was precisely its lack of transparency. Even as state actors continually invoked popular power and made the state incessantly visible in popular media and everyday interactions with the popular sectors, they often did not reveal the state's backstage organization and processes as to how many decisions were made, who made them, and to what extent popular voices and input shaped its decision-making. This lack of state transparency facilitated the illusion of revolutionary magic. As Coronil (1997, 2) notes, the Bolivarian state appeared to have powers that instantaneously came from itself, including its power to suddenly unfreeze genuine popular-sector claims for inclusion, assistance, and justice that the state had suspended within its bureaucratic apparatus. Indeed, the state's lack of transparency enhanced its magical appearance, because its subjects could project onto it their desires for and understandings of its internal machinations as well as the degree to which they were included within the state's orbit. The state's opaqueness lent to the generation of an environment in which rumors about its actions and inactions could flourish. I approach the rumors I encountered in Bolivarian Venezuela as not just imaginations of the state but also as subjects' understandings and experiences of the state.[30] Where I was not able to access state data, I took a more hermeneutical approach, focusing on how such rumors and perceptions of the state shaped popular women's interactions with it. Further, drawing from Gupta (1995, 2005), I contend that such representations of the state by its subjects were part and parcel of the Bolivarian state itself; these rumors in part constituted the state. The widespread circulation of rumors about the Bolivarian state—many of which contradicted each other—reveals how the state was structured around its lack of transparency to those outside its internal realms of decision-making powers.

The story ahead combines what is known and not known to reveal how popular women's unpaid labor shaped the Bolivarian state and how this magical revolutionary state affected their individual, social, and political power. Coronil (1997) notes:

> The persuasiveness of a historical account, like that of a magical performance, depends on rendering invisible the artifice of its production. Just as history refers ambiguously to the past in its completeness and to the selective remembering of stories about the past, magic alludes to an extraordinary reality as well as to the selective presentation of the elements that create the illusion of its existence through invisible tricks that exploit distraction and diversion. Like history, magic hangs suspended between fiction and fact, trick and truth. (3)

In the following pages, I aim to render visible a fundamental facet of the artifice of the Bolivarian state's production by illuminating how popular women and the gendered division of labor buttressed the Bolivarian state.

Chapter Outline

Chapters 1 and 2 provide a historical account of contested claims for state recognition of unpaid housework and homemakers' social security in Venezuela from *Puntofijismo* through the Bolivarian Republic's first eleven years. These chapters analyze these claims within the broader context of *Puntofijismo* and its breakdown, the rise of Hugo Chávez to power, the refounding of the republic through the 1999 National Constituent Assembly process, and the Bolivarian regime during Chávez's tenure. They examine how women organized around these claims for recognition of and redistribution for homemakers throughout these regimes and how broader political processes shaped women's movement organizing and these particular claims. Chapter 1 explains the processes that culminated in Article 88's inclusion in the 1999 Constitution. Chapter 2 examines how the political polarization and government radicalization that followed the 1999 Constitution's enactment affected claims for Article 88's implementation. It analyzes how Article 88's formulation in the Constitution interacted with larger processes of political conflict, executive centralization of power, the development of a parallel welfare state apparatus, and the government's (lack of) political will to enact women's rights legislation to shape the ways in which its implementation was contested and at times sidelined.

Chapters 3 and 4 focus on Madres del Barrio Mission, the discretionary conditional cash transfer (CCT) program targeting poor homemakers, through which the Bolivarian government claimed to enforce Article 88. Both chapters draw from Molyneux's (2006, 2008a) argument that CCTs in Latin America are maternalist programs, which both reinforce and resignify motherhood through the conditionalities they impose on women beneficiaries. I examine how Madres del Barrio intersected with Bolivarian notions of popular power to resignify motherhood within the context of the revolution and produce a revolutionary maternalism. The government set the expectation that, in exchange for a temporary monthly cash transfer, poor homemakers would extend their reproductive roles from their households to their communities to become the mothers of their *barrios*, in addition to developing collective productive projects and participating politically in the revolution. These chapters highlight dialectical tensions between popular women and the state that this social program generated. Through the mission, the Bolivarian state assisted popular-sector women in meeting their own and their dependents' welfare needs, yet it demanded popular women's social and political participation while also exercising its power and control over them.

Chapter 3 details how Madres del Barrio was created and managed by the national executive within the context of the revolution's radicalization, the development of a parallel welfare state apparatus, and the government's imaginations and empirical reconfigurations of state–society relations. This chapter also explains how Madres del Barrio's nontransparent structure reveals the kind of top-down state–society relations the mission was fostering with popular-sector women.

Chapter 4 provides a bottom-up examination of fieldwork carried out with Madres del Barrio and state gender institution actors who worked with Madres del Barrio. It shows how Madres del Barrio's revolutionary resignification of motherhood had regulatory effects for the *madres* who did not fulfill all the mission's conditionalities. Such resignification, in addition to the mission's selective and exclusive targeting mechanisms, served to generate new forms of social and economic divisions among popular-sector women. This chapter also examines how the mission's production of a revolutionary maternalism incorporated and occurred alongside a structural and discursive paternalism within the Bolivarian revolution. That is, the structure of the mission, the Bolivarian state's broader (non)intervention in care work, and general popular discourse and expectations assumed that the *madres* could intensify their labor in the absence of men's and state support in caring for their dependents. The *madres*, in turn, were blamed for depending on the state and not assuming their revolutionary role, even though the state expected them to perform unpaid community and political labor in addition to their housework. Disregarding popular women's unpaid labor, both the structure of and popular discourses about Madres del Barrio belied the constitutional provision upon which the Bolivarian state claimed that the mission was based.

Chapter 5 continues exploring popular women's unpaid labor from the standpoints of the women carrying it out, by focusing on women in a *barrio* who had not been incorporated into Madres del Barrio. These women continued performing unpaid reproductive labor mostly as they did before the Bolivarian state created new welfare programs, because state services did not reach them sufficiently. Some of these women—the poorest among them—waited for the state to reach them and provide services when it had promised and raised expectations that it would. This chapter analyzes how these women's experiences of waiting for the state interacted with their experiences of community disorganization and disintegration, everyday violence, and persistent gender roles to produce a negative feedback loop of nonsubstantive recognition of their unpaid labor. This negative feedback loop reinforced the gendered division of labor and individual family mechanisms of survival, wherein these women filled in gaps in social reproduction where the Bolivarian state did not reach.

Chapter 6 focuses on dialectical relations between popular women and the Bolivarian state by examining how the tension between radical democratic and populist political practices affected the struggle to advance popular women's labor rights and legislate Article 88 during the 2012 presidential election year. It contrasts instances of bottom-up participatory women's organizing driven by social movements with top-down instances of women's organizing controlled by the state. At the same time, it highlights where these conflicting modes of popular women's organization converged for the revolution's broader interests and analyzes the implications of this convergence for advancing women's labor rights. Their convergence as popular women in defense of state authorities' vision of the revolution's broader interests reveals the type of popular women's participation that the Bolivarian state was promoting. That is, the state held popular women's organization and mobilization as central to the revolution's continuation, yet it attempted to limit their autonomy and marginalize the advancement of their particular interests within the Bolivarian process.

Chapter 7 summarizes the book's key findings and raises broader issues of the spatial, temporal, and moral organization of the magical revolutionary Bolivarian state and how gender shaped and was shaped by these facets of the state. It concludes that gender analysis troubles notions of the Bolivarian state's promotion of popular power and construction of a post-neoliberal project. For a more equitable turn beyond neoliberalism, it calls for an alternative understanding of popular power and women's positioning within it based on everyday realities of women's work and interactions with the state.

CHAPTER 1

Out of the Margins: The Struggle for the Rights to State Recognition of Women's Unpaid Housework and Social Security for Homemakers

In 1999, Venezuela became the first country in the world to constitutionally recognize the socioeconomic value of housework and specifically entitle homemakers to social security. This chapter examines the historical and political processes that culminated in gaining these and other gender rights for women—a social group largely excluded from participation in and the benefits of the *Puntofijista* regime in Venezuela—in the 1999 National Constituent Assembly (*Asamblea Nacional Constituyente*, or ANC) that rewrote the Venezuelan Constitution.[1] Focusing in particular on the rights to state recognition of housework's value and social security for homemakers enshrined in the 1999 Constitution, I trace the genealogy of these rights demands within Venezuelan women's movement organizing. I situate the historical development of the politics of unpaid domestic labor and women's movement organizing in Venezuela within the larger context of state-building (1958–1989), state crisis (1989–1998), and state transformation (1999). Women's rights activists first demanded social security for homemakers in the 1980s. They finally encountered a political opportunity structure that was favorable to this demand when the old elite-controlled party system collapsed in 1999. The electoral mandate for the creation of a participatory and social democracy in the 1999 constituent process was a master frame through which women's rights activists could legitimate their demands.

In spite of women's underrepresentation in the ANC, the women's movement was able to use the new political opening in 1999 generated by rapid political upheavals to gain leverage in political parties, the state, and the ANC. A few key women's rights activists rose to positions of power within these structures and incorporated the broader women's movement in crafting constitutional proposals that addressed women's gender interests. Uniting across political and ideological divides, they used and further developed a conjunctural coalition-building strategy that they had previously honed. This strategy enabled them to successfully lobby and pressure the male-dominated ANC to include most of their proposals in the final constitutional product, and in particular their demands for state recognition of unpaid housework's socioeconomic value and homemakers' right to social security. The women's movement was able to harness this gendered political opening to exercise its power and influence as a social movement and set a framework for redistribution of gendered power—and specifically the redistribution of wealth toward women who worked without pay—in the Bolivarian Republic that the 1999 Constitution ordained.

Women's Rights Interventions in Constitutional Change Processes

In recent decades, insurgent demands from historically excluded social groups have shifted understandings of the possibilities, limits, and legitimacy of democracy. Constitutional design in many postcolonial countries tends to no longer be limited to elite decision-making (Waylen 2006, 1209), as was the case with the 1961 Venezuelan (*Puntofijista*) Constitution. Rather, emphasis is now placed on the constitution-making *process* and its openness to inclusion and democratic participation of the people (1209) whom a constitution will govern and protect. Since the 1980s, in many Latin American countries, social movements' democratic demands, combined with responsive state leaders, have opened constitution-making processes to civil society participation through constituent assemblies. Changing constitutions through constituent assemblies has been central to a number of Pink Tide regimes' attempts to pursue post-neoliberal national projects, such as in Bolivia, Ecuador, and Venezuela. These constituent assembly processes have marked new political openings for social groups, such as women, who were previously marginalized from power in corporatist[2] and neoliberal regimes. Social movements in the region have responded to these new political openings by developing new forms of contention and strategies for collective action (Hochstetler 2000, 170) to demand that their interests be codified into rights in these new constitutions.

Constitutions are not only about creating state structures, granting rights, and imposing obligations; they are also about epitomizing a country's fundamental aspirations (Dobrowolsky and Hart 2003, 2) for state–society relations. "A constitution," Dobrowolsky and Hart (2) explain, "is intended to stand above everyday politics, authorizing the rules of the game and legitimating the processes and outcomes of government." Because a constitution institutionalizes a governance framework and a citizenship regime—a regime of inclusion and participation within the political community—its production is the outcome of social groups' struggles to enter into and determine the rules of the political game. Constitutions, then, are ultimately about power—about outlining who has access to power and how power is distributed and exercised (2).

For women, who have been marginalized historically within constitutional republics across the world and excluded from enjoying full citizenship rights, constitutions can be important instruments (Waylen 2006) that omit and/or include their gender interests. As women experience gender inequalities in both public and private spheres, constitutions matter because they can "define the relationships between the state and its citizens as well as among citizens themselves" (1210). The status of women's rights within constitutions therefore can deeply challenge the gendered distribution of political, social, and economic power (Rakowski 2003, 415).

Because constitutions construct frameworks for power and citizenship, their production, effects, amendments, and transformation are constantly contested (Dobrowolsky and Hart 2003). Just as a constitution is the outcome of political contestation, it too sets the framework for future contestation over political, social, and economic power. And women's rights interventions in constitutional processes have the potential to both alter and set frameworks for future contestations over gendered power.

The political context (and also social and cultural norms) in which a constitutional change process occurs shapes the constitutional process and product (Dobrowolsky 2003). Particular cultural and material factors can converge to create new political openings for "constructing new political ideologies within which movements can frame feminist goals" (Viterna and Fallon 2008, 681) in constitutional change processes. Yet, a gendered political opening that enables women's mobilization for constitutional change does not necessarily guarantee that change in favor of their gender interests will be codified in a final constitution. For this to occur, the political opportunity structure during a constitution-making process must be relatively transparent, open, and favorable to women's rights interventions. This includes the willingness of actors within political parties, legislatures, governments, and state institutions to take up women's gender issues and form alliances with women's rights activists outside the state (Waylen 2006).

Such an enabling context for codifying women's constitutional rights includes the legacy of women's previous mobilizations, because it can set a recognized frame for women's collective action and contestation (Viterna and Fallon 2008, 684–685). Women's rights activists' prior achievement of positions of power within state and political party channels can be key to legitimating feminist constitutional demands. From these positions, activists can use their power to gain allies within political institutions and build cohesive, conjunctural coalitions that can effectively lobby and pressure state and party representatives during a constitutional change process. In her cross-country assessment of successful women's interventions in constitutional change processes, Dobrowolsky (2003) found that such an organizing strategy combining forces within and outside the state appears to be most favorable for the inclusion of their gender interests.

In addition to a favorable political opportunity structure, the timing of women's rights activists' constitutional interventions matters. Dobrowolsky (2003) finds that the earlier women intervene in a constitutional design process, the better, because it gives them more access to opportunities to voice their demands and exercise influence over political processes. Furthermore, where the political moment of constitutional change falls, in terms of a spectrum of incremental reform to complete transformation, shapes the potential for change in favor of women's gender interests:

> In periods of rapid change, when new institutions are being constructed and wholesale change is possible, women's capacity to influence political discourses and institutions becomes more likely . . . times of political upheaval, with the potential to create new institutions and structures, and the capacity to be creative and engage in *adaptation* appear particularly auspicious for women's constitutional activism. (Dobrowolsky 2003, 238–239; emphasis in original)

Five key factors then help to explain when, how, and why women's rights mobilizations are successful in changing constitutions: (1) timing and nature of constitutional change; (2) relative openness and transparency of constitutional design process; (3) legitimation of current demands through legacy of women's past activism; (4) cohesive conjunctural coalition-building; and (5) openness and willingness of officials within the state and political parties to take up women's gender concerns. These factors shed light on the gendered political opening in which women were able to mobilize successfully for gender rights—including the rights to recognition of unpaid housework's socioeconomic value and social security for homemakers—in Venezuela's 1999 National Constituent Assembly.

Transformations in State–Society Relations and the Gendered Distribution of Power under *Puntofijismo*

The 1958 Punto Fijo Pact signed by Venezuelan political and economic elites and the 1961 Constitution established the return to civilian rule after ten years of military dictatorship and paved the way for the consolidation of formal democracy and "rentier liberalism"[3] in Venezuela. The ensuing "pacted democracy," commonly termed *Puntofijismo*, was premised on this power-sharing agreement between the two main political parties—the social democratic party, Acción Democrática (AD), and the Christian democratic party, Comité Independiente Electoral (COPEI).[4] *Puntofijismo* promoted individual and collective welfare through state distribution of oil revenues (Coronil 1997), and it contained class conflict through centralized, political party–based, corporatist, and clientelist forms of interest mediation (Gómez Calcaño 1998; Grindle 2000; Hellinger 2003).[5] The *Puntofijista* regime used oil revenues to build and finance a large state apparatus that served as Venezuela's largest employer, the largest investor in industrial development, and that contributed to poverty reduction and middle-class growth (López Maya, Lander, and Ungar 2002; Rakowski 2003). In so doing, it generated expectations among citizens of entitlement to state-provided social security, perpetual progress, social mobility, and collective integration (Coronil 1997; Ellner 2003; Lander 2005; Levine 2006; López Maya, Lander, and Ungar 2002).

However, such expectations were part of an "illusion of harmony," which "was premised on reformist control of the oil industry and the forceful exclusion of radical demands" (Coronil 1997, 127). From its very inception, *Puntofijismo* "was an exclusionary regime" (Friedman 2000b, 4), because AD and COPEI closed off from power-sharing and representation many of the popular forces that helped to bring down the military dictatorship. In spite of the important contributions of the Communist Party, students, and women activists to the struggle against the dictatorship, the foundations of *Puntofijismo* explicitly excluded the Communist Party and largely kept out popular sectors and women and other non-class-based interest groups from political participation, leadership, and many citizenship benefits (Cannon 2009; Ciccariello-Maher 2013b; Friedman 2000b). Because of these foundational exclusions, which were quickly met with popular resistance followed by state repression of political dissent, a segment of the Left chose to take up arms and engage in a guerrilla struggle, beginning in 1961, to bring down the *Puntofijista* regime.[6]

Yet steady economic growth in the 1960s, the international oil crisis, and subsequent oil price surges in the 1970s aided in perpetuating the Venezuelan magical state and the corresponding illusion of social harmony that it inculcated, leaving existing social, political, and economic cleavages obscured (Cannon 2009; Coronil 1997; Hellinger 2003; Roberts 2003).[7] Coronil (1997, 301–302) terms this an "oil-supported subsidization of consensus" that served to "lessen the political cost of state decisions" and "artificially" prolong "the life of conflicting social actors." And as the *Puntofijista* regime consolidated and defeated the guerrilla struggle, it developed a policy of "pacification," in which nonarmed leftist groups could become legalized.

The exclusionary political opportunity structure of the transition to democracy originally foreclosed women's political organization. In the struggle to bring down the dictatorship, women had both worked within the structures of the banned parties and united as women across party political lines—a model of conjunctural coalition-building that Venezuelan women activists had begun to develop in previous legal reform campaigns (Friedman 2000b). Yet, in the transition to a pacted democracy, which was in part based on the exclusion of communist and radical leftist activists, women's very unity across party lines prevented their ongoing organization (Friedman 2000b, 126). *Puntofijista* party leaders viewed women's pluralist organizing as a threat to their strategy of excluding and isolating the Left (Friedman 2000b). Through adopting a democratic centralist organizing model, AD and COPEI were able to demand their women members' demobilization.

Yet this marginalization of women within traditional channels of interest representation ultimately provoked them to establish alternative and unique forms of representation, political organization, and collective action (Friedman 2000b). Even though the corporatist *Puntofijista* regime marginalized them, the prolonged period of liberal democratic consolidation opened up spaces for women's political organizing. They were able to safely develop and fine-tune their strategies for engagement with the Venezuelan state (Rakowski 2003).

When women activists did first unite across party lines under *Puntofijismo* in 1968 at the First Seminar for the Evaluation of Women in Venezuela (Friedman 2000b), they drew attention to women and work—both their paid and unpaid work—and the barriers to women's incorporation into paid labor. They made demands of the state to recognize care work and provide socialized care services that would enable them to undertake paid labor and enjoy the same labor rights as men. They also called for men to share in household labor ("Mujer Hazte Presente" 1968).

Even though no immediate gains came from the First Seminar, women's work and double shift emerged as central themes for the women's movement platform of engagement with the state, which it took up continually since then—throughout *Puntofijismo* (until 1998), into the National Constituent Assembly (1999), and under the Bolivarian regime during Chávez's tenure (1999–2013). The women's movement focus on work since the 1970s was on women's paid labor and reconciliation between paid and unpaid labor so as to enable women's equality in the labor market (Second Interview with Adicea Castillo). However, throughout this time, the issue of homemakers' unpaid labor, its value for society, and how to protect homemakers remained on the movement's agenda—albeit more often as a secondary focus.

Indeed, Venezuelan state recognition of unpaid housework began well before the 1999 Constitution, during *Puntofijismo*'s height, when Yolanda Poleo de Baez, a judge and leader of the Venezuelan Women Lawyers Federation (Federación Venezolana de Abogadas, or FEVA),[8] set the judicial precedent in 1975 that unpaid housework has an economic value.[9] This precedent, which could have had a landmark significance for the Venezuelan women's movement and gender equality struggles, was not popularly known or disseminated (Llavaneras Blanco 2017) because it was set before the movement had solidified and strengthened (Second Interview with Gioconda Espina). Yet it did inform future demands by women's movement leaders for recognition of unpaid housework and homemakers' social protection.

The mid-1970s marked an important political conjuncture for Venezuelan women's rights activists, as international legitimation of women's rights, promoted by the UN Decade on Women (1975–1985), coincided with Venezuelan women's growing dissatisfaction with political parties and the rise of middle-class and popular-sector women's organizations (Rakowski 2003). As a result, many Venezuelan women activists formed nonhierarchical, noncentralized alliances across their political and class affiliations to advance their gender interests. "Over time, this became known as a strategy of unity in diversity, focusing on common goals and avoiding issues that were divisive" (Rakowski 2003, 391), which they used to make effective demands of the state.

Venezuelan women's rights activists successfully organized around the demand for a national state women's agency,[10] which was founded in 1974 and later strengthened when it was transformed into the Ministry for Women's Participation in Development in 1979. Their organizing across class and partisan lines through the 1970s and into the early 1980s culminated in gender and children's equality gains in the 1982 Civil Code reform (Friedman 2000b).[11] Their victory in uniting to reform the Civil Code emboldened them as they drew lessons from their past organizing experiences and the political opportunity of the 1985 UN Conference on Women to create a national umbrella network of nongovernmental organizations (NGOs)—the Coordinadora de Organizaciones No-Gubernmentales de Mujeres (CONG), or the Coordinating Committee of Women's Non-Governmental Organizations.[12] Women activists within and outside the state used UN conferences, organizations, reports, and legal mechanisms, such as the Convention on the Elimination of All Forms of Discrimination against Women, to fuel their coalition-building and legitimate their demands. The model of conjunctural coalition-building that women's rights activists used and that they honed during the mid- to late-1980s rejected clientelist forms of interest mediation, while allowing women within and outside the state to work together "around particular issues without demanding organizational or ideological coherence" (Friedman 2000b, 284).

The institutionalization of the Venezuelan state women's agency (described in the previous paragraph) in the 1980s and influence of the national and international women's movements enabled further work on state recognition of unpaid housework to be undertaken. The Ministry for the Participation of Women in Development commissioned the Venezuelan Central Bank (Banco Central de Venezuela, BCV) to undertake a study determining how much unpaid housework contributed to the country's GDP (Caldera 1981). The study found that including women's unpaid labor would increase Venezuela's GDP anywhere between 20 and 63 percent.[13] It concluded that even the lowest estimation of the value of women's unpaid labor equaled petroleum production's contribution to the national economy (Banco Central de Venezuela 1983). The BCV study also consisted of a time-use study with households in Caracas and inland Venezuela, which found an overwhelming pattern of a traditional domestic division of labor, with women almost exclusively performing unpaid household labor,[14] even in cases where they worked in the paid labor force. Yet, just as the Poleo de Baez judicial sentence that preceded it, the BCV study was not popularly known nor disseminated (Llavaneras Blanco 2017).[15] Yet the study did inspire some women's movement activists throughout the 1980s and 1990s to continue to call for the inclusion of unpaid housework in Venezuela's GDP accounting and for broader recognition of the value of women's unpaid housework (Caldera 1986; Comité "Juntas por Venezuela Camino a Beijing" 1995; Ferrara 1989).

The Venezuelan women's movement took advantage of the political opportunity structure of the mid- to late-1980s, when women's rights discourse was legitimated in international and Latin American regional forums and within the Venezuelan state (Friedman 2000b), to organize and lobby for women's gender interests in labor law reform. When this campaign began, the state women's agency brought together women's rights activists inside and outside the state. They agreed on the need to address workplace discrimination against working women and protections for working mothers. Yet they disagreed on whom the labor law should protect, and the disagreement revolved around class differences, primarily around whether domestic workers and home-based workers should be entitled to the same labor-based social protection that the middle class and the formal working class enjoyed. The CONG then decided to draft its own proposal to ensure that perspectives of women outside the state were included in the reform process (Friedman 2000b). Yolanda Poleo de Baez, judge, lawyer, and FEVA leader, who had previously set the judicial precedent that unpaid housework had a socioeconomic value, facilitated the CONG proposal-generation process. The CONG proposal included the demands for equal labor rights for domestic workers and social security for domestic workers, home-based workers, and homemakers (CONG de Mujeres 1986; El Comité de Mujeres Ucevistas "Cipriana Velásquez" 1985; Las Organizaciones No Gubermentales 1986). Both the Círculos Femeninos Populares (CFP, or Popular Women's Circles)[16] and the Red Todas Juntas[17] (All [Women] Together Network), two popular-sector women's organizations, organized within and outside the CONG to demand social protection for domestic workers, homeworkers, and homemakers in the labor law reform (Círculos Femeninos Populares 1986; La Red Nacional de Apoyo de Organizaciones Populares de Mujeres "Todas Juntas" 1986).

The labor law reform passed by the Venezuelan Congress in 1990 banned sex-based discrimination and increased maternity protections for working women. Yet the dominance of middle- and upper-class women in the women's rights reform effort precluded the extension of equal labor-based social protection to domestic workers and homeworkers (Friedman 2000b). In addition, during the reform process, the women's rights activists and organizations who were demanding social security for homemakers dropped this demand when they realized that in the context of neoliberalism's ascendance in Venezuela, *Puntofijista* state and authorities would not accept it (First Interview with Gioconda Espina; First Interview with Marelis Pérez Marcano). Yet, just as the labor law was about to be passed, the CONG publicly stated both its support for the final draft of the reform and its determination to carry on with its demands for universal social security for domestic workers, homeworkers, and homemakers (La Coordinadora de ONG de Mujeres 1990).

Puntofijismo in Crisis

Venezuela's oil-subsidized consensus unraveled in the 1980s when the Latin American debt crisis and the fall of world oil prices precipitated the country's long-term economic decline and shift from a corporatist import-substitution industrialization development model to that of neoliberalization. Extant social, economic, and political cleavages subsequently were exacerbated. In response to its debt burden and IFI pressures, the Venezuelan state introduced a series of structural economic changes from the mid-1980s to the mid-1990s, redirecting much of the national budget from social and economic development to debt reservicing. These policy changes reduced the state's role in social protection, spurring the expansion of the informal economy, weakening organized labor, increasing the cost of living (Ellner 2008), decreasing real incomes (Coronil and Skurski 2006), and widening income inequalities (Roberts 2003). The socioeconomic crisis triggered by the imposition of neoliberalism in Venezuela was both more severe and more prolonged than neoliberal crises elsewhere in Latin America (Lander 2005; López Maya, Lander, and Ungar 2002). From the beginning of the 1980s to the late 1990s, Venezuelan poverty and extreme poverty rates almost trebled. By the end of the 1990s, almost half of all Venezuelan families were poor and more than a quarter were extremely poor (López Maya, Lander, and Ungar, 2002). The "material bases of consent that undergirded both the elite political pacts and the class compromise" (Roberts 2003, 58) of *Puntofijismo* thus decomposed as the nation was split into "an internationally connected upper class and its local associates . . ., and an impoverished majority" that included an ever-shrinking middle class (Coronil 1997, 383–385).

During this neoliberal shift, Venezuelan president Carlos Andrés Pérez suddenly implemented a structural adjustment package in 1989,[18] termed "El Gran Viraje" or "The Great Turnaround,"[19] in compliance with International Monetary Fund mandates and without any national consultation or debate. On February 27 and 28, 1989, Venezuelans from popular sectors rose up in protest against these reforms, and the state responded with massive military repression that resulted in numerous civilian deaths.[20] These events, which came to be known as the *Caracazo*, set off *Puntofijismo*'s delegitimation. As Ciccariello-Maher (2013b) asserts, the uprising of the popular classes and their violent repression by the state both "exploded the prevailing 'myth of harmony'" (13) and "revealed the bankruptcy and the violence of the existing system for all to see" (89). These watershed events of 1989 burst the magical veneer that had sustained *Puntofijismo* since the 1960s.

The *Caracazo* emerged as a direct reaction to neoliberal reforms shaped by global forces and international financial institutions, yet it also constituted "the culmination of building pressures" from popular sectors that had experienced steady socioeconomic decline and lacked access to powerholders (López Maya, Lander, and Ungar 2002, 199–200). The *Caracazo* illustrated that the *Puntofijista* corporatist institutions and party-based and clientelist forms of interest mediation that had been constructed to contain class conflict could no longer do so. *Puntofijista* institutions proved incapable of adapting to the socioeconomic changes in the Venezuelan population, which occurred with the prolonged neoliberal crisis, and of incorporating the growing marginalized popular classes' interests (Ellner 2003; Levine 2006; Roberts 2003).

The Venezuelan government responded to the *Caracazo* with a series of measures attempting to restore *Puntofijismo*'s legitimacy within a neoliberal framework.[21] Yet Venezuelans were particularly resistant to accepting neoliberal restructuring of the state and the economy precisely because it violated expectations of entitlement to oil rent redistribution and ongoing social protection that the *Puntofijista* magical state had inculcated in them (Ellner 2008; López Maya, Lander, and Ungar 2002). Following the *Caracazo*, as living conditions continued to worsen, protests by marginalized popular sectors experiencing the brunt of structural adjustment escalated throughout Venezuela, and state repression continued (Ciccariello-Maher 2013b).[22] This combination of ongoing structural and physical violence by the state made "increasingly public the view that people had been betrayed by their leaders and that democracy had become a façade behind which an elite had used the state for its own advantage" (Coronil 1997, 378). No longer inducing fantasies of collective integration, the Venezuelan state could not secure the compliance of the majority of its subjects.

Attempting to resolve its legitimacy crisis, the Venezuelan government undertook several initiatives aiming to reform and democratize political representation,[23] including installing a commission to amend the *Puntofijista* Constitution. However, in February 1992, the Movimiento Bolivariano Revolucionario-200 (MBR-200; the Bolivarian Revolutionary Movement-200), which emerged from within the military and was headed by a mid-level military officer, Hugo Chávez, staged a coup attempt. The attempt failed, and the movement's leaders, including Chávez, were arrested.[24] Afterward, the MBR-200 published a document explaining its motivations and its call to return sovereignty to the Venezuelan people through a national referendum on convoking a constituent assembly to rewrite the constitution. This was a position shared by a number of civil society organizations marginalized by *Puntofijismo* (García-Guadilla 2003; López Maya 2003). Yet AD and COPEI suspended the constitutional reform commission in 1992. AD and COPEI therefore furthered the conditions that facilitated their own demise by creating opportunities for new and antiestablishment and antiparty political actors, such as Chávez and the MBR-200 and urban social movements, to emerge to fill the vacuum in political legitimacy and representation (García-Guadilla 2003; Levine 2006).[25] Societal support then grew for the MBR-200's call for an immediate constituent assembly (Maingon, Pérez Baralt, and Sonntag 2000) as the only way to resolve the multiple crises that plagued Venezuela in the neoliberal era.

The 1999 National Constituent Assembly: A Gendered Political Opening to Reframe the Gendered Distribution of Power

The MBR-200, its electoral front—the MVR (Movement of the Fifth Republic)—and their leader, Hugo Chávez, emerged from outside the established *Puntofijista* party system and capitalized on popular sentiment against it to come to power. In uniting a diverse range of social, political, and economic actors and forces against *Puntofijismo* under the broad rubric of Bolivarianism, *Chavista* populism did not originally have a definitive ideological agenda (Ciccariello-Maher 2013b, 236). Chávez's successful 1998 presidential campaign centered on calling for a National Constituent Assembly (Asamblea Nacional Constituyente, ANC) in order to transform Venezuelan democracy from representation toward participation and resolve the systemic crises the country was facing. Chávez also framed the ANC and the institutional overhaul that it would enable as a necessary prerequisite for transforming the state's role in the economy from a facilitator of neoliberalism to a more social and interventionist function.

Although working-class and poor women in Venezuela bore the brunt of the shocks set off by neoliberalism (Castillo and De Salvatierra 2000; Friedman 2000b) because of persistent gender inequalities in productive and reproductive spheres,[26] the mutually reinforcing crises also provided a gendered political opening for women's mobilization and recognition as an interest group (Rakowski 2003).[27] During the 1998 presidential campaign, women from around the country organized in support of a new constitution (Jiménez 2000). After he took office in 1999, Chávez fulfilled his promise to prioritize the ANC in his first year as president.

Yet Chávez's campaign and election threatened the women's movement's previous gains vis-à-vis the state. Chávez showed very little interest in women's issues, employed a paternalistic gender-normative discourse, and initially named no women to his government, and his administration threatened to severely cut the budget of the state women's agency—the National Woman's Council (Consejo Nacional de la Mujer, CONAMU) (Rakowski 2003). Nor did the MVR initially promote women's issues (Second Interview with Marelis Pérez Marcano).

This potential for retrogression in women's rights, institutions, and power spurred women's rights activists into a new phase of coalition-building (Rakowski 2003). Venezuelan women's movement activists turned their initial lack of representation in the state heading into the watershed constituent assembly process into an opportunity to organize and mobilize women to defend their gender interests. A core group of women's rights activists[28] united to defend CONAMU and propose that María León, a long-proven activist on the Venezuelan left and in the women's movement, be named CONAMU president (García Maldonado et al. 1999). León's leftist background and recent activism within the MVR's women's department gave her political clout within the Bolivarian movement. Chávez, in turn, appointed her president of CONAMU in 1999 and restored the agency's funding. He then transformed it into the National Woman's Institute (INaMujer) in 2000, as had been previously stipulated by law.[29] This development not only preserved the institution but also strengthened it as a base for raising feminist demands within the state (Rakowski 2003). In addition to León, several key feminist leaders began to enter the state, including the ANC, and maintained their ideological position against gender discrimination (Espina and Rakowski 2002).

Once Chávez assumed the presidency in February 1999, the ANC became the centerpiece of his first year in office[30] and also transformed how Venezuelans could engage in constitutional change. In April 1999, Venezuelan voters participated in a national consultative referendum in which the majority voted for convoking an ANC "with the aim of transforming the State and creating a new juridical order that allows for the effective functioning of a social and participatory democracy" (*Gaceta Oficial No. 36,364*).[31] The simple majority system for electing ANC delegates combined with the opposition's fragmentation[32] enabled Chávez's electoral bloc, Polo Patriótico (Patriotic Pole),[33] to gain disproportionate representation in the ANC, while opposition interests won very little power within it.[34] As García-Guadilla and Hurtado (2000) and Segura and Bejarano (2013) conclude, this disproportionately favorable electoral outcome for the Patriotic Pole also meant that there would largely be no need for extensive negotiations within the ANC.[35,36]

Chávez's call and the mandate from the electorate for the creation of a "social and participatory democracy" framed the constituent moment, how people could participate in it, and what demands were considered legitimate within it. This constituent moment was embedded in a longer process in which not only *Puntofijista* political parties but also the concept of political parties had lost legitimacy (Molina and Pérez 2004). Yet the emerging dominant concept of the sovereign people's participation interpellated the Venezuelan people as protagonists in the making of their own constitution. Thus, popular participation was framed as both the process and product of the constituent moment, signifying a fundamental rupture with the past of elite and party control of constitution making and governance. The inclusion of formerly marginalized groups without substantial contestation with the political opposition characterized the 1999 constituent assembly process (Segura and Bejarano 2013). This meant that the majority of ANC delegates were not open to participation by and demands emerging from *Puntofijista* parties and organizations controlled by them, but they were open to demands from organizations not specifically associated with the *Puntofijista* parties. This dominant concept of participation within the ANC that excluded the old elite and instead included sectors previously marginalized by them (García-Guadilla and Mallén 2012) represented a political opening for recognition of women's rights demands. In addition, the mandate to construct a social democracy and to expand rather than contract the welfare state signified a political opening for women's social rights demands. Concepts of participatory democracy and social democracy constituted master frames through which women's rights activists could legitimate their demands in the ANC process.

The ANC delegates treated popular participation in the constituent process as a mandate, and they created participatory mechanisms to gather and channel people's proposals for the new constitution from across Venezuela (Asamblea Nacional Constituyente 1999d). Chávez also urged the assembly delegates to listen to everyone so that "all Venezuelans feel that they are participating and protagonizing this revolutionary process" (Asamblea Nacional Constituyente 1999a, 40).

Yet a fundamental tension between popular participation and speed also marked the constitution-making process. The referendum mandate allotted the ANC six months to complete the new constitution. From the ANC's opening in August 1999, Chávez urged the assembly both to act swiftly and to enable popular participation in this time-bound process (Asamblea Nacional Constituyente 1999a). Ongoing conflict between the *Puntofijista* elite and the emerging *Chavista* elite also constrained the extent of popular participation in the ANC.[37] Once the first draft of the new constitution was complete in mid-October 1999, Chávez urged the assembly to complete the drafting process within a month so that the final draft could go to popular referendum before the end of 1999. The ANC delegates stuck to the president's directive and approved the final draft of the constitution by mid-November 1999.[38]

Women's rights activists united to organize around the ANC—they were clear that they did not want to be marginalized in the new regime as they had been in *Puntofijismo*'s formation. They saw the constituent process as a gendered political opportunity to make their interests central to the new regime's construction. Women's rights activists organized around the idea that the only way to overcome their marginalization in the new constitutional framework was by mainstreaming a gender perspective throughout the constitution[39] and not just organizing for the insertion of a few specific women's rights in it.[40] This way gender interests would be a fundamental axis and not a footnote within the new constitution. They termed this strategy "making women's gender interests visible" (*visibilización*). Marelis Pérez Marcano, an ANC delegate who advocated for women's rights, explains:

> If the new political system that is longed to be created is a democratic system—a full democracy—women's rights had to be made visible in that whole space in an integral way . . . it meant that we were not entering through the back door asking for concessions, but that it was really essential that women's rights would be able to be incorporated in the constitution as part of this new democracy. (First Interview with Marelis Pérez Marcano)

Making women's gender interests visible throughout the constituent process meant rendering visible gender issues and women's contributions to the country that political society had traditionally rendered invisible by relegating them to the private sphere. Women's rights leaders, activists, and organizations continually pressed for the redrawing of boundaries between private and public spheres, specifically invoking household issues as of public concern in which the state should intervene to promote women's well-being.

This strategy of not narrowly defining women's gender interests also incorporated an intersectional perspective of gender, ethnicity, and class. Part of making visible women's gender interests from the household level up revolved around popular-sector women's everyday needs and experiences of struggling to maintain their households because of the intersection of their gender with their class. In addition, women's rights activists worked in solidarity with other organizations (not specifically working on women's rights) generating proposals for and mobilizing around the ANC (Asamblea Nacional Constituyente, Subcomisión Familia, Mujer, Infancia, Juventud y Anciano 1999a), such as indigenous organizations. This strategy strengthened support for women's rights demands, and it served to position women's rights as part of the broader, general popular struggle for recognition of and redistribution of power and resources to previously marginalized sectors in the new regime.

Women's rights activists seized this opportunity to potentially refound state–society relations from a gender perspective by deploying and adapting the conjunctural coalition-building model they had developed under *Puntofijismo*. They utilized their previously developed organizations, networks, tactics, and agenda to generate proposals and consensus around them, and also to organize within and across their organizations at multiple territorial and political levels—from community levels up to Latin American regional levels. Unlike the general drive to exclude actors associated with *Puntofijismo* that characterized the constituent process, women's rights activists united across all political tendencies and included women leaders associated with the old regime in the struggle to achieve women's rights and visibility in the new regime. This is because they understood that they would have greater power (and programmatic unity) if more women participated. María Auxiliadora Torrealba from the Popular Women's Circles reflects: "There was . . . a whole solidarity, really a sisterhood . . . with a lot of respect. . . . There were differences of course—nor was it heaven—but differences that could be settled on. . . . The common . . . themes and priorities could be agreed on, and very easily common spaces arose. And because of this, we were able to sign a document together" (Interview with María Auxiliadora Torrealba). Unlike in other social sectors, women's rights activists' sense of gender solidarity enabled them to unite across partisan divides during the constituent process.

Women's organizing activities for their gender interests in the constituent process proliferated both before and during the ANC. They saw the ANC not just as a moment or a constitutional product. They also understood it as a *process* wherein they would need to continually unite and make themselves visible in order to begin to effect the changes in gender and state–society relations that they desired. As Nora Castañeda, a former CONG member and later head of the Bolivarian state Woman's Development Bank, explained, such a process of constructing a new republic began within the home (Asamblea Nacional Constituyente, Subcomisión Familia, Mujer, Infancia, Juventud y Anciano 1999a). Further,

a constituent process is a process in which the organized people in many ways has the floor. It's like the very constitution says: the people, our people, is a subject, is a subject of power, it does not delegate its power, but it exercises it in a process of constitution of the new society. Constituent signifies to constitute something, and that something is not constituted in a lone product that is the constitution. The constitution serves as a instrument . . . like a fundamental program of struggle for the people, with it in their hand, so that they can constitute the new Republic. (Interview with Nora Castañeda)

A core group of women's rights activists began organizing around the constituent process at the end of the 1998 presidential campaign—months before the ANC was approved and ANC delegates were elected. Activists and organizations outside the state[41] presented their "Women's Political Agenda"[42] to the presidential candidates in 1998 and saw the forthcoming ANC as an opportunity to push for this agenda in the constitution (Interview with Nora Castañeda). Marelis Pérez Marcano—an MVR leader, feminist activist and scholar, and recently elected congressional representative and president of the congressional Bicameral Women's Rights Commission—was active in early conjunctural coalition-building for the ANC. With other MVR women leaders, she drew on their connections with women's rights activists inside and outside the state to draft women's rights proposals for the constitution (Duran 1999; Espina 1998). And within a week of Chávez's assumption of the presidency and decree of a popular referendum on whether to convoke an ANC, the CONG convened a participatory public forum in Caracas in which it presented and discussed a preliminary women's movement proposal for the new constitution (Jiménez 2000). In June 1999, the CONG published a popular booklet containing its proposals for the new constitution, which was also designed to promote popular women's participation in the constituent process.

Women's rights activists within the state and CONAMU strongly supported the conjunctural coalition-building work for women's rights and a gender perspective in the constitution. As soon as María León (who had been a CONG member) assumed power of CONAMU, she asserted that that state gender institution's primary objective was to promote women's participation in the constituent process ("Visita a la redacción de *El Mundo*. Participación proporcional a la del hombre pedirá Consejo de la Mujer en la Constituyente" 1999). León created a CONAMU constituent commission that worked both to unify all the women's rights proposals and to promote women's participation within the process (León 2000). CONAMU, the Bicameral Women's Rights Commission, and several regional and municipal state leaders and organizations held events with women in civil society, incorporating and publicizing women's demands for the new constitution.[43] By June 1999, CONAMU completed its first draft of a combined women's movement proposal for the constitution, which it presented for public debate (Jiménez 2000). This combined proposal was refined, subscribed to by a coalition of women's labor, popular, NGO, academic, and state organizations and networks,[44] and published by CONAMU several months later.

Women's rights activists were clear in their early 1999 organizing about their demand for a gender perspective within the new constitution, but they had not reached consensus on the demands for state recognition of unpaid housework's socioeconomic value and homemakers' social security. Yet, early in this organizing process, María León and other labor leaders signaled this was an outstanding demand from the women's movement that would be raised again (León and Tremont 1999). As women's rights activists developed their overarching demands to make women and their gender interests from the household level up visible, they came to agreement to revive the demands for recognition of unpaid housework and social security for homemakers. Inocencia Orellana, CONG member and former activist within the All Women Together Network, explains:

We had come along working on the theme of the invisibilization of women, and that one way in which we are seen as a minority is the fact that supposedly we are not productive. . . . Because we are not in the paid labor market, but in domestic work. It is unpaid work, but if you have to do it outside [one's own house] they have to pay you for it. . . . We saw that this work had to be valued because it was the way of making ourselves visible . . . and recognizing that, yes, we women contribute to the country's economy. (Interview with Inocencia Orellana)

They recognized that the revolutionary political conjuncture of the constituent process marked a unique gendered political opening for enshrining this demand.

Women's rights activists organizing around the ANC were clear on their demand that homemakers contributed to society through their unpaid labor, but they did not formulate a corresponding proposal on how to finance and implement the social security for homemakers they were demanding.[45] Some activists within the coalition were resistant to assigning economic values to their constitutional demand; they believed that couching it in maternalist and affective arguments would be more successful (Llavaneras Blanco 2017). Yet this lack of a financing proposal would later prove to be a fundamental challenge to fulfilling homemakers' social security under the new constitutional dispensation, given that the social security system was premised on monetary contributions from workers and their employers, and homemakers did not have an employment relationship through which they could contribute to the system. By May 1999 though, the women's rights coalition agreed on the demands for state recognition of unpaid housework's value and homemakers' social security (del Mar Álvarez and Castañeda 1999). The coalition published these demands in their proposals and promoted them as they organized around Venezuela in the run-up to the ANC's August 1999 installation (Castillo and De Salvatierra 2000).

All of this pre-ANC conjunctural coalition-building work at multiple levels throughout Venezuela meant that women's rights activists reached consensus on their constitutional proposals before the ANC began. Once the ANC started, the challenge for the women's rights coalition was to ensure that their proposals were heard and included. Even as some women's rights activists were also activists in the Patriotic Pole, some of their demands, such as recognition of unpaid housework's value and homemakers' social security, were not contained in President Chavez's proposal (5 August 1999)[46] or the Patriotic Pole's proposal (Polo Patriótico 1999)[47] for the new constitution.

As an essential part of representing women's gender interests in the constituent process, the women's rights coalition also publicly supported several of its activists' candidacies for the ANC and candidates sympathetic to women's movement concerns. Although most of these candidates were unsuccessful, Marelis Pérez Marcano, a Patriotic Pole candidate who campaigned on women's and family rights and whom the CONG supported (Zapata 1999), did win an ANC seat. Women constituted only 16 out of 131 delegates (12 percent) elected to the ANC. Yet, out of this small number, several women peripherally tied to the women's movement were elected, including Blancanieve Portocarrero, a lawyer and FEVA member who had taught women's studies and researched homemakers' contribution to the national economy.

Even though women were very underrepresented descriptively in the ANC, Pérez Marcano and Portocarrero made their commitments to women's gender interests clear to the assembly from the outset. The ANC more broadly, though, did not begin with an explicit commitment to a gender perspective. These two delegates used their positions within the assembly and the Patriotic Pole to carve out spaces to specifically address the multiple constitutional demands that the women's rights coalition had formulated and to push the women's rights agenda within the ANC more broadly.

Delegates to the ANC divided into commissions to work on specific constitutional thematic areas, and Pérez Marcano and Portocarrero utilized these spaces to promote a gender perspective and women's rights. Portocarrero joined the Constitutional Commission, arguably the most important commission because it edited all the proposals that the other commissions drafted and determined which would go the ANC plenary for final deliberation. In that commission, Portocarrero ensured that state recognition of housework and homemakers' social security went onward to plenary discussion (Llavaneras Blanco 2017). Pérez Marcano and Portocarrero also joined the Social and Family Rights Commission, and they proposed the creation of a Women's, Children, Youth, and Elderly subcommission within it so that women's rights proposals could specifically be addressed. Portocarrero was elected the subcommission's coordinator, and a subcommission technical assistance team staffed by key actors in the women's rights conjunctural coalition was then formed.

Taking advantage of the ANC's master frame of popular participation, the subcommission engaged in a consultation process with women's rights activists from civil society, academia, and multiple levels of the state, including leaders from the old regime. Since the women's rights coalition had already reached consensus on a set of proposals, it used consultation events not only to explain and discuss the proposals' significance but also to strategize on how to ensure their inclusion in the new constitution given women's underrepresentation in the ANC. They decided to submit their joint proposal to all the constituent commissions and to use Pérez Marcano's and Portocarrero's standing within the ANC to open up space for women's rights activists to speak about it in as many commissions as possible (Asamblea Nacional Constituyente, Subcomisión Familia, Mujer, Infancia, Juventud y Anciano 1999a, 1999b). The women's rights activists' approach to the ANC as a process in which they had to make women's gender interests visible meant that their work did not finish with submitting their proposals, but it carried on with being physically present within the ANC so that they could constantly pressure and monitor the delegates. Even though the women's movement did not have large numbers of activists at that time, it maintained a daily presence within the assembly, with anywhere between several dozen to several hundred activists interacting with ANC delegates and articulating their demands on a given day (First Interview with Adicea Castillo; Interview with Morelba Jiménez). Their constant presence thus lent the movement the appearance of organizational strength and density.

This joint approach of women's rights activists from within and outside the ANC pressuring the male-dominated assembly paid off. María Iris Varela, an ANC delegate and Constitutional Commission member who was not tied to the women's movement, stated that women "have been so fundamental in this whole process, that . . . the way in which we are carrying ourselves and the different commissions, . . . that vision of gender is . . . immersed in each one of the 131 delegates . . . and is being passed onto the constitutional text" (Asamblea Nacional Constituyente, Comisión Constitucional 1999). Increasingly, male delegates, including the ANC president, defended women's rights and a gender perspective in plenary debates. Crucially, several did so when the first full draft of the new constitution contained an article defining life as beginning from conception, which signified that voluntary abortion would become a fundamental human rights violation (Asamblea Nacional Constituyente 1999c). Significantly, the debate that ensued around this definition of the right to life—which the majority of delegates then voted against—was the only substantial debate within the ANC plenary on the draft constitution's contents as they related to women's rights. No substantial debate emerged within the plenary around including state recognition of housework's value and homemakers' social security,[48] and the plenary approved this draft article with support from the majority of delegates (Asamblea Nacional Constituyente 1999b).

Conclusion

As a result of women's rapid and intense conjunctural coalition-building and mobilization prior to and during the ANC, the Constitution of the Bolivarian Republic of Venezuela ratified by the electorate in December 1999 met almost all the demands for rights made by the women's movement since the late 1970s (Rakowski 2003). These new rights and obligations included sexual and reproductive health rights (Art. 76), the state's obligation to guarantee reproductive health (Art. 76), coresponsibility between fathers and mothers in raising children (Art. 76), gender equality and equity at work (Art. 88), the right to protection of maternity and paternity through the social security system (Art.86) regardless of the marital status of the parents (Art. 76), state obligation to protect maternity from the moment of conception (Art. 76), and both the recognition of housework's socioeconomic value and homemakers' right to social security (Art. 88). In addition, the 1999 Constitution employed a gender perspective throughout the text in its use of both masculine and feminine subjects.

For many women's rights activists, Article 88's enshrinement was of watershed significance, as the 1999 Constitution became the first constitution in the world to specifically recognize the value of women's housework for society and entitle homemakers to social security. Pérez Marcano, for example, asserted that "because patriarchal culture undoubtedly made . . . the home its great area of relations of subordination, then having conquered Article 88 was precisely an expression of the visibilization of women in their battle flags" (First Interview with Marelis Pérez Marcano). According to her, Article 88 generated a rupture with the "paradigm that the home is private and that the state did not have to intervene at all there" (Second Interview with Marelis Pérez Marcano). The achievement of Article 88 signified a crucial landmark for the struggle to recognize women's unpaid labor and transform the gendered distribution of power. In addition to making housework visible, it set a framework for the state to intervene in favor of the workers who performed such work by redistributing wealth to them.

Venezuelan women's rights activists were able to make these gains because they encountered a political opportunity structure that was favorable toward their mobilization around and codification of women's gender rights within the 1999 Constitution. Rapid political upheaval and transformation of the political structure and state institutions characterized the timing and nature of political change during the constituent process. The outcomes of these swift changes were uncertain and galvanized women to organize both to defend and advance their gender interests. At the same time, the Venezuelan constituent process marked a crucial political opening for social movements, and the women's movement in particular, as popular participation constituted a master frame that legitimated women's organizing and rights demands. Women's rights activists utilized their preexisting political agenda and began formulating proposals for constitutional change well before the ANC began, placing them in a strong position to consolidate, disseminate, and popularize their proposals during the rapid ANC. The old elite was largely excluded, but the constitutional design process was relatively open and transparent to women's pluralistic organizing and interventions. In spite of women's underrepresentation in the ANC, women's rights activists used the institutional footholds they had gained within the state, political parties, and the ANC to open spaces for a cohesive conjunctural coalition to mobilize within and outside of the state and successfully pressure political party, state, and ANC officials to take up women's rights proposals. Moreover, they drew on lessons they had learned and contributions from their past activism, and they incorporated many of the same activists from their past initiatives to make their conjunctural coalition an effective lobby for constitutional recognition of women's gender rights.

The Venezuelan experience of women's rights organizing for the 1999 Constitution empirically illustrates how the political opportunity structure of a constitutional change process can enable women's rights gains. In addition to timing and nature of constitutional change, relative openness and transparency of constitutional design process, legitimation of current demands through the legacy of women's past activism, cohesive conjunctural coalition-building, and openness and willingness of state and political party officials to take up women's gender concerns, the Venezuelan experience points to social movement participation in constitutional change processes as an emergent factor that can influence the extent to which women can bring about constitutional change in their favor. This new factor emerged as democratizing forces from below within Latin America more broadly increasingly pressured for their interests to be represented in the state, and, as such, they were contesting and expanding the very nature and shape of democracy and constitutional change. A constitution "authorizes the rules of the political game" (Dobrowolsky and Hart 2003, 2), and the Venezuelan women's movement participation in the political-institutional game during their country's constituent process also formed part of a larger collective action master frame that contested the rules of the old political game and opened spaces for popular participation in political decision-making processes. Women's participation in this process represented a broader shift in the Latin American region from elite-controlled, clientelist, and exclusionary forms of interest mediation to direct, participatory forms that empowered citizens and social movements as political subjects who could collectively transform the political distribution of power.

CHAPTER 2

Between Fruitless Legislative Initiatives and Executive Magic: Contestations over the Implementation of Homemakers' Social Security

Heading into the Bolivarian Republic (once ratified, the 1999 Constitution renamed the country the Bolivarian Republic of Venezuela), women's rights activists now had a constitutional framework to legitimize their demand for homemakers' incorporation into the social security system and thus for wealth redistribution to women who worked without pay. Yet Article 88 was not immediately enforceable, because it stipulated that homemakers had "the right to social security in accordance with the law." A legal framework giving shape to this constitutional mandate would have to be developed in order for homemakers to receive the social security to which they were entitled. Focusing on legislative struggles to implement homemakers' constitutional right to social security following the ANC, this chapter assesses the extent of political–institutional change in Bolivarian Venezuela from a gender perspective.

Women's successful mobilization for their rights in a constitution in and of itself does not transform a country's gendered distribution of power. The achievement of equal rights is "the indispensable prerequisite of a thoroughgoing transformation in women's condition" (Verucci 1991, 567), but it is not enough to stem gender inequalities. A thorough transformation in women's conditions, and thereby the deepening of democracy, hinges on women's ongoing participation in political processes. Their participation, and that of other traditionally marginalized groups, would help to ensure rights are enforced and enjoyed after they are codified within constitutions. Turning the rights within a constitutional text into concrete practice therefore "requires deep institutional and political changes" (Htun 2002, 748) beyond a constitution's enactment. Such deep changes include allocating resources to institutions committed to enforcing women's rights in all areas of state policy and action (Htun 2002). Women's pressure on states to enforce their rights also must persist within a new constitutional dispensation, because women's history of organizing for political change in Latin America has proven that states often grant women rights in order to co-opt women's movements, and they enforce women's rights only when organized women's movements pressure them (Alvarez 1994; Friedman 2000b).

Similar to the ANC the year before, women emerged very underrepresented in the first elections for the Venezuelan National Assembly (2000) that followed the enactment of the 1999 Constitution—only 9.6 percent of legislative deputies. Their representation rose to 14.2 percent in the second term of the legislature, beginning in 2005 (Aguirre and Testa 2010). Marelis Pérez Marcano, who had continually championed recognition of unpaid housework and homemakers' social security in the constituent process, was elected deputy to the National Assembly in 2000, became the first president of the assembly's Permanent Commission on Family, Woman, and Youth, and was reelected to the assembly in 2005. From the outset in her positions of legislative power, Pérez Marcano spearheaded the drive to legislate Article 88. She employed the women's movement's conjunctural coalition-building strategy by drawing in activists within and outside the state to assist her in developing a legislative proposal.

In addition, under President Chávez's tenure, women's organizing within, with, and outside the state proliferated. The Bolivarian government created and strengthened state women's and gender equality institutions, some of which were demanded by organized women: for example, CONAMU, which later became the National Woman's Institute (INaMujer) (1999); a national toll-free hotline for women experiencing gender violence (1999); the Woman's Development Bank (BanMujer) (2001); the National Public Defender of Women (2004); the Woman's Issues Ministry (2008), which later became the Ministry for Woman's Popular Power and Gender Equality (MinMujer) (2009); and district attorneys for violence against women (2011). And many women joined both new mixed-gender and women-only popular social and political organizations, many of which were organized, promoted, and/or financially supported by the state.

Yet Pérez Marcano and other women's rights activists within and outside the state working together for Article 88's implementation encountered a very different political opportunity structure from that of the constituent process. The way in which Article 88 had been drafted interacted with the larger and constantly shifting political context to constrain possibilities for the article's legislative implementation in the first eleven years of the Bolivarian Republic.

This chapter analyzes the implications of the 1999 Constitution for the contestation and enforcement of women's rights, and homemakers' right to social security in particular, during the Bolivarian regime's consolidation. Examining post-ANC legislative initiatives to implement Article 88 between 2000 and 2011,[1] I shed light on how these initiatives were shaped by larger social and political processes, including persistent gender-biased ideologies and practices of subordinating women's gender interests. Increasing political conflict and polarization, the Bolivarian regime's radicalization and consolidation, presidential centralization of power, and the executive's development of state institutions parallel to those enacted and overseen by the legislature also constrained initiatives to legislate Article 88. These larger political processes interacted with each other, and in turn the openness and transparency of legislative processes diminished, women's conjunctural coalitions declined, and the openness and willingness of officials within the state to take up and legislate women's rights waned. After the landmark ANC, the gendered political opening for the legislative advancement of women's rights became narrower, and redistributing gendered power by enforcing homemakers' constitutional right to social security was largely sidelined.

Political Polarization, Government Radicalization, Centralization of Power, and the Development of Parallel State Institutions under *Chavismo*

Political polarization, government radicalization, executive centralization of power, uncertainty about the role of representative democracy, the development of overlapping parallel state institutions, and lack of consolidation of democratic institutions and channels of interest mediation marked the larger national political context in which women's rights activists attempted to legislate Article 88 from 2000 to 2011. These larger political tendencies existed in dialectical tension with each other and produced a constantly shifting, conflictual political field. The electoral ratification of the 1999 Constitution and persistent *Chavista* electoral victories[2] signaled the end to the *Puntofijista* regime and its elite political-party-dominated form of (il)liberal democracy, but a new form of democracy did not consolidate under the Bolivarian regime during Chávez's presidency.[3] Rather, a constant struggle over the form democracy would take within Bolivarian Venezuela occurred, and this struggle was shaped by contestation from opposition forces and contestation by conflicting forces and currents within *Chavismo*.

From the outset of his presidency, Chávez's rhetoric was anti-neoliberal in orientation. Political and economic moderation, increased public and so-cial spending (Buxton 2009; Ellner 2008; Lander and Navarrete 2007), and opposition fragmentation largely characterized the first years of Chávez's government (1999–2001). At the end of 2001, Chávez decreed forty-nine special laws that were marked by an anti-neoliberal focus, most notably in the oil and fishing industries and in agrarian reform (Ellner 2008). Seg-ments of the opposition interpreted these forty-nine laws as endangering private property rights, thereby provoking them to unite against Chávez and the Bolivarian regime (Lander and Navarrete 2007).

Ensuing political polarization and conflict marked the second stage of Chávez's government (2001–2004), in which a "battle for state control" (Lander and Navarrete 2007) occurred, as the opposition used a myriad of tactics to try to bring down the government and the Bolivarian regime. The opposition convened a series of general strikes, which culminated in a coup d'etat and the 1999 Constitution's annulment in April 2002. The coup proved to be short-lived, in large part because of pressure from military forces and popular sectors loyal to Bolivarianism. Following his restoration to power, Chávez made attempts at reconciliation with the opposition, but they remained intent on unseating him from power.

In December 2002, opposition forces, including executives of the state oil company, Petróleos de Venezuela (PDVSA), declared an indefinite gen-eral strike in order to force Chávez from power by shutting down the oil in-dustry. The strike amounted to an employer lockout, but most workers did not support it and continued working, and in the case of PDVSA, work-ers and community members worked together to restore oil production dur-ing the lockout (Ellner 2008). As a result, the lockout petered out after eight weeks, and the government regained control over PDVSA management and revenue (Raby 2006).

Recovery of PDVSA proved crucial: even though the lockout had failed to unseat Chávez, it had unleashed an economic crisis. In addition, the op-position's intransigence and the role of the popular sectors in defending Chávez and the Bolivarian regime showed that the revolution both enjoyed and largely relied on popular-sector support (Ciccariello-Maher 2013b). The Bolivarian government immediately responded by instituting pro-poor so-cial and economic policies (Buxton 2009), initiating a process of govern-ment radicalization wherein it increasingly transformed state oil revenue into goods and services for the popular sectors. In 2003, with this newfound control over state oil revenue, Chávez exercised the Bolivarian petrostate's magnanimous sorcerer powers to create the missions, a set of emergency so-cial programs targeting the popular sectors. Through bypassing the extant state bureaucracy, the missions quickly began to address effects of the crisis and longer-term social policy shortfalls on the popular sectors.[4]

Yet the opposition remained recalcitrant in the wake of the failed lockout. In early 2004, certain opposition sectors staged open and aggressive confrontations with state security forces in the streets (Ellner 2008). Opposition forces also united to gather enough citizen signatures to convoke a popular recall referendum on Chávez's presidency in August 2004. Chávez emerged victorious from the referendum, with a sizable majority in support of his presidency. The recall referendum signaled a clear defeat of the opposition and the exhaustion of its tactics to bring down the government.

The defeated recall referendum and subsequent opposition fragmentation also signaled a political opportunity for both consolidating and further radicalizing the Bolivarian regime. The opposition's persistent yet failed insurgency and consistent popular-sector support for the regime taught Chávez that moderation was not an appropriate strategy for addressing the opposition (Wilpert 2007, 28). At the same time, he faced demands from loyal popular social movements and organizations to extend and deepen revolutionary changes and promote and sanction participatory popular democracy (Lander and Navarrete 2007). Propelled leftward, Chávez announced in 2005 that he and his government would be pursuing twenty-first-century socialism—a form of socialism that would recognize and promote popular participation and direct democracy, and institute a new production model for Venezuela. The period between the defeat of the recall referendum and 2007 marked the third phase of Chávez's government—a rapid and intense period of radicalization of the Bolivarian revolution's rhetoric, goals, programs, and state–society relations.

During this period of radicalization, the government initiated an economic reorientation to steer the country toward socialism, which aimed to promote "endogenous development" and transformation of production relations toward relations based on "social property" (Presidencia de la República Bolivariana de Venezuela 2006, 11).[5] The government increased state ownership of companies through expropriation, nationalization, and renationalization; redistributed land; radicalized and extended the missions; promoted forms of collective ownership; and institutionalized comanagement in state companies (Ellner 2008; Meltzer 2009). Yet this new production model did not become hegemonic; rather, it developed alongside and in tension with extant capitalist institutions.

To support the construction of twenty-first-century socialism, Chávez called for the establishment of a "revolutionary protagonistic democracy" based on republicanism and Bolivarianism in the "First Socialist Plan for

Economic and Social Development of the Nation." Though critical of liberal democracy, these outlines did not address the role representative democracy would take under this new form of democracy; rather, they focused
on and privileged direct democracy and popular participation (Presidencia
de la República Bolivariana de Venezuela 2006). Further, they stipulated
that under "revolutionary, protagonistic democracy, justice is above the law;
and the conditions to guarantee the welfare of everyone . . . are above the
simple formality of equality before the law and commercial despotism" (15).
Following these outlines, the government moved both to promote and to
institutionalize forms of popular power and participatory democracy. The
formation of local popular organizations and their action in coresponsibility with the state were key to its vision for reconfiguring democracy and
state–society relations. The government delegated legally binding decision-
making authority and provided material support to various forms of community organizations, such as communal councils, technical water tables,
and urban land committees. These newly legalized, territorially based organizations did not replace extant local and regional representative democratic
institutions; rather, they developed parallel to and in tension with them.

Alongside this shift toward decentralization and popularization of power
during the Chávez regime's third stage, a concomitant centralization of
power occurred. In 2005, the opposition boycotted the National Assembly
elections, alleging electoral partiality, thus enabling *Chavista* forces to gain
complete control over the legislature. Even with complete *Chavista* control,[6]
the National Assembly granted Chávez enabling powers in 2007 to decree
laws over a period of eighteen months in order to accelerate changes deemed
necessary to transition toward twenty-first-century socialism (Bruce 2008).

Further, the United Socialist Party of Venezuela (PSUV) was created
in 2007 to replace the MVR and develop and strengthen the political-
organizational base of *Chavismo* (Ellner 2011). Yet the PSUV developed
largely under the charge of state leaders and not its base (Ellner 2011). This
in turn limited rank-and-file control over the party, the ability of the party
membership to hold state leaders to account,[7] the establishment of pluralistic internal mechanisms of discussion and debate (Ellner 2008; Spronk and
Webber 2011), and a concomitant clarification of the politics and ideology of
the movement (Ellner 2011). Centralization of power combined with lack of
party consolidation meant that the programmatic content of twenty-first-
century socialism remained "vague and subject to ad hoc and pragmatic
change led by Chávez" (Buxton 2009, 73).

This lack of separation between party and state and weak internal and
decentralized democracy rendered the channeling of demands from the

party's base up to party leadership difficult, including women's specific demands around their gender interests. Chávez's support for state women's and gender equality institutions and public endorsement of feminism as essential to twenty-first-century socialism did create a gendered political opening for the PSUV to discuss and endorse gender equality and equity as party principles (I Congreso Extraordinario del PSUV 2010). However, this intraparty discussion on gender appears not to have extended to endorsing specific demands from the women's rights agenda[8] as part of the party's platform. Neither the "Declaration of Principles from the First PSUV Extraordinary Congress" (2010) nor the party's "Strategic Lines of Political Action" (2011) that emanated from this congress incorporated these demands. For example, María León noted that the PSUV had not substantially deliberated on at least one of the demands from this agenda—abortion decriminalization (cited in León Torrealba 2012, 157–158).

Such deficiencies in the development of participatory popular democracy carried on through and shaped the next (fourth and final) stage of Chávez's government (2007–2013), in which *Chavismo* suffered its first significant electoral defeat. In 2007, Chávez proposed a reform of the 1999 Constitution in order to construct a socialist democracy, which would be submitted to the electorate in a popular referendum. Chávez developed his thirty-three constitutional reform proposals with assistance from a select group of advisors. The National Assembly later developed an additional thirty-six constitutional reform proposals, which included some women's movement demands. Very little popular consultation and participation occurred in the proposal-development process (Webber 2010). The sixty-nine constitutional reform proposals were narrowly defeated in the referendum in December 2007. Chávez accepted the results, but he noted that the proposals remained "alive" and that he and his government would continue working for their enactment, alongside continuing to construct socialism within the existing constitutional framework (Prensa Presidencial 2007).

Following the referendum defeat, Chávez and the *Chavista*-controlled National Assembly did insert some of the constitutional reform proposals into the national legislative agenda by passing them individually as laws (López Maya 2011). Yet, linked to the political opportunity structure's shift away from popular power toward centralized power, these *Chavista* legislative initiatives generally did not include women's movement constitutional reform demands for women's gender rights.[9] The *Chavista*-controlled National Assembly, just before its term was to expire in 2010, granted Chávez enabling powers for eighteen months.[10] Both the National Assembly and Chávez continued to sanction laws promoting popular democracy, participation at local levels (Lalander 2012), and the construction of a communal state (López Maya 2011).[11]

In spite of these new laws promoting direct democracy, a new form of democracy did not consolidate during Chávez's presidency. Rather, the Chávez government utilized, renounced, and dismantled liberal democratic mechanisms at the same time. It avoided corporatist[12] and alternative structures of social dialogue (Ellner 2011) and halted decentralization of powers to municipal and regional governments (Ellner 2011). At the same time, it relied "heavily on elections rather than popular consultation in order to legitimize its programs and policies" (Buxton 2011, xvi–xvii). In addition, although the Chávez government granted legally binding decision-making powers and authorities to community organizations and allowed them to proliferate throughout the country, it tied the disbursement of funds to support them to the executive branch. Further, in all stages of Chávez's government, the National Assembly legitimized the executive branch's centralization of power as it granted legislative authority to the president in order to take urgent actions (enabling powers),[13] and over his tenure it granted him enabling powers for increasing amounts of time.[14] Though the granting of enabling powers did not signify that the National Assembly ceased to function, this meant that when Chávez did have these powers, he legislated just as much as the legislative branch.[15] Thus, a tension between liberal electoral democracy, participatory democracy, and revolutionary populist democracy marked Bolivarian governance during Chávez's presidency, especially during the third and fourth stages.

This tension around the emergent shape of Bolivarian democracy occurred because these multiple political currents existed within Chávez's discourses and actions and at all levels of the Bolivarian movement (Ellner 2005). Further, Bolivarianism first emerged not as a socialist movement but as a nationalist, anti-imperialist, anti-neoliberal movement. As Buxton (2009) explains, "the Bolivarian revolution should be understood more as a case of socialism by default than design" because of how the dialectical conflicts of popular support and domestic and foreign opposition forces later triggered the government's left turn, which remained vague, contested, and in constant flux (57–58).

Bolivarianism was characterized by social movement alliances with the government (Valencia 2015), yet it developed to be an internally differentiated movement driven not just by tensions from outside it but also by tensions from within it. As Ellner (2005, 2008) explains, these internal tensions included both top-down and bottom-up approaches and soft-line and hard-line currents. The tension between soft- and hard-line forces within

Bolivarianism revolved in large part around parallel institutions' role in the revolution, such as communal councils, the missions, social production companies, the communes, and popular militia. The soft-line viewed these new, parallel structures as necessary to fill in gaps that old institutions did not address, while envisioning new and old institutions as complementary, with their relations regulated. The hard-line envisioned new, parallel structures eventually replacing old institutions, and swift initiatives as necessary to develop them and achieve a revolutionary rupture with *Puntofijismo* (Ellner 2005). Although "this intra-revolutionary conflict, this dialectic within a dialectic" gradually pushed Chávez and his government leftward (Ciccariello-Maher 2013b, 236–237), these tensions within the Bolivarian movement were not resolved during Chávez's presidency. Indeed, they were exacerbated as the "bureaucratisation of the political sections" of *Chavismo* became "dominant" (Sara Motta, cited in Spronk and Webber 2011, 244) and popular resentment toward this tendency grew.

Yet conflicts from outside the Bolivarian movement at times served to gloss over these tensions within it. Even though the outcomes of events in 2004 and 2005 proved that the opposition forces were exhausted, permanent political polarization marked Bolivarian Venezuela, as opposition forces also proved that they could continually unite against the Chávez government. Given the opposition's historical aggression and willingness to use extralegal tactics to delegitimize and bring down the Bolivarian government and constitution, *Chavista*-aligned forces tended to continually view opposition forces as a bloc of enemies of the revolution, against which they defined themselves. Conflicting tendencies and actors within *Chavismo* were able to cohere as a movement in large part through their common opposition to the *escualidos* (Ciccariello-Maher, cited in Spronk and Webber 2011), the "squalid ones"—a *Chavista* term grouping together all opposition actors and forces. In spite of their ideological and strategic differences, *Chavistas* took their unity as necessary to defend and sustain their revolution against its adversaries.

However, this unity among different forces and tendencies contained within *Chavismo* also obstructed the movement's ideological clarification, because the (perceived) need to close ranks in the face of their adversaries hindered internal debate (Azzellini 2010; Ellner 2005). Moderate *Chavistas* attempted to hold back internal confrontation for fear that its exposure and exposure of government wrongdoing could be used politically against the movement (Ellner 2011). Further, because the extremely polarized *Chavista*-opposition dynamic rendered elections to be popularly interpreted as plebiscites on the regime (López Maya 2011), and elections were held most years

Chávez was president, the demand for unity and holding back internal confrontation was ever-present. This imperative to unify during election times to defend the revolution manifested itself in state and party leadership instructing social movements to delay their specific demands in order to campaign for the regime and/or not detract from the broader campaign. Such instruction fell in line with Chavez's strategy and directive of "carefully selecting targets rather than striking out on different fronts at the same time" (Ellner 2008, 158).[16]

This exigency to unify to defend the revolution, especially during election times, also constrained women's rights organizing within *Chavismo*. State and party leaders tended to view women's specific demands and organizing for gender rights as potentially divisive and vulnerable to appropriation by the opposition.[17] For example, during the 2012 presidential election campaign period, María León, former minister of women's popular power and gender equality and then National Assembly deputy, argued that *Chavista* women should prioritize Chávez's reelection and the revolution's epic and broader goals. She asserted that women's specific struggles for rights, such as abortion, should not be central to the campaign:

> We women believe as Chávez believes, that in this moment of history, the primary thing is independence, for us women, to be independent of the empire comes first. . . . Then for that historical discrimination to begin to be overcome, as is happening, the first is independence, the sovereignty of the homeland, and in that we are immersed, including ready to give our lives. . . .
>
> I'm not saying that women renounce their struggles; however, we can't place them as a central theme of politics. At least those of us women who are political, in this moment we have to dedicate ourselves to Chávez winning, and then there, my pains, my anguishes and my things are pending on him winning. (cited in León Torrealba 2012, 158–159)

León's words reflect a dominant *Chavista* state and party view that women's specific gender struggles (for bodily and economic independence) must be subordinated to the popular unification necessary for Venezuela's geopolitical independence and ongoing revolutionary transformation in the face of the revolution's adversaries. Further, León's discourse posited that women's specific gender demands both must be delayed for the revolution's benefit and hinged on Chávez and his maintenance of power; women must wait to make their demands and have faith that Chávez's victory would provide an opening for them to be heard.

Subordination of Struggles to Advance
Women's Rights Legislation under *Chavismo*

The Bolivarian state leadership's dominant approach of subordinating women's rights struggles to the revolution's broader goals in a politically polarized context, in addition to uncertainty around the role of liberal democracy, shaped the National Assembly's actions and inactions on women's and gender issues from 2000 to 2011. The National Assembly opened in 2000 with *Chavista* majority control. At its inception, the assembly created the Permanent Commission on Family, Woman, and Youth (Comisión Permanente de Familia, Mujer, y Juventud, CPFMJ), which, although it linked women to the family, provided women's rights activists with a stable institutional-legislative base through which they could draft and lobby for women's rights legislation. Yet, within the assembly, *Chavista* deputies viewed the CPFMJ and its work as insignificant. Former *Chavista* deputy Pérez Marcano (2000–2010) explains that other *Chavista* deputies referred to it as the "Siberia commission," because no one wanted to join it and it was where deputies were sent to work as a form of punishment for poor performance (Third Interview with Marelis Pérez Marcano). This devaluation among *Chavista* deputies of the CPFMJ was because of what Pérez Marcano describes as their "very restricted and limited and unfortunately in some cases even condescending conception of what a women's rights commission meant" (Third Interview with Marelis Pérez Marcano). General political will among *Chavista* National Assembly deputies to carry forward the mainstreaming of women's gender interests from the constituent process into legislation did not exist. Even as Chávez's progressively opened his discourse to feminism, the majority of *Chavista* deputies did not view the transformation of gender power relations as a priority of the revolution. Nor did the majority of opposition deputies view the transformation of gender power relations as a legislative priority. This left work on legislating and advancing women's rights within the assembly contingent on a very small number of legislators—both *Chavista* and opposition deputies (Rakowski and Espina 2010; Second Interview with Gioconda Espina).

Pérez Marcano recounts that opposition deputies did not view the CPFMJ and its work as having no strategic importance, yet their primary focus was youth and children's issues, not women's rights, or Article 88's legislation in particular (Third Interview with Marelis Pérez Marcano). In the first legislative term (2000 to 2005), Pérez Marcano therefore was situated as a president and later vice president of a commission populated by opposition deputies who did not share her primary legislative focus.

In the second legislative term (2006 to 2011) when *Chavistas* possessed complete control of the assembly, Gabriela Ramirez became CPFMJ president, and her legislative focus was also family and children (Second Interview with Gioconda Espina). Pérez Marcano became the president of the subcommission working on women's rights within the broader commission. Pérez Marcano returned to the commission's presidency in 2008, but she was not reelected in the 2010 legislative elections.

The CPFMJ's focus on family and children's issues and lack of attention to women's rights carried on into the third legislative term (2011–2016), wherein the opposition reentered the National Assembly and gained the CPFMJ presidency (Interview with Master's Student in Women's Studies). This emphasis on family and children translated into structural changes with the commission during this term; it was renamed "Permanent Commission on Family" and women's issues were dropped from its core legislative focus. This meant that, within the legislature, the structure for and thus the work of specifically promoting women's rights, gender equality, and affirmative action measures for women were subordinated.[18]

Women's Organizing outside the National Assembly for Rights and Power during Chávez's Tenure

Without the National Assembly's general political will to advance women's rights that would challenge gender power relations,[19] inside-out articulations between state feminists, such as Pérez Marcano, and activists outside the assembly combined with activist pressure on the assembly for women's rights would be have to be key. Yet ongoing political polarization also hampered women's conjunctural coalition-building to advance their rights under Bolivarianism, as broader struggles for or against the revolution tended to divide women's rights activists. During the first stage of the Chávez government, women's rights activists within and outside the state continued to work together across class and partisan lines, yet heightened political conflicts during the government's second stage obstructed them from uniting (Espina 2007). As Rakowski and Espina (2010) note, the increasing saliency of class divisions among women's rights activists and the "politicization of the national women's agency"—the dedication of its resources to partisan support of Chávez, the PSUV, and the revolution—rendered coalition-building across class and political divides for women's rights difficult (261).[20] Because of ongoing political polarization and regime radicalization, the participation of women who did not identify with Bolivarianism in state gender institutions' programs also tended to decrease.

After the defeat of the 2004 presidential recall referendum, women did come together across political divides as the "Broad Women's Movement."

Together they formulated an agenda for legislative action, which included the demand for the regulation and implementation of homemakers' social security (UNIFEM, MAM, and CEM [UCV] 2006), and which they submitted to the National Assembly in 2005 (García and Valdivieso 2009); drafted and successfully lobbied for the passage of the 2007 Organic Law of Women's Right to a Life Free from Violence (García and Valdivieso 2009); and drafted a penal code reform proposal (León Torrealba 2012).

Yet these initiatives were not the marks of a sustained coalition (they were often short-lived), and after the 2007 constitutional reform referendum defeat, women's rights cross-partisan organizing fell away (Rakowski and Espina 2010). Non-*Chavista* women's rights activists did not participate in the drafting and discussion of the Social Protection for Homemakers Bill introduced to the National Assembly in 2008 or the drafting of women's rights proposals in the organic labor law reform process from 2010 to 2012.[21] This meant that the knowledge and experience on advancing women's rights accumulated among activists who did not identify with *Chavismo* were no longer directly contributing to legislative and policy discussions.

The falling away of women's coalition-building across political divides for the advancement of their rights did not signify that women ceased to organize and lobby for their gender interests. Yet the focus of their organization generally was not the legislative advancement of their rights. During Chávez's tenure, popular women's social and political organizing and articulation with the state proliferated, as various new Bolivarian-aligned (semi)autonomous and state-led popular women's organizations emerged. And networks of women's rights activists and organizations not aligned with Bolivarianism, such as the Venezuelan Observatory of Women's Human Rights, continued organizing and using UN and international legal mechanisms and processes to legitimate their claims. In addition, new coalitions of women's organizations emerged within *Chavismo*, such as the Araña Feminista,[22] which formulated and submitted a number of women's rights proposals to the National Assembly and for which it lobbied the government. These new feminist organizations aligned with Bolivarianism employed new discursive tactics: rather than drawing on UN mechanisms to warrant and strengthen their claims, they tended to appropriate frameworks and concepts circulating and promoted in the revolution's broader discourse, such as socialism, sovereignty, and social justice in addition to the 1999 Constitution, and use them to legitimate their demands for women's rights. Yet, reflecting the broader context in which popular organizations allied with Bolivarianism proliferated and focused largely on local levels, the locus of organized popular women's contestation for the advancement of their gender interests was generally not the legislative sphere, but rather in gaining social and material power in their communities and within their mixed-gender organizations.[23] Homemakers' organizations aligned with Bolivarianism did emerge in regions throughout Venezuela during Chávez's tenure, but their articulation with the state did not include mass organizing to press for Article 88's legislation. The state gender institutions organized large numbers of popular-sector women through a broad range of community- and regionally based organizations,[24] which it mobilized for marches and public events primarily in broader support of the revolution and generally not to contest gender power relations (Espina 2009b; Friedman 2009).[25] Espina (2009b) also points out that both *Chavista* and opposition women organized and rallied in record numbers—but for or against the government, not for their specific gender interests and the advancement of their gender rights.

The deficit of sustained women's rights organizing and pressure, particularly around Article 88's legislation and implementation, was not merely a result of state–society relations under Bolivarianism and the ways in which the revolution and state gender institutions incorporated popular women. Along with the general barriers under Bolivarianism to advancing women's rights that would transform gender power relations, the struggle to advance Article 88 faced additional and historical barriers. Unpaid housework and homemakers had never been at the forefront of the women's rights agenda in Venezuela—under *Puntofijismo* or Bolivarianism. Nor had economic issues been central to the development of the Venezuelan women's movement and its organizing. Across these regimes historically, few women's rights activists occupied positions of power within state economic and financial institutions from which they could push for gender mainstreaming in economic policies. Nor had a gender perspective and recognition of women's unpaid labor been mainstreamed in these institutions' work (Interview with Adicea Castillo).[26] In addition, Article 88's inclusion in the 1999 Constitution did not result from a sustained struggle for recognition and redistribution led by homemakers (Interview with Red Todas Juntas Cofounder). Sustained movement and organization both in the state and society around recognizing unpaid housework that could propel Article 88's legislation forward under Bolivarianism therefore did not exist.

Initiatives to Legislate Article 88

Within this broader polarized, radicalizing, and constantly shifting political opportunity structure in which general will to advance women's rights legislation did not exist, a core group of women's rights activists began working to propose Article 88's legislation from the Bolivarian regime's out-set. Believing in Article 88's transformational promise and the new constitutional framework of gender mainstreaming, they came together during the Bolivarian regime's first phase (before heightened political polarization and conflict set in) to formulate a proposal for putting the article into concrete practice. As they emerged from the constituent process, broader political events provided an immediate context for them to carry forward developing Article 88.

Just prior to Chávez's assumption of power, President Caldera utilized enabling powers to decree a new social security law along neoliberal lines and according to IFI mandates. While campaigning for the presidency, Chávez denounced this social security system restructuring, and once in power he repealed measures contained within the Caldera law (Méndez 2006). In addition, the constituent process had reconfigured the constitutional framework for social security, enshrining it as a public, universal, integrated, unitary, participatory system covering all people, whether they could contribute monetarily or not, through solidarity financing (Art. 86 of the 1999 Constitution). The need to reform the social security system according to the new constitution therefore was urgent. Multiple sectors quickly responded by drafting bills for a new Organic Social Security System Law (Ley Orgánica del Sistema de Seguridad Social, LOSSS), which would set a new social security system framework for Venezuela.

This immediate legislative initiative provided a political opening for women's rights activists to demand legislation of homemakers' right to social security. Yet no women's rights activists were on the National Assembly commission charged with drafting the final LOSSS. And given the urgency for constructing a new social security framework and the fact that women's rights activists had no specific proposal for Article 88's implementation coming out of the constituent process, the time within which they had to formulate and lobby for such a proposal was short.

Within the National Assembly, Pérez Marcano spearheaded the initiative to include homemakers in the new LOSSS, insisting that it be of primary concern for the CPFMJ. As the commission's president, she convened state actors and institutions and women's rights activists to develop the proposal. Pérez Marcano also appointed Gioconda Espina, a longtime feminist and women's studies professor, as her advisor on Article 88. Deploying the conjunctural coalition strategy developed in the past, Espina invited a core group of women's rights activists inside and outside the state and across partisan divides, many of whom were involved in the constituent process, to assist in developing the legislative proposal.

This core group needed to quickly develop a proposition for who would be covered, what contingencies would be covered, and how they would be covered under Article 88's legislation. Some activists envisioned all women benefiting from this constitutional mandate, given the general disproportionate burden of unpaid housework on women (Interview with Adicea Castillo). However, the core group agreed upon a proposal to reduce the potential population of homemakers to be covered so as to protect homemakers most in need and thus make the proposal more financially feasible. They agreed that homemakers who carried out essential tasks for household maintenance and development and who were not already affiliated with any social security regime either directly or indirectly as dependents should be included. The granting of a retirement-age pension had always constituted the spirit behind women's rights activists' demand for homemakers' social security. Yet the core group did not reach consensus on the subsystems of social security in which homemakers should be included, because the social security system covered other contingencies through other subsystems, such as health, housing, and labor risks, alongside covering the contingency of old age through the pension subsystem. Even though the core group generated several ideas for financing Article 88's implementation, they did not reach consensus on how homemakers' social security should be financed.

The latter point proved to be the most determinate, because the pension system was funded by monetary contributions by employers and workers. Because homemakers had no employers, and poor homemakers—who were this legislative initiative's target group—did not have money to make social security contributions, the money to finance their social security would need to come from elsewhere. Yet this social security money for homemakers could not magically appear from converting minerals beneath the nation's soil into revenue: the 1999 Constitution stipulated that income from the extractive industries should finance production, health, and education (Art. 311). During the LOSSS drafting process, state leaders also indicated that they thought financing homemakers' social security would be too costly a burden on the state, and this judgment went up to President Chávez, who stated that homemakers would have to wait (Subcomisión de Derechos de la Mujer, Comisión Permanente Familia, Mujer y Juventud 2001). However, Pérez Marcano and the core group attempted to work with state economic and financial institutions on formulating viable means to finance poor homemakers' social security. Yet they were not able to devise a concrete, feasible financing proposal before the National Assembly passed the new LOSSS at the end of 2002. Nor did their efforts have a strong influence on the assembly and the president's Special Social Security Commission.

Rather, heightening political conflict strongly influenced the LOSSS's drafting and passage. Chávez pressured the National Assembly to review the various proposals and draft and pass the LOSSS as quickly as possible (Interview with Absalón Méndez). The bill was then redrafted and underwent limited public consultation before it was sent to the National Assembly plenary for discussion in December 2002, just as the employer lockout began (Méndez 2006). Taking advantage of opposition deputies' absence from the assembly because of their participation in the lockout, the *Chavista* deputies did not substantially debate the bill and quickly passed it into law (Interview with Absalón Méndez).

Some earlier LOSSS drafts did not specifically include homemakers, but the law that the National Assembly passed did. This inclusion was due not to women's movement and CPFMJ pressure on the assembly and the commission drafting the final LOSSS, but to articulations between Pérez Marcano, Espina, and Absalón Méndez (one of that commission's technical advisors). Méndez insisted on homemakers' inclusion in the LOSSS because Pérez Marcano and Espina had presented the core group's proposal as emanating from Article 88. Méndez, in turn, recognized that the law must obey the totality of constitutional mandates (Interview with Absalón Méndez; Second Interview with Gioconda Espina).

Yet homemakers were not included in this foundational law in the way in which Pérez Marcano and the core group had proposed, namely, as *workers* who were equal to workers who made monetary contributions to the social security system. Rather, LOSSS Article 17 grouped homemakers who lacked economic protection together with disabled peoples and indigenous peoples as "other categories of persons" who would be granted special protection in the development of social security subsystems and regimes that emanated from the LOSSS. Pérez Marcano interpreted homemakers' inclusion in this way as a "political defeat that the women's movement suffered" (Third Interview with Marelis Pérez Marcano). For her, such a categorization of homemakers denied Article 88's spirit, which recognized that through their work homemakers contributed indirectly to Venezuela's wealth and welfare. She notes that

> in that moment unfortunately it was not possible that the parliamentarians understand the revolutionary significance of that article. And clearly, since we had an enormous weakness in the commission—there was no gender vision, the members of the commission did not come from a tradition of struggle for women's rights—then it was very difficult to be able to defend that in the parliament in that phase. (Third Interview with Marelis Pérez Marcano)

Because of the National Assembly's general lack of political will to advance women's rights, the legislature included homemakers within this framework social security law only on terms that subordinated homemakers.

Yet Pérez Marcano and women's rights activists did not interpret this legislative "defeat" as the end to the struggle to legislate homemakers' social security. Rather, from the institutional foothold of the CPFMJ, they continued to work with state economic and financial institutions on a proposal to finance and implement homemakers' social security within the new LOSSS framework. However, their work was disarticulated from the Social Development Commission, which was simultaneously drafting bills to regulate the social security subsystems enumerated in the LOSSS (Interview with Absalón Méndez; Interview with Ana M. Salcedo González). The Social Development Commission appointed a technical advisory team to draft a noncontributory benefit regime for the elderly and "the other categories of persons" named in Article 17 of the LOSSS (Interview with Ana M. Salcedo González). Neither the CPFMJ nor women's rights organizations participated in this bill's development (Interview with Ana M. Salcedo González), yet homemakers were explicitly included within it as beneficiaries.

In 2005, the National Assembly passed the Law of Social Services (Ley de Servicios Sociales, LSS), which outlined the noncontributory social security regime. The LSS entitled all elderly people sixty years and older without contributory capacity to an economic benefit between 60 and 80 percent of the minimum-wage salary, in addition to homemakers of any age in "a state of need" (Arts. 32, 39, and 41). The LSS defined a "state of need" as a state of lack of economic, personal, familial, or social protection, which merited either temporary or permanent social security system protection (Art. 7). Although this legislative advancement did not entitle homemakers to a pension equivalent to the minimum wage to which workers who contributed monetarily to the social security system were entitled, it did provide a legislative framework for poor and elderly homemakers to receive state economic assistance.

Yet, for poor homemakers to receive this assistance, the LSS needed to be regulated and state social services needed to be restructured. For these reasons, the LSS explicitly stipulated that the Venezuelan Social Services Institute (Instituto Venezolano de Servicios Sociales, IVSS) present a plan to integrate the benefits and services enumerated in the LSS within six months of the law's enactment and that the integration of these benefits and services take place within two years of the plan's presentation (Title IX, chap. 1). Following the LSS's passage, the LSS drafters and the IVSS president held a forum on the law's regulation and invited women's rights activists and organizations to participate in the development of the law's regulations (Espina 2006a). Yet women's rights organizations did not submit a proposal for the law's regulation (Second Interview with Gioconda Espina), organizations and movements outside the state did not pressure the state to regulate the law (Interview with Absalón Méndez), and the state did not comply with the legislative mandates to develop and implement LSS regulations because the political will to do so did not exist (Interview with Ana M. Salcedo González). Thus, the law that could potentially enable the extension of social security to all poor homemakers throughout Venezuela was technically on the books but in reality dead on arrival.

Instead, in the 2006 presidential election year, during the time period in which the LSS was mandated to be regulated, Chávez decreed Madres del Barrio Mission. Enacted in parallel to the social security system outlined by social security law, Madres del Barrio was a discretionary social program, financed by the state oil company, targeting a narrower band of homemakers in a "state of need" (approximately 100,000 women) with an economic benefit between 60 and 80 percent of the minimum-wage salary.[27] Unlike with the National Assembly and its legislative process, Chávez made social assistance money for homemakers and elderly women suddenly and magically appear by converting minerals beneath the nation's soil into public revenue. In 2007, Chávez also exercised these magnanimous sorcerer powers when he issued two separate decrees establishing "exceptional and temporary programs" granting pensions to 150,000 elderly people in total, with the second decree granting pensions to 50,000 poor elderly women in particular, some of whom were homemakers.[28]

Once again, these executive developments did not signal the end to women's organizing for Article 88's legislation and implementation. Yet the next initiative came from outside the National Assembly, as feminist activists seized the political opportunity of the 2007 constitutional reform referendum process introduced by Chávez to organize and demand women's and LGBTTI rights in the referendum. Early in 2007, feminist and LGBTTI activists from both within and outside *Chavismo* formed an alliance in Caracas called Grupo Ese, which invoked its participatory democratic rights to engage in the constitutional reform process. Gioconda Espina, who had served as Pérez Marcano's Article 88 legislative advisor, was a member of Grupo Ese. She used the knowledge she had gained from that forestalled process to inform the group's demands for refining Article 88. As Espina explained, Article 88 did not explicitly guarantee homemakers a monthly pension, and this wording enabled state authorities to circumvent the spirit behind the article. Grupo Ese therefore proposed reforming the article's wording in order to make it enforceable (Second Interview with Gioconda Espina). The group proposed changing Article 88 specifically to contain the beneficiary eligibility requirements that women's rights activists had previously formulated (i.e., homemakers of retirement age who were not directly or indirectly affiliated with a pension regime were entitled to a pension no less than the minimum-wage salary). Grupo Ese also proposed the execution of LOSSS Article 17 and LSS Article 41, in addition to the implementation of homemakers' social security within ninety days of the constitutional reform's promulgation (Grupo Ese 2007).

Grupo Ese submitted its proposals to the National Woman's Institute (INaMujer) and the Constitutional Reform Commission (Espina 2009b). Chávez did not include any of Grupo Ese's proposals in his constitutional reform proposals. However, he did propose the creation of a contributory social stability fund for own-account workers, which would cover retirement, pensions, pre- and postnatal periods, and rest periods (Article 87, in Chávez Frías 2007). Homemakers could potentially be included in this fund if they could afford to contribute to it. Grupo Ese and María León, president of INaMujer, met with the Constitutional Reform Commission to discuss their proposal for Article 88's reform in addition to the rest of Grupo Ese's constitutional reform proposals (Second Interview with Gioconda Espina). Thereafter, the National Assembly did include several of their proposals in its thirty-six proposals for constitutional reform,[29] but not the proposal for Article 88's reform. Yet the electorate rejected both sets of constitutional reform proposals in the December 2007 national referendum. And Grupo Ese's organizing fell away afterward.

While feminist and LGBTTI activists were organizing for Article 88's reform in the 2007 constitutional reform process, Pérez Marcano continued meeting with state institution representatives to discuss mechanisms to legislate and implement Article 88. Inclusion of women's rights activists and organizations outside the state in those discussions was very limited (Interview with Alba Carosio), but women's studies professor Alba Carosio officially assisted Pérez Marcano in this process. These meetings carried on through 2008, and by the middle of the year the CPFMJ had drafted the Social Protection for Homemakers Bill.

This bill began to overcome deficiencies in past proposals for financing Article 88's implementation and got around the legal stumbling block of granting a pension equivalent to the minimum wage to retirement-age homemakers who did not have contributory capacity. It overcame these obstacles by proposing that homemakers who were to receive minimum-wage pensions would contribute 4 percent of their monthly state pensions to the pension fund until they fulfilled the number of necessary contributions (Comisión Permanente de Familia, Mujer, y Juventud de la Asamblea Nacional 2008). In this way homemakers could be defined as direct contributors to the social security system and be legally entitled to a pension equivalent to the minimum wage. The bill also aimed to legislate Madres del Barrio Mission by aligning it with the LSS framework and transforming it into a universal social assistance program for all working-age homemakers in a state of need.

The Social Protection for Homemakers Bill reached the National Assembly plenary floor in July 2008, where it underwent a first round of discussion[30] with deputies' unanimous support. Pérez Marcano addressed the assembly and introduced the bill, stating that it aimed to fulfill Article 88 and "settle a historic debt with Venezuelan women, with the homemakers of Venezuela" (Sección de Edición 2008, 3). She used both the constitutional framework and the framework of the Bolivarian revolution to justify the bill, arguing that it constituted part and parcel of constructing twenty-first-century socialism. Almost all the deputies who stood up in the plenary and spoke in support of the Social Protection for Homemakers Bill that day concurred in framing the bill as revolutionary. Invoking a magical revolutionary discourse, Cilia Flores, president of the National Assembly, spoke of the bill as part of a set of "revolutionary laws" for gender justice that the National Assembly had passed or was currently discussing (16). She stated to the assembly: "Women do not have a reason to complain because they are in the Constitution and now they are protected in the laws, as it should be, and with all the political will that the laws can be effectively developed and do not convert into dead letters" (16). The National Assembly then unanimously approved the bill in first discussion.

After this first-round approval of the Social Protection for Homemakers Bill, the CPFMJ held ongoing technical discussions to further develop it, but the commission struggled to refine it and move it forward through the legislature. In spite of the assembly's unanimous approval in the bill's first discussion, assembly deputies resisted the bill's development. Alba Carosio insists that this resistance in part stemmed from their gender bias, as they employed a "perverse form of utilizing the concept of equality," wherein instead of recognizing the bill as a positive discriminatory measure to achieve gender equity in social security, they argued that it discriminated against men (Interview with Alba Carosio). In the legislature's resistance to develop the bill, persistent gender bias intersected with the magical revolutionary state's nominalism of which Coronil writes: the boundaries between *representations* of gender justice and *real* gender justice were confused. Many of the assembly deputies whose public discourse hailed the bill as demonstrating the Bolivarian revolution's commitment to advancing women's gender interests did not support the bill's backstage development and passage into law. In addition, the Social Development Commission, which had previously been a stumbling block to Article 88's advancement, held more weight within the assembly, and was specifically charged with developing social security legislation, was against the bill (Interview with Alba Carosio). That commission argued that there was no need for the bill, since homemakers would be included in the pension law that it was going to draft (Third Interview with Marelis Pérez Marcano).

The CPFMJ also struggled with creating a feasible formula for financing the rest of homemakers' pensions beyond its proposal of homemakers' own contributions of 4 percent and state contributions of 10 percent. State financial institution representatives participating in actuarial assessments of funding proposals continued to argue that implementing homemakers' pensions would not be economically feasible. The National Assembly's Economic and Financial Research and Advice Office, for example, stated that the bill's approval would significantly affect inflation and GDP (Dirección de Investigación y Asesoría Económica y Financiera 2008, 2009). It estimated that the implementation of homemakers' pensions would be equivalent to 2.5 percent of the national budget—which was approximately one and a half times the total annual budget for the state ministry charged with all social protection (Dirección de Investigación y Asesoría Económica y Financiera 2008, 2009). However, Carosio contends that such resistance from state financial authorities and the calculations they gave as justification for not passing the bill into law were informed by their gender bias and not necessarily from reliable statistics (Interview with Alba Carosio). Yet, Pérez Marcano admits that "unfortunately" the National Assembly women deputies pushing the bill allowed themselves to be "co-opted" by such assessments (Third Interview with Marelis Pérez Marcano).

Pérez Marcano also admits that the failure to develop and push for the passage of the bill was due to the women's movement not coming together around it (Third Interview with Marelis Pérez Marcano). At the same time, no conjunctural coalition around the Social Protection for Homemakers Bill existed: women's rights activists beyond a limited number of state gender institution authorities did not participate in discussing or drafting the bill, nor was the bill that the assembly approved in first discussion disseminated broadly to the women's movement outside the state. Between the scarce knowledge and support from popular women constituents and the resistance from National Assembly deputies and state economic authorities, little pressure both within and outside the state existed to overcome the gender bias and funding barriers and to propel the bill's development and passage.

Once Pérez Marcano lost her seat in the 2010 National Assembly elections, work within the assembly to push forward the Social Protection for Homemakers Bill petered out. The bill became a set of dead letters, which ironically Flores had forewarned. Homemakers by and large remained unprotected by the social security system. Yet, once again, the national executive acted magically, swiftly appearing with an abundance of oil money that the National Assembly could not access to take up forestalled social security expansion. At the end of 2011, less than a year before the 2012 presidential election, Chávez announced that he was creating a new mission, a "great mission"—Great Mission in Elderly Love (Gran Misión en Amor Mayor)—to establish a special minimum-wage pension regime not just for excluded homemakers but for all elderly adults living in households with incomes less than the minimum-wage salary. And suddenly, with the president's 2011 decree, the state that for years had insisted it could not fund and sustain poor homemakers' pensions appeared to have funds to include all the nation's elderly poor in its social security system.[31]

Conclusion

Legislative contestation after the National Constituent Assembly over the gendered distribution of power illustrates that although the 1999 constituent process and 1999 Constitution laid the foundations for homemakers' entitlement to social security, these foundations were not strong enough for women's rights activists to rely on to impel state enforcement of this constitutional mandate. The political opportunity structures of the ANC and the Bolivarian regime during Chávez's tenure were both characterized by rapid changes. Yet the ANC represented a political opening for women's rights advancements, but the post-ANC period of regime contestation and consolidation largely represented a political sidelining of the legislative advancement and enforcement of women's rights. Unlike the transversalization of gender in the 1999 Constitution, a fundamental commitment to gender mainstreaming and gender equality promotion did not transverse state policies and state and party actions under Bolivarianism. The Bolivarian government created new women's and gender institutions, formed new organizational articulations with popular-sector women, and incorporated a discourse of feminism as central to twenty-first-century socialism, yet the state more broadly did not undergo deep and thorough institutional changes in terms of its commitment to mainstream, advance, and enforce women's gender interests. Popular women lacked equal descriptive representation in governance, and they especially lacked substantive legislative representation to champion and forward their gender rights. Moreover, unlike the ANC process, when women were able to take advantage of the unique political moment to unite across partisan and class divides to further their gender interests, broader political polarization and conflict under Bolivarianism tended to hamper women's rights conjunctural coalition-building—the saliency of partisan and class differences generally rendered their gender solidarity insufficient to unite them. This larger political context often turned the focus of women's organizing and coalition-building from their specific gender interests toward actions for or against the revolution and/or the government. No mass movement existed to compel the state to legislate and implement Article 88. Pressure from within and outside the state for women's rights enforcement, and Article 88's enforcement in particular, was not sustained. Thus, during Chávez's presidency, popular-sector homemakers in Venezuela had the constitutional right to social security but largely without legal mechanisms and institutions to enable them to enjoy their newly won right.

Moreover, state recognition of homemakers' right to social security was profoundly shaped by executive centralization of power under *Chavismo*. When the state did channel social assistance to popular homemakers, it did so outside the legislative arena—where legislation partially recognizing Article 88 had been passed and women's rights activists had been developing a fuller proposal for Article 88's implementation—and through executive action. On several occasions, Chávez acted suddenly and magically with the state's oil money to expand social protection for popular women through the missions and executive decrees. The Bolivarian state, under Chávez's charge, recognized popular homemakers (though not all of them), but they and the women's rights activists supporting their interests did not control the terms of this recognition and redistribution.

State Imaginations of Popular Motherhood within the Revolution: The Institutional Design of Madres del Barrio Mission

The legislative initiatives aimed at implementing homemakers' constitutional right to social security that did not bear fruit did not signify a vacuum of state action around Article 88 during Hugo Chávez's presidency. Rather, the Bolivarian government's executive branch acted in parallel to the national legislature and the extant welfare state apparatus when it invoked Article 88 in a new social policy targeting extremely poor homemakers throughout Venezuela. In 2006, Chávez decreed Madres del Barrio Mission—a discretionary conditional cash transfer (CCT) program claiming to recognize the value of popular homemakers' unpaid housework.

Analyzing Madres del Barrio Mission's relation to Article 88, this chapter locates this mission's design within the Bolivarian government's development of the missions as a parallel welfare state apparatus integral to the revolution's radicalization during Chávez's presidency. Through this new mission, the government drew on preexisting maternal gender roles and gendered divisions of labor and resignified them to advance its goals for constructing a new social contract between the Venezuelan state and society. The institutional design of Madres del Barrio Mission shows how the Bolivarian government, under Chávez, *imagined* the role of popular-sector motherhood and women's unpaid labor within the revolution.[1]

Similar to other CCT programs—state programs transferring cash to poor citizens in exchange for their performance of certain duties—in Latin America, Madres del Barrio Mission constitutes what Maxine Molyneux (2006, 2008a) terms a maternalist program. Like other CCTs in the region, this mission incorporated women as mothers and reinforced their role as caregivers and the gendered division of labor. Drawing from Molyneux's conception that CCTs resignify motherhood through the conditionalities they impose on women beneficiaries, I argue that Madres del Barrio also resignified popular motherhood according to state goals for the Bolivarian revolution. The gendered assumptions underpinning Madres del Barrio's conditionalities intersected with state notions of popular power in the revolution. In addition to expecting them to carry out their housework, the mission framed the *madres* as revolutionary subjects—"protagonists"—who were expected to articulate popular power through the fulfillment of community, political, and productive coresponsibilities. These conditionalities that Madres del Barrio set for poor women produced a notion of revolutionary maternalism to which they were expected to conform in exchange for their cash transfer.

At the same time, the mission's design was not clearly related to Article 88, and this uncertain relationship can be traced to the mission's nontransparent structure. The mission's lack of transparency indicates its development of top-down state–society relations, which call into question the potential for the Bolivarian state's promotion of popular women's power through Madres del Barrio.

Gendered Assumptions Underpinning CCTs in Latin America

At the end of the twentieth century, as Venezuela experienced multiple crises associated with neoliberalism, poverty rates remained high and socioeconomic inequalities widened throughout Latin America more broadly. In response to such failures associated with neoliberalism, many states in the region, with the assistance of IFIs, began designing and implementing CCTs targeting poor people in the late 1990s and 2000s. In exchange for money, CCTs require recipients to perform certain duties or "coresponsibilities," such as ensuring their children's schooling, nutrition, and medical visits and performing community work. Aiming to "reconfigure state–society relations" (Molyneux 2008b, 793) while not abandoning neoliberal market fundamentalism, CCTs were formulated to alleviate the social and institutional barriers that were believed to have been keeping people in poverty and out of participating in markets (Taylor 2009). Addressing the fallout generated by neoliberal state retreat from social reproduction, these new social programs have brought states back into social protection of the poor. Yet they have done so in ways that sought to overcome Latin American welfare state "assistentialism"[2] associated with the post–World War II era, which had been identified as inculcating a culture of dependency and passivity among the poor (Molyneux 2006, 2008b). Premised on notions of "participation," "active citizenship," "empowerment," and "coresponsibility" between the state and citizens,[3] CCTs target the poor and expect them to share responsibility with the state for managing socioeconomic risks (Bradshaw and Quirós Víquez 2008; Molyneux 2006, 2008a, 2008b). These social programs specifically target families and households, positing the family/ household unit as the locus of the agency necessary to overcome poverty (Barrientos, Gideon, and Molyneux 2008). CCTs frame their conditionalities, or "coresponsibilities" between the state and families, as investments in human development, especially in poor children, which would help the poor to develop lifelong capacities to participate in markets, take care of themselves, and escape poverty (Barrientos, Gideon, and Molyneux 2008; Escobar Latapí and González de la Rocha 2009; Luccisano and Wall 2009; Mahon and Macdonald 2009; Molyneux 2006, 2008b; Razavi 2009; Tabbush 2009). Analysts have found that CCTs in Latin America have constituted more inclusive social protection measures than during neoliberalism's peak: they have mitigated poverty by granting certain vulnerable groups minimal social rights to basic welfare (Escobar Latapí and González de la Rocha 2009; Luccisano and Wall 2009; Molyneux 2006; Razavi 2009; Tabbush 2009).

At the same time, Latin American CCTs' "emphasis on strengthening and 'responsibilizing' the family has gone along with a largely unacknowledged dependency on women for the fulfillment of programme goals" (Molyneux 2008b, 793). For example, studies of CCTs in Mexico (Bradshaw 2008; Escobar Latapí and González de la Rocha 2009; Luccisano and Wall 2009; Molyneux 2006, 2008a),[4] Argentina (Tabbush 2009),[5] and Nicaragua (Bradshaw 2008; Bradshaw and Quirós Víquez, 2008)[6] have shed light on these programs' underlying gendered assumptions and the gendered implications of their targeting mechanisms and conditionalities. These countries' CCTs were designed to target mothers in particular, as the cash transfers that mothers have received have been in exchange for fulfilling their reproductive functions and thus support them in their reproductive role (Molyneux 2008a). These CCTs have not targeted fathers for sharing responsibility in meeting household reproduction needs (Bradshaw and Quirós Víquez 2008; Luccisano and Wall 2009; Molyneux 2006). Such gender-specific targeting of women to fulfill family needs is based on notions of gender differences in how resources are allocated and used within households (Bradshaw 2008). Women are understood to be the family members who make choices that can improve the whole household's welfare rather than merely their own. These CCTs have therefore positioned mothers as "policy conduits, . . . in the sense that resources channeled through them are expected to translate into greater improvements in the well-being of children and the family as a whole," and the benefits that mothers derive from the programs "are a by-product of servicing the needs of others" (Molyneux 2006, 59–60). Sarah Bradshaw (2008) and Constanza Tabbush (2009) note that in positioning beneficiary mothers as policy conduits, CCTs have been underpinned by an "ideology of maternal altruism." Such ideology informing CCTs has promoted a "model of the 'empowered' woman based on her alleged altruism and commitment to family welfare" and willingness to conduct unpaid family and community labor (Tabbush 2009, 311). Similarly, Molyneux (2008a) concludes that such CCTs are maternalist programs, which have served to resignify motherhood, in that their coresponsibilities are normative devices that have promoted specific notions of motherhood to which states have expected women beneficiaries to conform. These gender analyses of CCTs in Mexico, Argentina, and Nicaragua have concluded that in actually targeting female heads of households, these programs have tended to reify traditional gender roles by reinforcing maternal modes of care and gender-differentiated social reproduction relations and modes of social protection. Instead of promoting gender equity in social reproduction, these CCTs have increased poor women's reproductive burdens. These programs have both relied on and tended to exacerbate gender differences and women's primary responsibility for family welfare. Although these CCTs have assisted in meeting the needs of poor women's dependents, they have not transformed the structural determinants of these women's vulnerability in relation to the market and the family.

At the same time as many Latin American states instituted CCTs, the Bolivarian government developed new social missions, which it claimed advanced the revolution through promoting the popular sectors' active "participation" in "coresponsibility" with the state. Important aspects of the Bolivarian government's social policy rhetoric therefore resembled the discourse of IFI-supported social policies in contemporary Latin America (Meltzer 2009). However, unlike CCTs claiming to enhance the poor's capacities to participate in markets, the Bolivarian government framed the missions as central to Venezuela's departure from neoliberalism, because they emphasized redistribution (of state oil revenue), a solidarity economy, and free public services (103). Yet, as with other Latin American CCTs, the Bolivarian government-instituted Madres del Barrio Mission specifically targeted poor women through their reproductive roles. Madres del Barrio therefore provides an important case study to analyze if the Bolivarian state, in its pursuit of post-neoliberalism, actually constructed a social policy alternative that was not predicated on inequitable gender power relations and the exploitation of the labor of poor mothers positioned within them.

The Development of the Missions within
the Bolivarian Revolution's Radicalization

From 1999 to 2003, the Bolivarian government made little headway in addressing the social policy shortfalls that it inherited from the *Puntofijista* regime,[7] because its social policy initiatives remained targeted measures and failed to reach the majority of the popular sectors.[8] Indeed, during the Bolivarian regime's first years, persistent social policy shortfalls perpetuated the social exclusion of large swathes of the popular sectors. For example, in 2003, 70 percent of people in Venezuela could not access health services, the majority of adolescents dropped out of the education system, close to 60 percent of households lacked adequate housing, and around 80 percent of people did not have social security for old age (D'Elia and Cabezas 2008, 1).

However, social policy did not dominate the Bolivarian government's political agenda during its first years. Rather, as chapter 2 details, intense and increasing political polarization and conflict, which in turn unleashed an economic crisis, marked the Bolivarian regime's first years. Following the failed April 2002 coup and the 2002–2003 employer lockout, the opposition moved to revoke President Chávez's mandate through a recall referendum that took place in 2004.

Responding to this conjuncture of mass social exclusion, an economic crisis, and an opposition intent on unseating him from power and rendering the country ungovernable in the process, Chávez announced the creation of the missions in 2003. The missions were a set of programs intended to augment already existing Bolivarian social policy initiatives and rapidly address welfare needs among the popular sectors. The missions began as emergency social policies, designed "to demonstrate the capacity of the revolution to reduce social exclusion" (D'Elia and Cabezas 2008, 4). In order to roll out the missions quickly and avoid resistance from the extant state bureaucracy, the government bypassed the existing state institutions charged with administering social policy.[9] Small presidential commissions quickly designed the missions and the executive financed them through extrabudgetary funds taken from state oil company (PDVSA) revenue. The government turned to the military, Cuban officials and workers, PDVSA workers, some state and municipal workers, and Bolivarian-aligned community organizations and volunteers to roll out the missions in popular-sector neighborhoods (D'Elia and Cabezas 2008). From 2003 to 2004, the government created and rolled out thirteen missions across the country to address welfare deficits. (See table 3.1 for an outline of these missions). These initiatives

Table 3.1. Development of the Bolivarian missions, 2003–2004

Name of mission	Date of creation	Focus of mission
Barrio Adentro	April 2003	Health
Robinson I	July 2003	Literacy
Sucre	July 2003	University education
Robinson II	October 2003	Primary education up to sixth grade
Miranda	October 2003	Organization of reserve military bodies
Ribas	November 2003	Secondary education
Mercal	January 2004	Access to basic food security
Milagro	January 2004	Correction of degenerative eye conditions
Identidad	February 2004	Official identity documentation
Vuelvan Caras	March 2004	Cooperatives and nuclei of endogenous development
Habitat	August 2004	Access to land and housing and home improvements
Guaicaipuro	October 2004	Food security and health, education, and housing services for indigenous communities
Piar	October 2004	Support to small-scale mineworkers

Sources: Adapted from D'Elia (2006, 207) and D'Elia and Cabezas (2008, 8).

resulted in the Bolivarian government quickly reaching and assisting many of the poorest members of Venezuelan society and meeting their basic welfare needs[10] in novel ways that invoked and depended on community organization and participation.

With Chávez's legitimacy reasserted by the electorate when he defeated the opposition in the 2004 recall referendum, he began to radicalize the Bolivarian state project. After this victory, Chávez stated that "the objective of this new phase [postreferendum] is to guarantee the definitive transformation of the inherited political and social structures and the economic and cultural model that sustained them, through the radicalization of revolutionary policies and especially the social missions" (Chávez Frías 2004). He moved to consolidate the missions as an institutional apparatus integral to the revolutionary state's transformation. In this framework, the missions would privilege social equality and popular participation in public policy and, in turn, reconfigure state–society relations. From 2004 to 2006, the government's objectives with the missions were the debureaucratization of state–society relations; the armed forces' incorporation in public programs; the social, political, and economic organization of communities according to the collective values of solidarity and revolution; and state control and management of oil revenue (D'Elia and Cabezas 2008, 5). This new social policy framework marked a further turn by the Bolivarian government away from reforming the welfare state apparatus inherited from *Puntofijismo*. The government aimed for this alternative, or parallel, welfare state apparatus to be broadened and strengthened; to implement social policy targeted specifically at the popular sectors; and to support, defend, and advance the revolutionary Bolivarian project.[11]

Although the missions began as emergency social policy measures, in their consolidation after the recall referendum, they did not transition out of an administrative logic of emergency. That is to say, they remained designed and managed by presidential commissions in an ad hoc fashion, financed by extrabudgetary funds from PDVSA revenue, and not subject to legislative approval and oversight.[12] This administrative structure enabled the missions to operate magically: through Chávez's masterful and decisive leadership, they could suddenly arise to address suspended claims for social inclusion and expand rapidly throughout Venezuela by almost instantaneously converting the country's oil wealth into massive goods and services for the popular sectors. Yet in maintaining the missions as discretionary social policy, this administrative structure meant that, just as they could magically appear on the national stage, they could easily and quickly disappear from it according to fluctuations in oil revenues and political whims (Wilpert 2007). Entrenching the missions as discretionary social policy in turn perpetuated the preexisting disarticulation between social policy and social rights, as citizens did not necessarily have rights to recourse if the missions did not reach them and/or fulfill their stipulated responsibilities (D'Elia and Cabezas 2008; Wilpert 2007). Furthermore, in continuing to operate as discretionary social policy subject to an administrative logic of emergency, the missions did not dismantle the extant welfare state apparatus that was enshrined in law and subject to legislative oversight. Rather, they developed parallel to it as "an integrated system in itself to attend to the . . . needs of the excluded sectors and consolidate within it the values and symbols of the revolution" (D'Elia and Cabezas 2008, 15).

State Imaginations of Popular Motherhood and Unpaid Labor within the Revolution: The Development and Institutional Design of Madres del Barrio Mission

Against this backdrop of developing a parallel welfare state apparatus to advance the Bolivarian revolution, Chávez announced the establishment of Madres del Barrio Mission during the 2006 presidential election year, in time for Venezuela's International Women's Day (IWD) celebration. Chávez (24 March 2006) decreed Madres del Barrio as a new mission that would specifically target homemakers "in a state of need" with a temporary or permanent economic benefit of 60 to 80 percent of the minimum-wage salary in order to "overcome poverty [and] exclusion and elevate their quality of life." Chávez issued this decree little more than six months after the National Assembly signed the Law of Social Services (LSS) into effect and just after the period in which the Venezuelan Social Services Institute was mandated to draft a plan to roll out this new law. The 2005 LSS stipulated that homemakers "in a state of need" would receive an economic benefit between 60 and 80 percent of the minimum-wage salary. Even though Chávez's presidential decree used the same wording in stipulating its target population and the economic benefit, it did not cite this law. However, the decree stated that Madres del Barrio was "in concordance" with Article 88 of the Constitution and "in accordance with" Article 17 of the Organic Social Security System Law (LOSSS) (Chávez Frías, 24 March 2006), which stipulated that specific social security benefit regime laws would establish the conditions under which "special protection" to homemakers who "lack personal, family or social economic protection" would be granted (Asamblea Nacional de la República Bolivariana de Venezuela 2005). The enactment of Madres del Barrio carried on with the framework set by previous missions in duplicating social policy through developing parallel welfare state institutions, which the 2005 LSS had explicitly prohibited (Asamblea Nacional de la República Bolivariana de Venezuela 2005).[13]

As with the development of previous missions, Chávez appointed a small presidential commission to design Madres del Barrio, which it devised within a few months. None of the five officials he appointed to this commission came directly from women's movement organizations and none had been directly involved in post-ANC organizing around legislating homemakers' social security. Rather, according to Gioconda Mota, who served on this presidential commission and then became Madres del Barrio's first president, the idea for the mission came from María Cristina Iglesias, the labor minister. Mota said that Iglesias saw a pressing deficit in homemakers' social security coverage and proposed that the mission would take an integrated and progressive approach of targeting extremely poor women "while more structural measures with relation to the issue of social security coverage were taken." Further, Mota stated that the commission designing Madres del Barrio viewed social security as a historical debt owed to homemakers, while noting that no legislation existed that implemented homemakers' right to social security as enshrined in the 1999 Constitution. The commission therefore conceptualized Madres del Barrio as a measure to begin putting Article 88 into effect (First Interview with Gioconda Mota).[14]

Yet, unlike the group of activists organizing to legislate and implement Article 88 by targeting retirement-age homemakers for a pension, the presidential commission designing Madres del Barrio decided to target with social assistance primarily extremely poor homemakers who were not yet of retirement age. To be eligible for the mission, a woman did not have to be of retirement age, but had to be a homemaker with "ascendant and/or descendent persons under their dependency" whose "family income was less than the cost of the food basket" (Chávez Frías, 24 March 2006). The economic benefit of 60 to 80 percent of the minimum-wage salary that beneficiaries would receive would be the same for all recipients, regardless of how many people were under their care. Madres del Barrio targeted only women as potential beneficiaries, and the decree enacting the mission made no mention of men. Mota stated that this targeting design intended to provide "an initial economic support that would level the life conditions of the family and at the same time develop some work with a humanistic, organizational and even socio-productive character that would allow the women to enter the work world in an individual and collective way" (First Interview with Gioconda Mota).

As with other conditional cash transfer programs in Latin America, the design of Madres del Barrio contained the coresponsibilities that mothers use their cash transfers to care for their families and ensure their children's schooling and nutrition.[15] Yet Madres del Barrio went further than other CCTs in the region by setting additional duties for mothers to fulfill, which included receiving occupational training to assist them in overcoming poverty. The mission's designers intended that the economic benefit would be temporary for working-age homemakers: the mission was meant to prepare its beneficiaries for productive occupations. This preparation would include state provision of microcredit for their productive activities once they completed their training. The executive envisioned that such support would in turn enable the *madres* to become independent of social assistance and "overcome their situation of extreme poverty" (Chávez Frías, 24 March 2006). The mission's design of occupational training and microcredit for the *madres* therefore fit into the general contemporary Latin American social policy paradigm of enhancing poor people's capacities to take care of themselves.

The presidential decree establishing Madres del Barrio did not stipulate a specific time limit for working-age homemakers' receipt of the cash transfer. Rather, the decree noted that the duration of the economic benefit would be determined by the particular conditions of each homemaker and her family. Neither the presidential decrees governing Madres del Barrio nor the official mission documents I accessed stipulated who in the mission would be responsible for making this determination and how they would make it. Rather, Mota informed me that the mission designers envisioned that "after a period of time, when the woman had sufficient levels of empowerment in all viewpoints—economic, social, humanitarian—she could hand over that benefit to another mother who in some way was at the point in which she started" (First Interview with Gioconda Mota).

The training and microcredit that the *madres* would receive to enable their independence were designed to fit into the larger state socioeconomic goals for the Bolivarian revolution. The *madres* would choose their "socio-productive" occupations. Yet their occupations would have not only to serve the individual *madres*' needs to overcome poverty but also to meet their communities' needs—the executive decree stipulated that they must fit into "their communities' endogenous development" (Chávez Frías, 24 March 2006). The concepts of "socio-productive inclusion" and "endogenous development" employed in the establishment and parameters of Madres del Barrio Mission were broader strategies employed by the Bolivarian state to achieve national sovereignty and construct socialism. The *madres*' socio-productive occupations were conceptualized as part of a larger process of "generating cultural dynamics that can overcome the logic of capitalist domination" and forming a "new social structure and the consolidation of a new economic model, that is driven by the National Bolivarian Government" (Misión Madres del Barrio "Josefa Joaquina Sánchez" 2007, 56).

In envisioning the *madres*' productive work as fitting into the broader national revolutionary project of supplanting capitalism and its organizing logics, the mission expected the *madres*' productive activities both to meet social needs and be collectively organized. Mission guidelines stipulated that the *madres*' socio-productive projects should be developed and carried out collectively, and the mission would grant loans[16] only to "economic associative units"[17] and cooperatives to finance their projects (Misión Madres del Barrio "Josefa Joaquina Sánchez" 2007, 1–2). Further, the mission would finance socio-productive projects only in productive areas that fit into the National Plans (Misión Madres del Barrio "Josefa Joaquina Sánchez" 2007) and that created production chains or added value to production chains (Misión Madres del Barrio "Josefa Joaquina Sánchez," n.d.).[18] The mission itself, or through referrals to other state institutions, would provide *madres'* collective enterprises with "socio-political and motivational" education, productive skills training, and technical advice so that they could successfully undertake their socio-productive projects (Misión Madres del Barrio "Josefa Joaquina Sánchez," n.d.).

Madres del Barrio Mission's design extended beyond occupational training and microcredit to multiple mechanisms for social inclusion. The mission's designers employed a multidimensional conceptualization of poverty as a social, "structural," and "spiritual" "problem" in addition to an "economic problem" (Misión Madres del Barrio "Josefa Joaquina Sánchez" 2007a), which affected not only women as individuals but also their family members. Since they viewed social exclusion as a crucial aspect of poverty, the mission designers envisioned a range of integrated public interventions to socially include beneficiaries and their families. The presidential decree enacting Madres del Barrio stated that homemakers and their families would receive state "support" in "health, food, education and training, culture, recreation and housing" (Chávez Frías, 24 March 2006).

The Madres del Barrio designers also viewed poor homemakers' lack of social and political participation as part of the structural problem of poverty that they faced. The mission guidelines stated that extremely poor homemakers would overcome poverty and exclusion only through their participation in the design, execution, and evaluation of activities carried out for their benefit (Misión Madres del Barrio "Josefa Joaquina Sánchez" 2007b). Through their participation in productive and community activities, in "co-responsible articulation" with the state, popular-sector homemakers would be empowered to take charge of their own welfare, overcome poverty, and "break with assistentialist" modes of welfare delivery (Misión Madres del Barrio "Josefa Joaquina Sánchez" 2007a). The presidential decree enacting Madres del Barrio stipulated that state support of *madres* and their families would be "carried out in co-responsibility between public institutions and the organized community" and the *madres* should "assume the commitment . . . to participate with their families in organizing processes of the communities to which they belong" (Chávez Frías, 24 March 2006).

Similar to other CCTs in Latin America premised on notions of active citizenship, participation, and coresponsibility, Madres del Barrio framed popular women's participation in coresponsibility with the state as integral to achieving the mission's goals. The notion of coresponsibility developed by the mission's designers included not just an articulation between individual women citizens, their families, and the state, as in other Latin American CCTs. Guided by an understanding of collective participation as pivotal to constructing twenty-first-century socialism, the Bolivarian government envisioned the *madres'* coresponsibilities as also including articulations between them and community-based organizations. The formation of local popular-power organizations and their action in coresponsibility with the state were central to the government's vision for reconfiguring state–society relations. According to mission's design, the *madres* would support the state and popular-power organizations (in addition to supporting their own families), the state and popular-power organizations would support them, and popular-power organizations would mediate between the *madres* and the state.

The Madres del Barrio designers framed popular power, in articulation with the state, as the "principal" means by which poor homemakers would come to be included in the mission. According to the mission guidelines, "the different politically organized forms of the communities"[19] would select "the mothers and families in the greatest condition of poverty and vulnerability" for inclusion in the mission (Misión Madres del Barrio "Josefa Joaquina Sánchez" 2007, 6). State surveyors would then assess these mothers in their homes to determine their and their family members' "socioeconomic profiles" and needs (Misión Madres del Barrio "Josefa Joaquina Sánchez" 2007a). Their data would be reviewed and verified by state institutions, and ultimately sent back to their communities, where "citizen assemblies" would have the final power to decide if they were really in a state of need and should be included in the mission (Misión Madres del Barrio "Josefa Joaquina Sánchez" 2007).

Under the mission design, Madres del Barrio committees, composed of ten to fifty homemakers (Chávez Frías 2006), would be the vehicle to articulate the *madres'* popular community organization and participation. The presidential decree stated that these committees "should contribute to" the following communal coresponsibilities:

1. Strengthening ties in the *barrio*, providing affect and help to the poorest mothers and families.
2. Looking after the care of children, youth, and elderly of their community.
3. Guaranteeing the schooling and contributing to better school performance of the children and youth of their community.

4. Watching over the smooth functioning of the feeding houses, school cafeterias, Mercal establishments, and ensuring that no member of the community experiences hunger.
5. Looking after health in the *barrio* and the health conditions of the community, paying special attention to the children, youth, and elderly.
6. Participating in the communal councils and articulating with the social services network.
7. Administering public resources for the attention to social security needs of the community.
(Chávez Frías 2006)

These decreed guidelines for the Madres del Barrio committees' work drew on gendered assumptions of poor women's maternal altruism, as did other Latin American CCTs. Further, they indicate that homemakers were expected to extend their reproductive role from their individual households to their communities by attending to vulnerable community members' welfare needs. In essence then, though the mission termed them "community promoters," the mission beneficiaries were expected to become the *mothers* of their *barrios* through their community organization and participation.[20] The *madres'* extended reproductive labor was also expected to include supporting the state's welfare services in their communities through monitoring, channeling, and administration of state resources. Later mission guidelines stipulated that the Madres del Barrio committees' spokeswomen should assume the additional task of socially and politically integrating other women from their communities who had been previously excluded; the committees were to serve as sites of popular women's incorporation into the Bolivarian revolution (Misión Madres del Barrio "Josefa Joaquina Sánchez" 2007b). The mission's designers imagined that the *madres'* reproductive labor and community-based organization would buttress the Bolivarian state and revolution.

Madres del Barrio Mission's coresponsibilities for *madres* to receive occupational training, engage in collective socio-productive activities, and organize socially and politically in their communities were framed as serving the government's broader geopolitical and economic goals of national sovereignty, socialism, and popular participation for the Bolivarian revolution. The mission posited the *madres* as policy conduits not just for their families and children but also for their communities and the revolution. As mothers of their *barrios*, the resources channeled to them were expected to translate into social, economic, and political improvements for their communities and the national revolution in addition to their individual families. The mission expected the *madres* to perform triple shifts of housework, productive work, and social and political community work in order to fulfill these coresponsibilities.

The Uncertain Relation of Madres del Barrio to Article 88

Madres del Barrio Mission's design targeted poor working-age homemakers, yet it did not exclude homemakers of retirement age. Rather, the mission's designers intended, as Gioconda Mota notes, for elderly homemakers to enter the mission, and from there eventually "trampoline" to a permanent pension equivalent to the minimum-wage salary, once the social security system underwent structural reforms and was broadened. According to Mota, the designers also conceived that working-age homemakers under "very adverse conditions," such as having prohibitive disabilities or heavy care burdens of family members with disabilities, would receive the mission benefit and eventually transition into permanent social security. Further, Mota stated that the presidential commission used the 2005 Law of Social Services as the juridical basis for Madres del Barrio Mission's allocation of an economic benefit to poor homemakers (First Interview with Gioconda Mota), even though the presidential decree enacting the mission did not state that it was in accordance with that law.[21]

Women's rights activists were divided over whether Madres del Barrio partially fulfilled Article 88, even though the presidential decree establishing the mission drew on Article 88 to legitimate it. The actors who designed Madres del Barrio were not the actors who had been organizing for Article 88's enforcement, and the Madres del Barrio proposal and design did not directly emerge from women's movement proposals for Article 88's legislation. Nor were forces outside the state pushing the state to create a mission as a vehicle to put Article 88 into effect. In addition, the subjects targeted by Madres del Barrio were largely different from those who were the intended social security beneficiaries in the Article 88 legislative initiatives. Both the means by which the mission was created and the mission's structural design contributed to a lack of consensus among women's rights activists on Madres del Barrio's relation to Article 88.

Gioconda Espina, who served as an advisor to the National Assembly on Article 88, contended that this uncertainty was a result of the vagueness of the article's drafting, because Article 88 does not state that homemakers of retirement age will receive a pension but rather that "homemakers have the right to social security in accordance with the law." This wording leaves homemakers' social security and its fulfillment open to a range of interpretations. Even though Chávez and the presidential commission did not base Madres del Barrio's design on the work that the women's movement had already done on conceptualizing Article 88's implementation, according to Espina, "one cannot say that Chávez lied. Chávez referred to the letter of the article, but not what we had been working on since 1999 as the 'spirit' behind the letter. He chose the interpretation of Article 88 that was most convenient to him." For Espina, who was not *Chavista*, this convenience was political, and she saw the mission as a clientelist vehicle for Chávez to strengthen his grassroots political support among young popular-sector women and their children—his electoral base (Second Interview with Gioconda Espina).

Marelis Pérez Marcano, the former *Chavista* deputy who had been the prime driver for Article 88's implementation within the legislature, also did not view Madres del Barrio as fulfilling Article 88. She argued that the mission did not recognize the added value that homemakers produced and thus was not a measure to achieve gender equity. Rather, according to Pérez Marcano, the mission incorporated "a perspective of social inclusion" of the most vulnerable in society—poor single mothers with children—in order to meet their immediate needs with temporary social assistance, incorporate them into productive processes, and thereby "combat extreme poverty" (Fourth Interview with Marelis Pérez Marcano). Espina and Pérez Marcano, who had worked together across political divides within the National Assembly to legislate Article 88, agreed that Madres del Barrio did not mark state fulfillment of Article 88.

However, other women's rights actors within the state viewed Madres del Barrio as partially fulfilling Article 88. Virginia Aguirre, a national-level feminist public official and the former Bolivarian Gender Observatory director, saw the mission as a form of state recognition of unpaid housework. Another national-level feminist public official I interviewed saw the mission not as a form of recognition of the value of poor homemakers' unpaid housework but as a means to incorporate them into the social security system. At the same time, two former Madres del Barrio municipal coordinators and a municipal gender institution worker I interviewed did view the mission as fulfilling Article 88. These former municipal-level mission workers referred to the economic benefit that the mission allocated to beneficiaries not as social assistance but as payment for their household labor.

The women's rights activists working on drafting and legislating Article 88 had been careful to avoid such an interpretation of Article 88 as payment for household labor because of the potential gendered regulatory effects associated with paying women for the housework they performed in their own homes. For example, Nora Castañeda, who was active in the CONG and ANC women's organizing and went on to serve as BanMujer president during Chávez's tenure, noted that the women's rights coalition explicitly discussed whether to demand a salary or social security for home-makers in the constitution. According to her, they decided against a salary "because the salary is an instrument to enslave the worker and it would come to constitute an instrument to enslave the women worker-homemakers," and that is why Article 88 explicitly enshrined homemakers' entitlement to "social security" and not remuneration (Interview with Nora Castañeda).

Madres del Barrio Mission's Nontransparent Structure and Its Price of Silence for Popular Women's Power

These differing views about Madres del Barrio and its relation to Arti-cle 88 among women's rights actors who had worked within the Bolivar-ian state arose not only because the idea for the mission did not emerge from women's movement Article 88 organizing and because of differing political perspectives among them. This lack of consensus also existed be-cause of the mission's nontransparent structure. Information about the mis-sion that went beneath the Bolivarian state's public transcript to evaluate its performance was not publicly accessible. The "public transcript" refers to James Scott's concept of what oppressed peoples say and do in the pres-ence of those who dominate them—their public ritual displays of compli-ance with power relations that seem to be "in close conformity with how the dominant group would wish to have things appear" (Scott 1990, 4). Under Chávez's tenure, Madres del Barrio beneficiaries were everywhere on the public stage set by the Bolivarian state: at state-led marches; in events with local, regional, national, and even presidential government figures; and in government print, digital, TV, and audio media. But reliable public infor-mation about the beneficiaries and what the mission had specifically done and not done for them was almost nowhere to be found.[22] This included even the most basic of information about the Madres del Barrio, such as how many of them existed. The few state documents that I was able to ac-cess that provided information about how many women were incorporated in Madres del Barrio contradicted each other. For example, both Aguirre, Bethencourt, and Testa (2009, 93) (from the Bolivarian Gender Observa-tory) and the National Assembly's Office of Economic and Financial Re-search and Advice (Dirección de Investigación y Asesoría Económica y Financiera 2008, 17) cite 2008 statistics from INaMujer on the total number of women incorporated into the mission at that time. Drawing from the same institutional source, Aguirre and colleagues state that Madres del Barrio incorporated 99,633 women, but the National Assembly office states that the mission incorporated 240,000 women. This lack of transparency helped to preserve the magical appearance of Madres del Barrio; the mission's opaqueness helped to generate an environment in which different understandings of its actions, inactions, and internal machinations could be projected onto it. The divergent views of the mission speak both to its uncertain relation to Article 88 and to how the mission's discretionary design was constructed around its lack of transparency to those outside its internal realms of decision-making powers.

Those internal realms of decision-making powers appear to have been closed off not just to those outside the Bolivarian state but also to those within it.[23] Since Madres del Barrio had been administered by the woman's ministry (MinMujer), led by Nancy Pérez from 2010 to 2013, the ministry and Pérez did not make information about the mission publicly available, even to leaders and workers *within the very same ministry*. For example, MinMujer denied the proposal to evaluate Madres del Barrio submitted by the Bolivarian Gender Observatory, the state institution charged with evaluating women-targeted public policies that was located within the same ministry (Interview with Virginia Aguirre).[24] A former MinMujer worker tasked with articulating the ministry's various programs, which included Madres del Barrio, also informed me that she struggled to access basic information about the mission. Even after several years in this role, she did not possess a clear understanding of how the mission worked (Interview with Laura). If national-level state gender institution workers could not access information about Madres del Barrio from within their own organization, what then was the fate of the public, who had the right to know how its resources were used? What does this indicate about the state of the public sphere in Bolivarian Venezuela and how popular-sector women were positioned within it?

The Madres del Barrio documents I was able to access were not readily accessible in the public sphere. They were provided to me not by MinMujer— the state institution charged with administering the mission since 2008— but by the National Assembly's Family, Woman, and Youth Commission. They were provided to me because Pérez Marcano, the commission's former president, asked the commission staff to furnish them to me. None of those documents were available in the National Assembly's public archival offices at the time of my research in 2011, and those documents covered only the first two years of the mission's existence, before it fell under MinMujer's administration. This brings into question how the Venezuelan public could even access the limited documentation I was able to access.

My experience as a researcher of persistently approaching the local, regional, and national gatekeepers of Madres del Barrio Mission addresses questions of access to the public sphere by demonstrating the lack of public access to information[25] about the mission and the popular women participants within it. In 2011, I moved to Falcón state, believing I would be able to interact with the mission participants—with beneficiaries, workers, and local and regional authorities. Subnational and national state gender institution authorities had granted me research preclearance prior to Nancy Pérez becoming MinMujer minister. However, when I approached the (new) Falcón regional (male) coordinator of the mission (who was appointed after I received my preclearance and Pérez assumed power), he informed me I would first need approval from Madres del Barrio's national authorities before I could begin my research with the mission. And so began what became a half-year process of engaging with regional and national state gender institution authorities in order to seek permission to conduct my planned research. Navigating this institutional maze eventually took me to the national Ministry of Woman's Popular Power and Gender Equality office in Caracas, where I was told that Pérez had rejected my proposal without providing any reason, only after I had been told that her vice minister had approved it.[26] A state authority then informed me that, without such national-level permission, I was not allowed "to touch the *madres*."[27] The magical, nontransparent structure of Madres del Barrio Mission enabled state authorities to block me from accessing information about the participants within it.

Gender inequalities in control over public resources for poor women also complicated hierarchies of power and knowledge within the mission's bureaucratic structure. In the above anecdote about the hierarchy of control of access to the mission's information and participants—of who was allowed "to touch the *madres*"—the regional coordinator's gender is relevant because Madres del Barrio was the only mission in Venezuela targeted only at women. In my research in 2011 and 2012, I found men leading the mission at the municipal level (Miranda municipality, where the city of Coro, Falcón, is located), the regional level (Falcón state), and the national level (the national director of attention to the Madres del Barrio). If Madres del Barrio was an institutional mechanism to articulate popular women's power, why were men leading it?

I persisted, however, in my endeavor to construct knowledge of Madres del Barrio Mission, its organization, and its effects on popular-sector women. I did this by piecing together a picture of the mission through documenting the words and experiences of those who had "touched" the *madres* in one way or another—as former mission workers or authorities, or state workers whose work brought them into contact with the mission and its participants.[28] I also attempted to access mission participants and workers without state authorities' knowledge, but I found that the Bolivarian state's disciplinary power cast a large shadow over them and constrained their voices. One mission worker in Falcón told me she could lose her job if her employer were to find out I interviewed her. And a mission participant revoked her participation in my study when she became convinced that her answers to my questions would endanger her status with the state and potentially endanger President Chávez in the run-up to the 2012 presidential election. Moreover, a former mission participant told me that when Madres del Barrio were interviewed on public television, their words were scripted for them by the mission's staff. The *madres'* public discourse upheld the magical Bolivarian state by following the mission's public transcript, which my research aimed to go beneath.

Several former municipal mission coordinators and mission participants insisted to me that Madres del Barrio imposed no obligations on women in order to benefit from it. Yet my experiences of attempting to listen to popular women's experiences of the mission in 2011 and 2012 suggest that at least one key condition existed to which program beneficiaries and workers at several levels and in several locations were expected to submit. At that juncture in the Bolivarian process, they were supposed to remain silent or, when they did speak in the public sphere, their words were not their own but scripted for them from above. These examples indicate that their participation was both demanded and controlled. The Madres del Barrio were constantly made visible on the local, regional, and national stages in government events, TV programs, and publications. Yet their presence in the public sphere was also concomitantly marked by the absence of their range of voices and experiences.

My blocked attempts to listen to the *madres'* voices beyond their participation in publicized events and their sound bites contained in government media raise important questions as to their power and control. What is the price of the silence of Madres del Barrio beneficiaries and workers, the silence of poor and working-class women whose labor ensured that the poor survived? What does it mean for how their unpaid labor and their voices were valued? Moreover, what is the price of their silence to the public sphere—a public sphere that was supposedly constituted by and for the popular classes under the Bolivarian revolution—about a *public* social program that supposedly put into effect a constitutionally enshrined right? What does this indicate about the public's right to know about its own political process? What would making public the mission's hidden transcript endanger? And, finally, since Madres del Barrio was discursively invoked as an articulation of popular women's power, what did it mean for the state of actually existing popular power that the *madres'* publicly expressed words were controlled by government administrators—by the same actors who controlled the *madres'* access to economic benefits?

My attempts to know Madres del Barrio Mission from the standpoints of its beneficiaries and workers may raise more questions than answers as to what the mission meant for poor homemakers' power and participation in the public sphere. However, the closed doors and silences I confronted do not automatically translate to a vacuum of knowledge about the mission. As Burawoy (1998, 17) states: "A social order reveals itself in the way it responds to pressure," and its "resistance . . . discloses much about the core values and interests of its members." My intervention in the world of Madres del Barrio, my very presence (even from just outside its gates), the pressure of my persistent desire to know it, and the resistance I encountered from actors within it all reveal properties of how the mission was structured. I originally set out to construct knowledge about Madres del Barrio by placing myself as a participant observer within it. My blocked attempts at knowing the mission and the homemakers within it exposed some of the most intimate and fundamental contours of the mission's structure and the top-down state–society relations it was fostering with popular women in spite of the program's rhetoric of articulating popular power.

Conclusion

The missions were a key institutional mechanism in the production of the magical revolutionary Bolivarian state. Bypassing the legislature and extant welfare state bureaucracy, President Chávez responded to mass social exclusion throughout Venezuela by enacting the missions suddenly and expanding them rapidly through converting state oil revenues into goods and services for the popular sectors. By privileging coresponsible popular participation in delivering these new public goods and services, the missions were an integral part of the Bolivarian government's vision for reconfiguring state–society relations and advancing the revolution.

Deeply entrenched assumptions about gender roles and the gendered division of labor were woven into the Bolivarian government's plan for re-configuring state–society relations through the missions. In its design and development of Madres del Barrio Mission, the Bolivarian government imagined the role of popular-sector motherhood and women's unpaid labor in line with its objectives for the revolution's radicalization. The mission drew on the extant hegemonic gender role of women as altruistic mothers and resignified it such that poor mothers were expected to be responsible for their communities' welfare and the revolution's advancement in addition to their families' welfare. Producing a revolutionary maternalism through Madres del Barrio was vital to the Bolivarian government's vision for radicalizing the revolution.

The Bolivarian state was a magical revolutionary state not only because it suddenly produced new institutions, goods, services, and visions for the roles and work of the popular sectors but also because it was opaque. Chávez and the Madres del Barrio Mission designers appeared to answer suspended claims for gender justice by invoking Article 88 in this mission's development. Yet Madres del Barrio was a discretionary program, constructed around its lack of transparency to those outside its internal realms of decision-making powers. The mission's nontransparent structure both limited what could be known about its relation to Article 88 and enabled the state to persist with its public transcript that the mission marked Article 88's fulfillment. Although it enhanced the Bolivarian state's magic, the mission's nontransparency reveals its development of top-down state–society relations with popular-sector women. The ways in which the mission held back the *madres'* range of voices and experiences from the public sphere calls into question the extent to which the mission was an institutional mechanism to promote popular women's power and control.

CHAPTER 4

Regulating Motherhood in Madres del Barrio: Intensifying yet Disregarding the Unpaid Labor of the Mothers of the Bolivarian Revolution

Continuing to examine Madres del Barrio Mission's resignification of motherhood according to Bolivarian state goals for the revolution, this chapter brings to light how the mission's structure and practices empirically intersected with popular understandings of the mission and of motherhood. Such resignification had regulatory effects for the *madres* who did not fulfill all their coresponsibilities. The imaginations of revolutionary maternalism that the mission produced and impressed upon the *madres* served to exacerbate existing divisions and generate new forms of social and economic divisions among popular-sector women. The mission's structure intensified popular women's unpaid labor while perpetuating nonrecognition of unpaid care work within the heart of the very social policy that Chávez decreed as applying Article 88.

To explore how Madres del Barrio Mission functioned in everyday practice and was popularly understood, I located *madres* who had been incorporated into the mission and had exited it.[1] Through the accounts of these former *madres*, I began to uncover a bottom-up perspective of how the mission worked and the effects it had on popular-sector homemakers' welfare, gender relations, and social and political participation. I was introduced to three former mission participants—Miriam, Aida, and Soraya—who had each exited the mission because they were running businesses with cooperatives that they had launched with the mission's assistance. The Bolivarian government had held up these three former mission participants as Madres del Barrio poster women because they had relinquished their economic benefits, were continuing to carry out their productive activities, and therefore had fulfilled the mission's objectives. Due to their achievements, they were already accustomed to media attention and publicly telling their stories of *echando pa' lante* (a popular colloquial term in Venezuela for "getting ahead") under the mission's tutelage.

I set out to listen to these three women's success stories and learn from them how they were able to *echar pa'lante* by fulfilling the mission's core-sponsibilities, when so many of their fellow Madres del Barrio had yet to do so. Both these former *madres* and state gender institution workers often employed these terms (*echando pa'lante* or *saliendo para adelante*) to describe them as the mission's success cases and to set them apart from the *madres* who had not exited the mission and gotten off state assistance. This discursive device differentiating "independent" from "dependent" mothers brings to light important popular understandings of women's and state roles and responsibilities for social reproduction within the Bolivarian revolution. Miriam's, Aida's, and Soraya's stories were not representative of the majority of Madres del Barrio; their stories do not represent the typical Madres del Barrio experience or the full range of the *madres'* experiences. However, their stories do reveal how the mission operated in practice, how popular women were positioned within it, and ways in which it was popularly understood.

Utilizing Dorothy Smith's (1987) "everyday world as problematic" methodology, I fleshed out these women's accounts of their everyday experiences within and outside the mission in order to explore the broader relations in which their experiences were embedded. Over the course of three months, I visited Miriam, Aida, and Soraya at work in their shops, talked with them and listened to them about their struggles, accomplishments, opinions, and frustrations, and conducted interview processes with each of them.[2]

This chapter thus begins with Miriam's, Aida's, and Soraya's individual stories. After telling each of their stories, I weave them together to reveal their common threads. I then extend these threads to include the voices, experiences, and interests of state actors and institutions and women's movement activists and analysts in order to show the structural forces and social and political dynamics that shaped their experiences of Madres del Barrio and popular understandings of the mission in general.[3]

Three Former Madres del Barrio Who Had *Echado Pa'lante*

Miriam

Miriam was from a *barrio*, had three children, and was a single mother in her forties. She had performed only unpaid housework and community work for the approximately twenty-five years that she was with her former partner. Prior to launching her business with her cooperative and the support of Madres del Barrio Mission, Miriam had only about two and a half years of paid work experience—in the retail and clerical sectors—and she never contributed to social insurance during that time. She cared for her partner when they were together, and she was responsible for caring for her father, who was disabled and ill before he died. At the time of the interview, she continued to care for her two youngest children and her adult brother, who had become disabled from an accident. At times, Miriam was also caring for her adult child and his children, as well as for her sister, who was sick with cancer and was also a Madres del Barrio beneficiary. Before she entered Madres del Barrio in 2006, Miriam lived off whatever money her partner gave her. However, she noted that this money was "a pittance" and rarely sufficient to meet her family's needs.

Miriam had participated in her community's neighborhood association before Chávez came to power. However, Miriam said that even though she had always been involved in her community and was a community leader, she became interested and involved in [formal] politics only when Chávez was in power. She said that she did not participate in the 1999 national constituent process (but she did vote in the referendum to approve the 1999 Constitution) and she did not read the Constitution before her participation in Madres del Barrio. Yet she noted that before her incorporation into the mission, while Chávez was in power, "we were always in agreement with the laws in everything that was to be beneficial for us, for the inhabitants of our country. . . . Not because I love and admire the president, but because I know that what he is doing is . . . a benefit for all of us and not for one person only, but for the collective—for all." Further, Miriam became interested in politics because she identified with Chávez, with his discourse and practice:

> The form of our president simply called my attention—the intellectual, the human being that he is with the people, with the children, with the elderly, with the people he wants to help, that he wants to benefit. Why? Because he is a person that comes from below, who knows and understands the needs of the people. Before . . . a president was talking and it made you sleepy; it did not provoke you. Now he is talking and one turns on the television to hear the things that he says.

She noted that it was Chávez's way of doing politics that triggered her to become politically involved. Miriam joined the PSUV, through which she worked with Madres del Barrio committees.

Miriam was already serving on her community's health committee for five years and acting as the committee's coordinator when Chávez announced

Madres del Barrio's establishment in 2006. When he launched the mission, her sector's[4] health committee was charged with carrying out the census of all the mothers living in extreme poverty in her sector, and she registered herself on the list. She assisted in registering women in her community by accompanying the mission surveyor in house-by-house visits and interviews. Of the list of forty potential beneficiaries in her sector drawn up by the health committee, Miriam was one of the twenty women that were chosen to benefit from the mission, whom she said her community approved in a validation assembly. She said she had to wait one or two months from the time she signed up for the mission to when she began to receive the mission cash transfer.

Miriam described the arrival of the Madres del Barrio cash transfer as "a help—one more complement to what the father of my kids gave me for their nutrition and for all their needs because from that I had to . . . make miracles . . . I believe that it arrived to me from heaven." Even though Miriam used most of her transfer to provide basic necessities for her children and grandchildren, such as food, clothing, and shoes, she noted the significance of the benefit for *her*, in that it belonged to her and did not come from her partner. "I had to spend my money, because it's mine then. And he did not go on supervising me. It was for my needs. In fact, I helped my eldest son, my grandchildren, what they also needed. . . . They benefited from that help." Miriam pointed out that how she spent the transfer was her choice because neither her partner nor the mission instructed her how to use the money. The mission benefit gave her a newfound sense of control in decision-making and over resources.

Although Miriam noted that her own and her family's welfare improved while she received the cash transfer, the gender roles in her household remained the same. She still remained responsible for housework and her partner did not assume household responsibilities, even when she was working with her fellow *madres* to launch their business.

While she was participating in Madres del Barrio, Miriam separated from her partner. The economic support that the mission had provided appears to have helped her when she made this decision, because she was economically dependent on him before she entered the program. In this sense, the mission cash transfer seems to have contributed to Miriam's autonomy, and it enabled her to survive independently of her former partner.

Miriam also benefited from other Bolivarian government missions. The missions provided Miriam with a degree of recognition of her housework by helping to lighten her reproductive burden. For example, with Madres del Barrio assistance, Miriam was able to access discounted credit from Mi Casa Bien Equipada Mission[5] for a refrigerator, and she noted that other Madres del Barrio also received discounted credit for refrigerators.

Yet Miriam's engagement with other Bolivarian missions shows the limited extent to which they recognized her reproductive labor and how this burden restricted both her time and her ability to benefit from them. For instance, Miriam viewed Mercal Mission as a huge benefit, and she had used the mission to purchase subsidized food for her family. Yet, she noted that her care burden prevented her from being able to utilize the mission regularly because she did not have time to wait in long lines to access food. And while in Madres del Barrio Mission, Miriam enrolled in Ribas Mission,[6] where she began to study for her high school equivalency. However, she was not able to complete her studies because the class schedules conflicted with her care work—her classes took place when she had to drop her son off at school. When I asked her, Miriam responded that she would still like to study and complete her high school diploma, but she did not see that as feasible, given that she now had her small business and had to work outside of the house up to six days a week in addition to carrying out her unpaid care work in her own and her family members' homes.

Seven of the *madres* in Miriam's sector formed a sewing cooperative the year after they entered Madres del Barrio, as per the coresponsibilities stipulated by the mission. Miriam continued to be involved in this project at the time I interviewed her, five years later. The *madres* in her sector received training from state institutions in accounting and cooperativism. After the training, Miriam's cooperative bought fabrics, worked individually on sewing assignments during the week, and came together on weekends to share their products. Miriam noted how she saw her own and others' sewing capacities grow through this process when she sewed a quilt out of a tablecloth: "I transformed it, I transformed it myself. And like this successively until each one saw that we could do it, that we could achieve it. We started like this, because it was useful for ourselves, and later we began to make things . . . to offer them to other people, to go on doubling, tripling the money until the mission gave us the credit." Madres del Barrio Mission then granted her cooperative a loan to acquire sewing machines and primary materials so that they could develop their business.

A Madres del Barrio promoter assisted Miriam's cooperative to start their business. At the time I interviewed Miriam, she said that a mission promoter continued to visit them, though less often because they no longer received the mission cash transfer and the mission personnel had changed. A former mission coordinator had linked her up with the local government to rent discounted municipal-owned retail space, from which she and Aida were jointly selling their respective cooperatives' products in 2012.

Miriam described her exit from the mission and her relinquishment of its cash transfer in 2011—five years after joining the mission—as voluntary, because she had determined that her business was established enough to sustain her without the mission's economic support. Yet, in interviewing Miriam after she had relinquished the benefit, it was obvious that she and her cooperative were struggling—they went days and sometimes weeks without sales, and she was exhausted. Her cooperative had lost members: from the original seven, four now remained: two lost their houses to natural disasters and were offered houses by the government in another community, and one member found employment, which offered her more stability than the cooperative could. Miriam was now the only cooperative member available to sell their products from the shop. This meant that Miriam had to work at the shop five or six days a week. Her cooperative and Aida's cooperative had a joint loan from a state bank, and after Miriam's cooperative paid off their monthly share of debt to the bank, she was often left with very little to get by on.

Miriam often had to run the shop and watch her youngest son there simultaneously. The Bolivarian state's full-day schooling program had yet to reach the *barrio* where Miriam lived. Her son therefore attended a half-day school, and she in turn relied on assistance from her sick sister, her disabled brother, and her eldest son in caring for him while she worked at the shop on weekday afternoons and Saturday mornings. But Miriam often found herself without their assistance, and, in such instances, she had to bring him with her to the shop.

When I interviewed Miriam in 2012, she had recently registered as an independent worker for social insurance, and she was waiting to begin contributing to this new public service. Miriam asserted that because of her participation in the mission, she felt more developed as a human being, she had acquired knowledge that helped both her and her children, and she possessed a stronger sense of self-confidence.

Aida

Aida was from a different *barrio* than Miriam. She had three children and was a single mother in her forties. She had previously performed paid domestic and cleaning work for twenty-two years. Aida withdrew from her paid work to carry out unpaid care work in her home when she became pregnant with her third child.

When Madres del Barrio was launched in 2006, Aida was already participating in her community's health committee. She signed up for the mission that same year through a community census conducted by her community's land committee, and she was one of the twenty-two women from her sector selected to benefit from the mission shortly thereafter. Aida noted her surprise at how quickly she received the cash transfer; she and the other mothers in her sector believed Madres del Barrio would turn out like other unrealized state promises in the past. She said that the mission cash transfer was a substantial help because she had no fixed paid work during that period, and it gave her temporary stability. She used most of the benefit to feed her family, but she was also able to use it to pay for her children's extracurricular activities and to assist her eldest son in attending university.

While participating in the mission, Aida organized with other women from her sector to take sewing classes and form a sewing project. They found a space in their community to work, and the mission gave them an interest-free loan to adjust the space and to buy machinery and primary materials. At the time I interviewed her, four years after their initial loan was granted, Aida's cooperative was still paying it off, even though the mission originally expected them to finish paying it back within two years.

As Miriam had, Aida had received low-interest credit for discount household appliances through Mi Casa Bien Equipada Mission, which helped to lighten her housework.

Aida described participation in Madres del Barrio as "an eye-opener" for the women within it: they received political education workshops and learned that a woman "not only served to be inside the home—taking care of the husband, of the kids—but also that she had to participate in society and that she had another place other than the home." In spite of her community and political participation prior to joining Madres del Barrio, she had not been aware of Article 88. Aida said that the mission educated the *madres* about their constitutional rights, including Article 88. She viewed the mission as a vehicle for women's social inclusion and participation in the public sphere. And she described the mission as a transformational program that had enabled her to "*surgir* [arise] as a person," because with her cooperative partners, she now had her own business, which she had never imagined she would have. Rather, she had previously imagined that her life would always be characterized by "having to be dependent on others." Aida spoke of Madres del Barrio Mission as facilitating her economic independence, but she neglected to mention how the mission had at the same time facilitated a new form of economic dependence in her life. She and her cooperative partners now were indebted to the bank,[7] and she noted it was hard to pay off the loan given her cooperative's slow sales.

Aida said that, prior to Bolivarianism, she and her fellow community members were not participating in any community or political organization because "for us that was something distant. The truth is that no one participated in anything that had to do with politics, the government or related with the community. We were apathetic to that: every one in their work, at their house. . . . Politics was distant from the popular sectors." She described a shift in her own and her community's political participation triggered by the national process that Chávez helped to unfurl: they supported the MBR-200 in its 1992 coup attempt. According to Aida, "beginning then, we opened our eyes and we understood that we had to become integrated in politics, that it was part of us." She began to get politically involved, and she assisted with organizing her community for the 1999 constituent assembly referendums. She noted that she could become informed prior to voting in these referendums, because beginning then, "nothing was hidden. That arrived to the communities, the parties took charge . . . to bring information to the sectors." And since then, her entire sector in her *barrio* was "100 percent *Chavista*."

With the missions' arrival to her *barrio*, Aida said that the mothers there learned that they could participate, express themselves publicly, and look for solutions to community needs. She described this as a process of awakening, wherein the people from her community realized that they were taken into account by the developing political process. She saw her community's political participation as a tool to create a better future for their children, and the mothers of her community as possessing the responsibility to make this future a reality for them. When she was in Madres del Barrio, Aida's Madres del Barrio committee elected her as its principal spokesperson, and in this position, she was tasked with regularly meeting with the mission staff and serving as the principal articulator between the *madres* in her sector and the institution. Aida now was participating in any political, cultural, and educational activities in and outside of her community that she could. At the time I interviewed her, she was her communal council's financial spokesperson, a member of her community's health committee, and a PSUV *patrullera* (patrol officer). (Aida had joined the PSUV when she was in Madres del Barrio.) The members of Aida's community now sought her out when they needed assistance and to be connected with state programs and services. Aida remarked that she now felt complete.

Aida described her exit from the mission and relinquishment of the mission benefit in 2007 as voluntary. She said that she chose to withdraw from the mission when she felt she could "more or less maintain herself, in order to make room for other people who really needed more." Here, Aida's own words reflect an internalization of an expectation articulated by Gioconda Mota (see chapter 3) in which she stated that the mission's designers expected the *madres* to relinquish their cash transfers when they were sufficiently empowered so that more needy mothers could receive them. However, Aida noted that when she gave up the benefit, she was left "hanging in the air": all of a sudden she found herself in a financially unstable position because her cooperative's customers accumulated tabs instead of paying on time.

Even with the shop, from which her cooperative was selling its wares, Aida was struggling economically. After her cooperative made its monthly loan repayment, there were times when she could barely afford transport to work. (Aida was the only member of her cooperative who staffed the shop that it shared with Miriam's cooperative.) In spite of being exalted by the state as a success story, Aida's cooperative had no contracts with the state, even though it produced textiles that they could easily tailor to meet the specific requirements of state institutions. Nor, Aida noted, had the state provided her cooperative with support in formalizing their business and navigating institutional apparatuses, such as banking, tax, and municipal authorities, with which she and her fellow cooperative members had no experience. After exiting the mission, the support that she and her cooperative received from the state was thin at best. Aida and her partners had launched their cooperative because of and through assistance from the state, which in turn was failing to connect them with other state institutions that could benefit from their textile services.

On the one hand, then, the state expected them to be the poster women of Madres del Barrio, and on the other hand, it had not completed its job of providing them with services that would guarantee their ability to sustain their business and not return to receiving state social assistance. Aida was quite aware of this contradiction, pointing out instances when the state would hold publicized events with Madres del Barrio where it would promise the *madres* forms of assistance (such as credit and procurement contracts with state institutions), and then after such events, the *madres* spent months waiting for the state to fulfill such "promises." And in times of patchy state support and poor business, Aida found herself having to turn to her female family members for assistance.

When I interviewed Aida in 2012, she was working at the shop five to six days a week for about five hours a day. Aida's sister and mother, who were also Madres del Barrio, helped to care for her children as they continued to work as unpaid homemakers. From time to time, Aida's two oldest children also helped her in carrying out household duties. During school holidays, Aida often had to bring her youngest child with her to the shop and care for her while she simultaneously ran the shop. Aida was returning home from the shop (which was an hour from her home on public transport) every day, not to rest but to care for her youngest child—she remained responsible for household care work—and to sew for her cooperative from home. At times, Aida labored from home under difficult conditions, such as completing sewing orders by candlelight when the electricity went out. Aida was returning home often from her paid labor to do unpaid community and political work. Aida's labor had intensified since her departure from the mission; she often performed her productive and reproductive labor simultaneously at home and at the shop. She carried out all of this work without ongoing assistance from the mission. She spoke of exhaustion as a common feature of her everyday life. Further, at the time I interviewed her, Aida was preoccupied by the fact that the following year her daughter would be attending a school with a shorter school day, which conflicted with the hours Aida had to be at the shop. She did not know how she could reconcile this added care burden with her productive labor.

Soraya

Soraya was in her fifties, had been a single mother for around thirty years, and had never received monetary assistance from her children's father after she had separated from him. She had four biological children and six orphaned and abandoned children whom she fostered. All of her children were now adults, and she took pride in the fact that all of them had finished high school and none of them had turned to delinquency.

Soraya was from a *barrio* that was extremely vulnerable to natural disasters, and because of this, displacement from her housing marked her life history. Soraya lost her home from natural disasters four times in her life. Such loss began when she was a child and an earthquake caused her family to lose their home and they had to move to another *barrio*, where they lived in a shack that was also vulnerable to disasters. Most recently, Soraya was displaced from her home during heavy rains the year before I met her. When I interviewed her, she was temporarily living in a state-administered refuge as she waited for the state to build and grant her the subsidized house in a middle-class neighborhood that it had promised her. (During the three-month period in 2012 that I engaged Soraya in my research, the state postponed the delivery of her house several times. But Soraya, unlike many of the other victims of the heavy rains who were living in refuges at the time, remained patient for her house to arrive.) Precarity and struggle for decent living conditions therefore ran throughout Soraya's life.

Soraya had previously performed skilled health work on a contract basis and often worked overtime to earn enough to maintain her family. She had to resign from this work after her last child was born because he demanded a lot of attention, and her mother, who had previously assisted with her children's care, had become elderly and could not help. From home then, while taking care of her children, Soraya also painted and sold ceramics, baked and sold cakes, and sold clothing in order to make ends meet. She never received public assistance to raise the orphaned and abandoned children whom she fostered.

While Soraya was performing paid health work, she contributed to social insurance, but she did not complete all her contributions to be eligible for a state pension. When Chávez decreed that workers such as she could complete their contributions,[8] Soraya finished contributing to social insurance. Soraya had recently begun to receive her state pension equivalent to a minimum-wage salary. After many years of income precarity, she now had a stable income.

Prior to *Chavismo*, Soraya was a leader in her community; she began her community organizing work when she was young, helping to organize cultural and recreational events and charitable activities. Between the time when Chávez initiated the missions and the launch of Madres del Barrio, Soraya worked half days as an unpaid volunteer, accompanying the Cuban Barrio Adentro[9] doctors on their house-by-house visits throughout her *barrio*.

Soraya said she never participated politically prior to Chávez's presidency, but then she voted in the 1999 constitutional referendums because she was in agreement with Chávez's proposals and believed that they would begin to make things better. She noted she had read the 1999 Constitution prior to voting for it, but she had not heard of Article 88 before becoming incorporated in Madres del Barrio. She later joined the PSUV. Soraya spoke of the new constitution and Chávez as bringing improvements to women's conditions. She asserted that Chávez valued women and took them into account where they were unrecognized before. For Soraya, this was part of Chávez's larger approach of "favoring" the popular sectors and improving their welfare.

Apart from receiving the Madres del Barrio cash transfer, Soraya had concretely benefited from other Bolivarian government initiatives to improve popular-sector welfare. She previously ate daily in her *barrio*'s popular cafeteria built by the Bolivarian state, and her children attended educational missions, where they did not have to pay for their learning materials.

According to Soraya, a government official she already knew came to her community in 2006 when Madres del Barrio was launched to identify and register the mothers most in need for the mission. Soraya signed up for the mission because she was unemployed at the time. She also assisted with registering mothers in her community for the mission; she asserted that because she was working as an unpaid community health worker, she knew the needs of the members of her community. Soraya waited a few months and the cash transfer arrived, and she was very happy because it was a significant help to her household and marked the beginning of improvements to her own and her family's welfare.

Soraya used her Madres del Barrio transfer to buy building materials to fortify her house over time, which was made only of zinc sheets and concrete. With her children's help, she improved her house. Sadly, this was the same house from which she was displaced the year before. Soraya also used her Madres del Barrio transfer to meet some of her children's basic material needs.

Soraya had served on her sector's Madres del Barrio committee as vice president and health spokesperson. As health spokesperson, she said she was alert to the health needs of community members, organized and assisted with community vaccination drives, and accompanied and assisted the Cuban doctor in his daily house visits to sick and disabled community members.

While in the mission, Soraya taught two occupational training courses to multiple groups of women—both from and not from Madres del Barrio. She was not paid for either of these teaching positions. Soraya made a point to note that she did not receive training as such while in the mission, but rather that she provided training to other *madres* and community members. She saw such training as enabling younger mothers to take care of themselves so that they would not have to depend on others to meet their own and their children's basic needs. For Soraya, then, the mission provided her with a venue to develop her teaching skills, assert her leadership skills, and assist other women in their processes of asserting their agency and independence.

Soraya said that the mission provided the Madres del Barrio with a broad education of the 1999 Constitution and their rights and focused on motivating them to *salir adelante*. While in Madres del Barrio, Soraya formed a household and industrial supplies cooperative with other women. At the time I interviewed her, she was the cooperative's president. The mission had linked her cooperative to the municipal government, which provided them with cooperativism training. Once their cooperative was established, they received a discounted rental from the municipality for their shop, which they were sharing with another cooperative assisted by Madres del Barrio. The mission assisted their cooperatives in accessing a state bank loan for their shop's start-up, which they were still paying off. As with Aida's cooperative, though, even as Soraya's cooperative was launched through state assistance, it had not received any state procurement contracts that could help them to sustain the cooperative.

In 2012, six years after her incorporation into Madres del Barrio, Soraya exited the mission and relinquished the cash transfer. Unlike Miriam and Aida, she described her withdrawal from the mission as a decision made by the mission staff. According to her, this occurred once her cooperative had obtained its shop and the mission staff saw she would be making more money through the cooperative's business than she was through the mission's cash transfer.

At the time I interviewed her, Soraya worked on manufacturing her cooperative's products between her old *barrio* and the refuge where she was temporarily living and the shop where she sold them. Her workdays were long, but she said she was earning more money with her pension and her cooperative's earnings than when she received the Madres del Barrio transfer. She could afford to work these long days because she was still in relatively good health and her children now took care of themselves. The two forms of state assistance—Madres del Barrio and her pension—had enabled Soraya to reach a sense of income security.

New State Presences Generate New State Absences

Miriam, Aida, and Soraya all spoke of the quick turnaround time between when they initially signed up for Madres del Barrio Mission and when they began to receive the mission's cash transfer. As Aida noted, the cash transfer did actually arrive to her and other *madres*, unlike other state promises of goods and services to the popular sectors in the past that went unfulfilled. For them and the approximately 100,000 women across Venezuela who were initially incorporated into the mission in 2006 and 2007,[10] the arrival of the cash transfer signified the presence of a state that fulfilled its promises to them.

However, for the popular-sector women that Madres del Barrio did reach, such as Miriam, Aida, and Soraya, their stories indicate that the mission also made them wait at times for the state to further fulfill its promises. Even though the mission had rapidly incorporated them, and they in turn worked to fulfill the mission's socio-productive coresponsibilities, the mission later made them wait for continued support to sustain their cooperatives and their independence from social assistance. The mission's absent follow-through generated frustrations among them.

At the same time, the Bolivarian state made many poor homemakers throughout Venezuela, for whom it had raised expectations of incorporation into Madres del Barrio, wait for the mission to reach them. Following Madres del Barrio's enactment, the mission reached only targeted geographic areas. According to Madres del Barrio Mission (2007), in 2006, women from 68 of Venezuela's 335 municipalities were included in it. The criterion for selecting these municipalities was based on the state's determination of the three poorest municipalities in each state. In addition, Madres del Barrio Mission stated that in 2006, it incorporated homemakers with "special cases"—specifically homemakers with disabilities or homemakers who had people with disabilities dependent on them—from 105 additional municipalities. In 2007, Chávez announced that 160,000 women would be newly included in the mission in the latter half of that year. In that same year, forty-four new municipalities were added to the mission's geographic coverage, and women from these municipalities were selected to benefit from the mission. However, the mission reported that funds were not transferred to it in time to transfer cash to selected beneficiaries from those forty-four new municipalities that year, and it had finished selecting only about 40 percent of the new beneficiary quota (Misión Madres del Barrio "Josefa Joaquina Sánchez" 2007). These numbers indicate the presence of a state apparatus that could not keep up with the pace that the president had publicly set for it and the popular women it was supposed to reach. Although I could not access Madres del Barrio documents that show the numbers of mission beneficiaries over time, various state gender institution workers informed me in 2011 and 2012 that Madres del Barrio had previously stopped incorporating new beneficiaries, and at that point, if the mission did incorporate new beneficiaries, it did so only when *madres* withdrew from the mission or were removed from it. One state gender institution authority informed me that the state had halted the mission's expansion and incorporation of new beneficiaries because of lack of funding for program growth.

From early on in Madres del Barrio Mission's trajectory, communities began to raise concerns they had about the mission not reaching them. For example, in 2007, the National Homemakers' and Assistance to Pregnant Women Association of Carabobo state told National Assembly representatives that it did not agree with the mission's selection methodology, because many homemakers lived in extreme poverty outside of the three Carabobo municipalities that had been chosen to be reached by the mission. The organization did not understand why the government had prevented such women from benefiting from the mission (Subcomisión de Familia 2007).

This phenomenon, in which popular women did not understand why Madres del Barrio had not reached their communities, extended beyond Carabobo and the first years of the mission's existence. In Falcón state in 2011 and 2012, the mission existed in only five out of the state's twenty-five municipalities. In my 2012 interview with Gloria, a Falcón state gender institution worker, she noted that women in the majority of the municipalities that she and her co-workers had been visiting had consistently complained about the mission not reaching poor women in their communities. Gloria said they raised this complaint because they did not know why the mission had not arrived in their communities. Apparently, the confusion about why the mission was absent in certain municipalities and why certain homemakers living in extreme poverty had not been incorporated into it had at least in part been generated by the mission's own practices. According to Gloria, Madres del Barrio representatives had visited all the municipalities throughout the state and compiled a list of women who could be eligible for the mission, but these women never received responses from the state as to whether and when they would be incorporated into it. So the state left them waiting.

This new state presence of Madres del Barrio concomitantly generated a new form of state absence—the state did not fulfill the expectations that it had spawned among many popular women of this new mission reaching and benefiting them. As new state institutions and services, such as Madres del Barrio, engendered new expectations for state articulation, when such articulations did not transpire, their absence did not go unnoticed, but rather was often felt most by the subjects they were supposed to reach. Such sustained state absence had triggered growing frustrations among popular women, as the Carabobo and Falcón cases illustrate.

Thus, in the absences and the unfulfilled expectations it raised for both the women it did not incorporate and those it did, and who in turn had fulfilled its goals, Madres del Barrio contributed to ongoing income precarity for many popular-sector women. Madres del Barrio Mission's "raising [of] expectations and then mutely crushing them," as Javier Auyero (2012) observes with state welfare services in Argentina, "induct[ed] poor people into a process they [could] neither understand nor control" (74). Similar to Auyero's conclusion, the mission's forcing popular-sector women to wait in uncertainty for initial or further assistance "constitute[d] an exertion of state power" (2)—an act of everyday Bolivarian state domination—in and through which popular women's "political subordination was reproduced" (2).

New Forms of Inclusion Generate New Divisions among Popular-Sector Women

The mission's targeted selection mechanism and lack of transparency served to generate new social and economic divisions among popular-sector women through a dialectic of simultaneous state presence and absence, social inclusion and exclusion, and rapid rollout of social assistance for some while making others wait in perpetuity for it. As Madres del Barrio brought popular homemakers together in community organizations and microenterprises, it also served to divide popular women between those touched and those not touched by the mission.

Miriam, Aida, and Soraya all were participating as leaders in Bolivarian government initiatives in their communities before the Madres del Barrio launch in 2006. Both Miriam and Soraya also assisted with the initial registry of women from their respective communities for the mission. And female family members of both Miriam and Aida were chosen to benefit from the mission. It is not clear if the mission originally chose Miriam, Aida, and Soraya (and their family members) to receive cash transfers because of their earlier participation in government initiatives in their communities (and not necessarily because of their socioeconomic "states of need"). However, the lack of transparency about why certain women were chosen to benefit from the mission while others were not raised broader questions both within and outside *Chavismo* of clientelism, patronage, cronyism, and nepotism in the mission's selection mechanism.

For example, a *Chavista* feminist working within a state gender institution told me that she believed the women who were initially selected to benefit from Madres del Barrio were chosen because of their social proximity to the state surveyors generating beneficiary lists and not necessarily because of their needs (Interview with Laura). And Paula, a former Madres del Barrio municipal coordinator, who was *Chavista*, shared with me stories of local "fiddling" with beneficiary selection. When she assumed her post in the mission, she found that many community organizations had already chosen women who were not extremely poor to benefit from the mission. She said that one city council member allocated the mission benefit in exchange for votes (Interview with Paula). Further, Adicea Castillo, a women's studies professor in opposition to *Chavismo*, noted the importance of the mission reaching very excluded women and families, and at the same time contended that the selection of beneficiaries was managed clientelistically. She asserted that only *Chavista* women had been chosen to benefit from the mission (Second Interview with Adicea Castillo). These interpretations of clientelism with Madres del Barrio Mission's selection mechanism coincide with past research concluding that targeted social spending programs can re-create and expand clientelist relations, because their limited nature allows state actors to exercise discretion in deciding who will benefit from them (Gay 2006).

Gioconda Mota, the mission's first president, contested such allegations of clientelist selection mechanisms. She asserted that, at least under her leadership from 2006 to 2008, the criteria for selection was always "the condition of extreme poverty independent of political orientation," and that women from the opposition were chosen to benefit from the mission. She insisted that Madres del Barrio was "a policy of social protection of the Bolivarian government toward the most excluded population" (First Interview with Gioconda Mota).

Without concrete data from the mission on who its beneficiaries had been and what their socioeconomic profiles were, these questions about clientelism and favoritism in the mission's selection of beneficiaries cannot be definitively answered. Even so, these questions constitute subjects' understandings and experiences of the mission, and thus were part and parcel of the mission itself.

These questions also prove difficult to answer because of the very nature of Madres del Barrio's selection mechanism, which depended on various forms of community organizations to act coresponsibly with the state in deciding who should benefit from the mission. The extent of transparency in selection mechanisms probably varied from community to community and according to existing webs of power relations within particular communities. The Bolivarian government represented this methodology for beneficiary selection as an articulation of popular power in that it was based on the premise that community members were experts in understanding problems within their own communities. However, such selection methodology rested on assumptions that communities were internally organized and would act harmoniously and ethically in ensuring that limited social assistance resources would reach women most in need. Carolina, a feminist public official, contended that such underlying assumptions were problematic because

there is scarce capacity for control. If you do not have capacity for control and you permit that the communities—which are not benevolent entities and free from internal conflicts—select and tell you that "these are the persons who are going to receive X or Y benefit," you can generate firstly power relations in the community that can mar relations and, moreover, generate leaderships based on government transfers in which you are politically usufructing the people that they are choosing. Imagine all the power that you have in an extremely poor community—now you decide who is saved. (Interview with Carolina)

Reliance on community organizations to implement targeted selection mechanisms for social assistance then could potentially serve as both a vehicle for particularism and a mechanism to divert resources from community members most in need. Such a communitarian selection process in turn could exacerbate already existing social, economic, and political divisions and/or generate new divisions within communities.[11]

Madres del Barrio Mission itself appears to have become aware of problems with its reliance on community organizations to select mission beneficiaries. Gioconda Mota admits "that there were tricks in the same bosom of the popular movement," wherein community members would get their female family members, who were not in extreme poverty, into the mission (First Interview with Gioconda Mota). And in the Madres del Barrio 2007 General Report, the mission stated that in 2006, "during the inclusion process, some popular power authorities fell into the political error of proposing women that were close to their groupings, but were not found to be in extreme poverty" (Misión Madres del Barrio "Josefa Joaquina Sánchez" 2007, 10).[12] The mission asserts that it took measures to address benefit maldistribution problems with community-managed targeting mechanisms, including the removal in 2007 of 293 women from the mission who were found not to be extremely poor (10). These statements indicate that, as the state positioned popular community organizations as mediators between it and popular women, some of these organizations and their leaders then used their authority to become vehicles for the maldistribution of benefits to women. That is to say, some popular power organizations became new mediums for patronage and corruption.

Gioconda Mota asserts that such "illegitimate practices" had been magnified out of proportion with what really happened (First Interview with Gioconda Mota). Even if that is the case, the absence of publicly accessible and reliable information about the mission's beneficiaries created the environment for perceptions of such practices to be magnified and gain a foothold in popular discourse and understandings of the mission. This is especially so in a context in which only a select number of poor homemakers received the mission benefit and more poor homemakers did not, yet they got to constantly watch those who did benefit in their own communities and/or through state media channels.

This simultaneous inclusion of some popular-sector women in and exclusion of others from Madres del Barrio Mission, combined with the absence of transparent selection criteria, served to generate resentment and stigma among popular women. For example, Miriam and Aida told me that some women from their communities were envious of them and other Madres del Barrio because they had waited to be included in the mission while they witnessed Miriam, Aida, and their co-*madres* receiving the cash transfer. And in Falcón state, Ana María, a regional-level gender institution worker, joked with me that a popular saying existed among older women who had not benefited from the mission: the mission beneficiaries were not

Madres del Barrio (mothers of the *barrio*) but rather *vagas del barrio* (slackers of the *barrio*). When I asked Ana María to explain this term, she noted that such women saw the young Madres del Barrio hanging around the *barrios* and remarked how the cash transfer was wasted on them.[13] This tension generated between popular women included in and excluded by the mission's incorporation process is similar to that described by Molyneux regarding Mexico's CCT program in areas where its coverage was more selective (Molyneux 2008a, 35), and shows that selective targeting measures can serve to divide popular women.

Processes of state disincorporation of beneficiaries from Madres del Barrio also generated and/or reproduced divisions among popular-sector women. For example, Paula, the former municipal mission coordinator in a Caracas *barrio*, said she encountered women who were not extremely poor receiving the mission benefit when she assumed her post. She stated that she then removed these women from the mission to ensure that the mission benefit arrived to women who were really in a state of need. Paula noted that she "gained many enemies" in this process of "purifying" the beneficiary list (Interview with Paula). And though this same former municipal coordinator recognized that in the context of the *barrios* many needs did exist, she blamed such maldistribution of the mission benefit on the lack of ethics of community members who chose the mission beneficiaries. Paula did not engage in an outwardly reflexive turn that linked the benefit's maldistribution to the mission's structural design—a design that relied on community organizations without first assessing their representativity, transparency, and accountability mechanisms. Rather, she attributed this maldistribution to community members' failure to ethically fulfill their coresponsibilities. This explanation extended beyond Paula to constitute a popular discursive phenomenon that placed blame on the *madres* and popular-sector organizations for the mission's failures, as she, other state gender institution workers, and several former mission beneficiaries consistently invoked such a discourse, which is examined below in the section "Dividing the *Madres* Who 'Get Ahead' from Those Who 'Stay Behind.'"

Improving Family Welfare, Fulfilling Their Role as Mothers

For the popular-sector women who had been incorporated into Madres del Barrio, the mission's cash transfer and services appear to have contributed to improvements in their own and their families' welfare. Miriam, Aida, and Soraya all remarked how their participation in the mission improved their own and their children's welfare. Both Miriam and Aida primarily used their cash transfers to meet their children's basic welfare needs and fulfill their roles as mothers and "policy conduits" for enhanced family well-being. In addition, Miriam and Aida were able to purchase discounted household appliances through their association with the mission, which also helped them to fulfill their maternal household roles more easily. Paula, too, stated that while she was serving as a mission coordinator, many *madres* purchased washers, stoves, and refrigerators. Adriana—the former municipal mission coordinator in Falcón state—noted how several *madres*, who had been living in overcrowded conditions, used their mission benefits to improve their housing, just as Soraya had used part of her mission benefit to gradually build her house. This is consistent with evaluations of Mexico's CCT program, where beneficiaries reported enhanced well-being and the means to enhance their assets to mitigate risks (Escobar Latapí and González de la Rocha 2009; Molyneux 2008a).

Madres del Barrio also appears to have contributed to improvements to the *madres'* and their children's welfare by linking them to the state health and educational systems. According to Adriana, this included family planning education and access to free birth control. Adriana stated that children of *madres* who had not been attending school entered the school system through the mission's intervention. Both she and Paula in Caracas noted that under their respective leaderships, they encouraged the *madres* to pursue their own education, and as a result *madres* enrolled in the various educational missions—at primary, secondary, and tertiary levels. And Adriana took great pride in the fact that five *madres* from her municipality had graduated from Sucre Mission with university degrees.

Yet, in targeting only women for improving family welfare, Madres del Barrio reified maternal models of care, as did the CCTs in Argentina (Tabbush 2009), Mexico (Molyneux 2006, 2008a), and Nicaragua (Bradshaw 2008; Bradshaw and Quirós Víquez 2008). As Tabbush (2009) asserts, the condition that beneficiary women use their cash transfers to care for their families functioned to "naturalize traditional female roles" and responsibilities "within the family around motherhood and care" (314). That is, Madres del Barrio conditionalities served to reinforce women's maternal altruism and household-level gendered divisions of labor.

Tensions in State-Based Provision of Political Education to the *Madres*

Unlike other CCTs in Latin America, Madres del Barrio Mission provided program beneficiaries with political education in addition to health and welfare education. Through their participation in Madres del Barrio, the bene-ficiaries received education about their rights, but the content and extent of this rights education appear to have varied across time and space. Both Aida and Soraya said that the mission provided the *madres* with education about their constitutional rights. Yet they could tell me only about general ideas, such as the right to equality, and nothing about specific constitutional rights and laws. Soraya noted that the mission did not educate them about specific constitutional articles or about Article 88 in particular. Both former munic-ipal mission coordinators I interviewed—from Caracas and Falcón—noted that under their leadership, the *madres* received education in the 2007 Or-ganic Law of Women's Right to a Life Free from Violence. And Adriana in Falcón stated that the mission educated the *madres* on Chávez's creation of Madres del Barrio Mission as a means to address extreme poverty among women and on Article 88 as the mission's constitutional basis.

Yet the planning, design, and evaluation of such political education and the extent of the *madres'* participation in it were not necessarily under the *madres'* control and driven by the *madres'* expressed needs, voices, and feed-back. Aida said that although the mission always provided *madres* in her community with workshops on women's rights, these were not participatory spaces for the *madres* to provide input on their design and evaluate them. I did observe a School of Socialist Formation for Gender Equality facilita-tor provide the space for the *madres* from one rural Falcón town to evalu-ate the workshops she was giving them, but she had no evaluation planned. She asked me to design and conduct the evaluation even though I had not attended all the workshops that needed to be evaluated. Nor did she docu-ment the oral evaluations that the *madres* did provide.

Madres del Barrio Mission's structure appears to have enabled it to be a space for participatory, critical education and for didactic, controlled, and nonreflexive education about women's rights, depending on who led the mis-sion at particular times and in particular places, who delivered the political education, and what their particular pedagogical and political frameworks were. For example, the School of Socialist Formation for Gender Equality (Escuela de Formación Socialista para la Igualdad de Género, EFOSIG), a MinMujer-administered political education school with branches in every state in the country, provided political education workshops to Madres del Barrio. Under María León's leadership of the national ministry from 2008 to 2010, the school's curriculum apparently focused on socialism, feminism, and gender. After Nancy Pérez assumed the ministry's leadership in 2010, the content of the school's curriculum shifted focus to commune construc-tion and the defense of national sovereignty, while retaining a component on feminism and gender.

With EFOSIG education delivered to Madres del Barrio in Falcón, I observed different facilitators employ didactic and participatory approaches in the political education workshops that they led for *madres* in different communities throughout the state. For example, in one rural town in 2012, I attended a workshop on violence against women that an EFOSIG facilitator gave to a small group of Madres del Barrio. She spent the first part of the workshop lecturing the *madres* on how to organize women in the "battle" to reelect President Chávez. She then used the second part of the workshop to quickly deliver a PowerPoint presentation on what violence against women was, how it functioned, what its consequences were, and the Organic Law of Women's Right to a Life Free from Violence. The facilitator encouraged the participants to know their rights and use such knowledge to help the women in their lives. But she did not provide them with copies of the law or other resources for women experiencing violence. Nor did she provide much space for the participants to discuss the concepts and rights she was presenting and how they applied to their own lives and their own communities.

However, the previous month, I attended a workshop on empowerment given by a different EFOSIG facilitator, Luisa, the Falcón EFOSIG director, to a different group of Madres del Barrio, where she employed both more participatory pedagogical methods and a more radical political framework. In this workshop, Luisa and the participants discussed empowerment as women's increased decision-making about their own bodies, in their own communities, and in political and economic arenas. They also discussed empowerment as the transformation of asymmetric power relations to relationships based on equality, beginning in the home with everyday practices and interactions and extending to national democratic institutions and the economy. Luisa stressed that because of women's role in social reproduction as "transmitters of culture," they were crucial actors in driving Venezuela's transformation toward a socialist, participatory, and protagonistic society. Likewise, in 2011, in the same Madres del Barrio office, I attended an accounting workshop led by a BanMujer facilitator who used participatory popular education methods to advance participants' numerical literacy and accounting skills. The facilitator linked that educational experience to women's constitutional rights to education and training, their insertion into socio-productive activities, and the larger national process of constructing a socialist society.

In these snapshots of state-provided educational workshops to Madres del Barrio in Falcón, the facilitators all emphasized that the *madres* were bearers of rights—a key part of which entailed the right to be central participants in their households, in their communities, and in national political and economic processes. Yet their facilitation styles and their workshops' content reflected a tension between state promotion of a form of popular participation controlled from above and from outside the *madres'* communities and a radical democratic popular participation from below, from the *madres* themselves.

When I asked Luisa, the Falcón EFOSIG director, about this tension in state-delivered political education for Madres del Barrio and its implications for the type of popular power the state was promoting, she recognized this tension between different actors within state gender institutions and the state apparatus more broadly. Within the contested space of the state apparatus, Luisa drew on Chávez's discourse to validate her advocacy for popular women's power in her own work. She stated that the work of the school was to promote socialism and feminism because "the lines of the school are the lines of President Chávez" (Second Interview with Luisa). In her strategic usage of Chávez to legitimate a radical political education project for popular women, her own words reflected this tension between popular participation from below and participation controlled from above, justifying this approach by stating that "popular power is decreed" (Second Interview with Luisa). At the same time, Luisa asserted that in educational programs with Madres del Barrio, "the idea that they are autonomous has to be encouraged. And that is a right, because it forms part of sovereignty: you decide the destiny of your country, not a third person. And when we talk of a participatory and protagonistic democracy, it means that I don't have an interlocutor" (Second Interview with Luisa). She contended that this type of education in radical democracy was well received by the Madres del Barrio, but resistance to it existed within the state institutions, because "when the population becomes conscious of its rights and the importance that it has within this process, you are putting in danger a status . . . of power that the institutions give you" (Second Interview with Luisa).

Mothers of the Bolivarian Revolution:
State Mobilization and Containment of Chávez's Women

This tension around popular power that the Bolivarian state was generating among Madres del Barrio—between popular women's participation from below and popular women's participation controlled from above—appears to have also run through the political activities in which the Madres del Barrio participated. Chávez often employed a discourse that revolutionary mothers' participation was necessary to advance social and political changes crucial for the Bolivarian revolution (Espina and Rakowski 2010). This revolutionary maternalist discourse both honored and reinforced women's maternal altruism, which extended from their households to performing unpaid community work in service of the revolution (Espina and Rakowski 2010). Sujatha Fernandes (2007) contends that Chávez's invocation of a revolutionary motherhood trope contained contradictory implications for the popular women it interpellated, such as the Madres del Barrio. According to Fernandes, such rhetoric both reinforced and challenged traditional gender roles for popular women because it "created the groundwork for new possible roles and identities to emerge" (102). With the Madres del Barrio, their participation in the mission opened up possibilities for developing new political roles and identities. Yet, their political protagonism often was based on, reflected, and reinforced their role as mothers. The mission's promotion of revolutionary maternalism served as regulatory device, wherein the *madres*' dependence on the mission benefit enabled the state to demand their political protagonism and to direct and contain their political identities and activities.

For Miriam, Aida, and Soraya, Chávez's leadership inspired them to take on new political identities, and they remarked that they became involved in party politics during Chávez's presidency. Many Madres del Barrio also appeared to have become involved in party politics; informal accounts from state actors indicate that many *madres* joined the PSUV since they joined the mission. And these new political identities provided opportunities for them to exercise leadership roles in local political organizing. For example, Aida became a patrol officer (*patrullera*) for PSUV and was assisting with organizing community members for the 2012 elections. Paula and Luisa stated that other Madres del Barrio had also become PSUV *patrulleras* and had conducted house-by-house electoral organizing drives in their communities. Luisa further asserted that she had noted a political maturation among some Madres del Barrio with whom she had been working over time: they were no longer "only Chávez's women, but they now also express other opinions about what is happening in their environment" (Second Interview with Luisa).

Yet, the *madres*' new political identities and activities as revolutionary mothers were vulnerable to state manipulation, as other Bolivarian state actors appear to have been keenly aware that the Madres del Barrio were "Chávez's women" and interpellated them as such. "Chávez's women" (*mujeres de Chávez*) was a term I observed employed by emcees and authorities at Bolivarian state events across times and spaces to hail the popular women in the audience. In other words, they consistently used this term as a shout-out to the popular women in the crowd. For example, the most common way they used the term at such events was "Where are Chávez's women?!" (¿Donde están las mujeres de Chávez?!) And I observed many women in crowds shouting back jubilantly in recognition of this hailing. In functioning as a call-and-response between the Bolivarian state and popular women, it therefore served to interpellate popular women's political identity as not just tied to Chávez but also belonging to him. Such authorities constantly called on the *madres* as revolutionary mothers to focus their political mobilization on supporting Chávez and thus to organize for his reelection. The gendered political opening for the *madres'* political participation, which was legitimated through a revolutionary maternalist discourse, also constituted an opportunity for the state to attempt to direct their political organization. Such an attempt to direct the *madres'* political participation is illustrated in the sixth anniversary celebration of the mission in Falcón described in the opening to this book (see my introduction). As that opening description shows, the male state coordinator of the mission stressed that the *madres* would be central to Chávez's successful reelection campaign because of their maternal altruism, their love for their commander, and their greater political protagonism (as implicitly compared to men). He framed the revolution's continuation as dependent on the *madres'* political participation. Yet on that day he and other state authorities announced they were "paying homage" to the Madres del Barrio, they staged the celebration to both mobilize and contain the Madres del Barrio by limiting their voices to supporting Chávez. The *madres'* state-directed mobilization and containment was in line with what Fernandes (2010) has described as a broader vertical and instrumental Bolivarian state approach to popular-sector political organization.

The Madres del Barrio present at the Falcón state sixth anniversary celebration of the mission responded jubilantly to state authorities interpellating them as revolutionary mothers organizing for Chávez, yet not all Madres del Barrio appear to have been content with the way state authorities were framing and, in some instances, controlling their political participation. One of the former *madres* reflected to me how she observed the state using the *madres* for its own political ends in 2012. For example:

> Former *madre*: It seems like a lie, but now it has turned into pure politics, a pure joke (*broma*) that people want to sign [into attendance registers at official events], show things that they are not doing. And the truth is that the *madres* are not being attended to as they should be.

Rachel: And what are they doing with the *madres* right now?
Former *madre*: They only use them when there is a march.

This former *madre*'s choice of the term "use" in analyzing the political dynamic unfolding between the state and the *madres* is apt, given that some of the state actors calling on the *madres* to organize and attend political events were the same officials who controlled the *madres*' access to the mission cash transfer. According to her, the *madres* she knew were quite aware of how the state was using them, and they were willing to participate in this arrangement as long as they continued to receive their cash transfers. This former *madre* said that the mission benefit's temporary nature lubricated this political dynamic. The *madres* were aware that the benefit was temporary, she noted, and some understood this to mean that if they did not participate in state marches and political events and prove that they had by signing attendance registers at them, then the state could take away their cash transfers.

With this former *madre*, I too observed the importance attributed to the *madres*' signatures on attendance registers at state-run political events. One afternoon, several months before the 2012 presidential election, we traveled together to a *barrio* to attend a government event/political rally at which President Chávez was expected to speak. When we arrived, the *madres* from her *barrio* were already in attendance, alongside local mission authorities, and waiting for the president to arrive. The mission appears to have expected the *madres* to attend this rally, and to arrive early at that, because the *madres* were signing attendance registers before the event began in order to prove to the mission staff that they were present.[14]

In addition, unlike the *madres*' stories of rapid incorporation into the mission, I heard stories among them about the state not transferring cash to *madres* for months at a time. Similar stories from various regions across Venezuela about mission cash transfers absent for months also appear on Bolivarian state media and comments sections on Chávez websites. In addition, I heard rumors circulating that *madres* would be disincorporated from the mission in the run-up to the 2012 presidential election.[15] Whether or not there was any truth to these rumors, some perceived the potential risk to be real. This was the case, for example, for one of the *madres* who was still in the mission in 2012 and who agreed to be interviewed by me then without the mission's knowledge. She subsequently withdrew her participation from my study less than two months before the presidential election because of fears that state authorities would discover what she told me.[16] Thus, as does Auyero (2012), I contend that the importance of these accounts does not lie in whether these rumors and fears about the state stripping *madres* of their benefits were verifiable, but in how the *madres* perceived the state and how such perceptions shaped their interactions with the state. What these accounts reveal is that *madres* understood the continuation of their benefits to be uncertain and linked to their political voice and participation in support of and in line with the Bolivarian state.

Even if state actors were not explicitly or implicitly threatening to strip *madres* of their benefits in the 2012 electoral year if they did not toe certain lines about how to participate politically, the lack of guidelines and transparency around how long and under what conditions *madres* were entitled to receive the mission cash transfer created the environment for the transfer to be used by mission officials, or at least understood by mission beneficiaries to be used, as a device to control the *madres'* political voice and participation. This indicates that not only was Madres del Barrio a social policy created, funded, and sustained at the president's discretion, but it could also serve as a discretionary tool for regional and local state authorities to determine under what conditions popular-sector women could and would continue to benefit from it. The discretionary and temporary nature of the mission's cash transfer could create what Fraser (1997) terms an "exploitable dependency" of the *madres* on the whims of state officials (46). Those conditions could be political, and in turn shape the political participation of mission participants, who may have depended on the cash transfer to support themselves and their families. Thus, the selective nature and uncertain duration of the cash transfer provided the grounds for state authorities to use the mission as a clientelist vehicle for the *madres'* political mobilization and containment.

Indeed, Adriana, the former Falcón municipal mission coordinator who served in this position after Gioconda Mota's presidency of the mission, informed me that part of the *acta compromiso*—the commitment agreement that the *madres* signed with the mission when they entered it—consisted of a "political commitment." She explained that this was a commitment by the *madres* to "active political participation," which included "giving support to the current system of government, which is that of President Hugo Chávez Frías" (First Interview with Adriana).

The politics of "giving" between the *madres* and the president appears to have both informed and facilitated the dynamics between the *madres* and the Bolivarian state. For example, Adriana referred to the mission cash transfer as a "benefit that the president gave to women of scarce resources to improve their quality of life" (First Interview with Adriana). Across several geographic regions of Venezuela, I heard *madres* refer to the cash transfer and services that they were receiving through the mission as things that

Chávez was "giving" them. In this discourse framing the Madres del Barrio cash transfer as an executive gift, the language of rights was absent, even though Chávez himself decreed that the mission was in accordance with the constitutional right to state recognition of unpaid housework's socioeconomic value.[17] Yet the cash transferred to poor mothers by Madres del Barrio could be popularly interpreted as a benefit Chávez had "given" them because it was enacted by executive decree and disarticulated from legislative processes and the long struggle by women's rights activists for state recognition of unpaid housework and homemakers' social security. In fact, the *madres* who referred to the president "giving" them the mission cash transfer appeared to be unaware of the legislative and women's movement processes for state recognition of unpaid housework and homemakers' social security. The fact that the executive granted the Madres del Barrio cash transfer to a select number of poor homemakers also enabled the benefit to be popularly interpreted as a gift and not a right by the women who received it and the state authorities who administered it. This historical disarticulation, coupled with the selective nature of the mission benefit, served to enhance Chávez's executive magic, allowing him to be understood as personally using his magnanimous powers to pull benefits/gifts out of his magician's hat for the select *madres*. Yet when economic benefits granted by the state to citizens are understood as gifts and not as rights, then they can also be understood as needing to be reciprocated by their recipients.

The discretionary design of Madres del Barrio Mission therefore intersected with popular interpretations of the mission cash transfer, ties between the *madres* and President Chávez, and revolutionary motherhood to create a context in which the mission could be—and appears to have been—used as a vehicle for clientelist exchanges between the Bolivarian state and the *madres* in the 2012 presidential election year. Because the cash transfer was not universally available to all extremely poor homemakers, mission authorities could use it politically and/or be understood to be using it politically. Where clientelist exchanges occurred, *madres* received and/or understood that they received crucial material benefits—or gifts—from the executive in exchange for their ongoing political mobilization in line with state expectations. The clientelist exchanges that occurred appear not to have been about traditional clientelist vote-buying—the Madres del Barrio I observed and heard spoken of appeared to have already supported Chávez and the Bolivarian government.[18] Rather, the clientelist exchange of the Madres del Barrio cash transfer appears to have constituted what Benjamin Goldfrank (2011) terms "participatory clientelism," because it was for the *madres'* continuous political presence, voice, and organization in support of the Bo-

Figure 4.1. "We are the Madres del Barrio, of the Socialist Homeland, Commander, we say to you, we Women are ready!"; sign at International Women's Day rally in Caracas, 2012 (photo by author)

livarian government. Thus, the exchange was also for the *madres'* time to devote themselves to such political activities. These accounts indicate that such exchanges were unequal—the state and not the *madres* controlled who had access to the mission cash transfer, and under what conditions and for what duration. And they indicate that the conditions and duration of the cash transfer were not fixed and clear but uncertain. This uncertainty about benefit conditions and duration positioned the *madres* as uncertain clients of the Bolivarian state.[19] With this uncertain status, *madres* appear to have understood that their ongoing receipt of the mission cash transfer hinged on their continuous political performance as revolutionary mothers in support of and in line with the Bolivarian state.

Mothers of the *Barrio*: Extending the *Madres'* Reproductive Labor from the Household to the Community

In spite of the Bolivarian state's expectations of the *madres'* continuous political performance, Miriam, Soraya and both the former municipal mission coordinators I interviewed asserted that women did not have to fulfill any obligations in order to benefit from the mission. Yet, when I probed further, all of them except for Miriam noted that *madres* were expected to perform volunteer community work.[20] Both Soraya and the former Falcón municipal mission coordinator said that such work formed part of the *acta compromiso* the *madres* signed when they entered the mission. In addition, the executive decree establishing the mission stated that the *madres* should "assume the commitment . . . to participate with their families in organizing processes of the communities to which they belong" (Chávez Frías, 24 March 2006). The Madres del Barrio committees were designed as the vehicle to articulate the *madres'* community organizing work.

The state actors who had worked or continued to work with Madres del Barrio I interviewed all spoke of the Madres del Barrio committees as spaces for previously socially isolated and excluded women to come together, share knowledge and experiences, build their self-confidence, organize, and develop their community leadership skills. For example, Gioconda Mota asserted:

> It was really beautiful, because we are talking about women who never left their house, never left their intimate circle. First to start to meet with the women in their Madres del Barrio Committee. . . . Already there is a giant feminist political step, which is to recognize oneself in the other, to start to make friends with others, and to start to do things in common. Then they begin to take charge of many other things like political participation, because they are highly combative women, the social participation in the seat of their communities, that then the responsibility of reproductive care is also extended to the care of the community. (First Interview with Gioconda Mota)

Both former municipal mission coordinators spoke of how such a process of meeting and organizing with other women built the *madres'* self-confidence by giving them spaces to exercise their voices and skills. As Soraya's story shows, the Madres del Barrio committee provided her with the space to share her professional and occupational knowledge and experience through training other *madres*, and, as such, to develop her teaching and leadership skills. And both former municipal coordinators and the Falcón EFOSIG director noted that many of the *madres* made use of their enhanced self-confidence and leadership skills by participating in their communal councils. Miriam insisted that *madres* she knew who were previously ashamed to speak and participate in social activities were now actively participating in their communities. Such community participation could serve to enhance the *madres'* status in their respective communities. Both Aida and Soraya, for example, remarked that members of their respective communities now saw them as leaders and sought them out for assistance. These accounts from former *madres* and gender institution workers are consistent with evaluations of Mexico's CCT program, where it was found to provide a space for women participants to boost their self-confidence, develop solidarity with each other, engage in expanded realms of activities, and thereby enhance their autonomy (Molyneux 2008a).

Miriam, Aida, and Soraya all participated in their respective community's Madres del Barrio committee, and in so doing they fulfilled their communal coresponsibilities by extending their reproductive roles from their individual households to their communities and attending to vulnerable community members' welfare needs. They all spoke of their respective committee as a vehicle to bring *madres* together and exercise leadership roles, as well as to organize to meet health, education, food, recreation, and transport needs of vulnerable community members. Aida described this community work performed by the Madres del Barrio committees as "collaborating with everything"—the health, education, and food systems in the community. They looked after these systems, ensuring that they were working and that community members in need were incorporated into them.

To facilitate this community work, each community's Madres del Barrio committee elected a spokesperson for each area of social welfare. In order to fulfill community work duties, Aida, Miriam, and Soraya all described carrying out what were termed "censes" or *diagnósticos*, or community needs assessments. Paula explained that the *madres* were well suited to conduct *diagnósticos* of community members' needs because they were the ones who spent the most time at home and in the community and, in turn, knew best the "reality of the household and the community" (Interview with Paula). This former municipal mission coordinator invoked the *madres'* maternal role, tying them physically and geographically to the household and the community to explain their positioning here as social policy conduits. Using the *diagnóstico* to inform her community work meant that as her Madres del Barrio committee's health spokesperson, Miriam said that she knew the names and addresses of everyone in her community suffering from an illness or disability. She used this information to assist and accompany the Barrio Adentro doctor in house-by-house visits or to channel such community members to more advanced medical services. Soraya was also her committee's health spokesperson, and carrying out this role had her working half days every day of the week during her time in the mission, accompanying the Barrio Adentro doctor in his house-by-house visits, and bathing, cleaning, vaccinating, and doing the washing for sick and disabled members of her community as well as vaccinating members of other communities. Performing Madres del Barrio community work therefore could constitute a substantial workload for the *madres*, and at the same time it could be essential to channeling many vulnerable community members to appropriate services and meeting their basic welfare needs.

The *madres'* community care work made an important contribution to rebuilding collective life and community in the *barrios*, according to women's studies professor and former advisor to the National Assembly, Alba Carosio. She notes that "Venezuelan society was very fractured . . . there was a great individualism, above all in the cities. That mutual collaboration, that sharing that has to be in social spaces was not there, and really the mothers of the *barrio* that are currently the Madres del Barrio have contributed to articulating those social spaces" (Interview with Alba Carosio). Thus, even as Madres del Barrio Mission was a dividing force between popular women in communities, it had simultaneously served as a unifying force in rebuilding social cohesion and collective life in popular-sector communities.

Yet this vital community work came with costs to the Madres del Barrio who performed it. Part of the coresponsibility of the Madres del Barrio community work appears to have consisted of *madres* contributing a portion of their monthly cash transfers to meet the welfare needs of other *madres* and vulnerable members of their communities. Soraya described how this worked within her community's Madres del Barrio committee: "We organized ourselves as a committee . . . when the mission [benefit] was paid." Out of the 300 Bolívares that they each received monthly, they each contributed 20 Bolívares to one pool. "Then we went to the Mercals and we bought all that in food . . . then we prepared bags—ten bags or more . . . and in each bag we put flour, sugar, rice, pasta, oil, sardines . . . and we took the bags to those who were poorest." Paula, the former Caracas municipal mission coordinator, and the three former mission beneficiaries I interviewed asserted that this economic contribution was not mandatory, but their responses showed that across times and spaces, the *madres* were contributing their own money to meet other community members' needs. And because such organizing occurred across times and spaces in Venezuela, it appears to have been a standard procedure within the mission. Adriana, the former Falcón municipal mission coordinator, spoke of such organizing as standard operating procedure in her municipality, saying that each committee in her municipality organized "solidarity pots" with a portion of each *madre*'s transfer, and the pots were used to cover medical, food, clothing, transport, and funeral costs of members of the *madres*' communities (First Interview with Adriana). Both former municipal mission coordinators and Miriam referred to organizing "solidarity pots" from the *madres*' transfers to cover community needs as "socialist" work. For example, Adriana said that this practice gave the *madres* a "socialist . . . vision": "in other words, the government is helping you, because of that, you can also help others" (First Interview with Adriana). And Miriam said that as a socialist, she needed to "look beyond her own interests also at the needs and concerns and problems that her neighbor or whatever person who needed" her had.

Although some referred to such community organizing as a socialist measure, in essence, the *madres* were organizing to make up for the shortfalls in the Bolivarian state's social policy measures. In the absence of progressive tax reform and universally substantive wealth redistribution from the rich to the poor during Chávez's tenure,[21] some of the economic burden for meeting the welfare needs of the poorest community members was not being offloaded onto members of society with sufficient economic capacity to contribute, but onto the Madres del Barrio—women excluded from the formal economy whose monthly income was 80 percent of the minimum-wage salary. Thus, where the state's social assistance programs did not reach, the poor mothers of the *barrios* reached into the state social assistance they received to organize mutual assistance for those even poorer and more excluded than they themselves. The discourse of the *madres*' socialist solidarity was invoked to justify this practice, which, in reality, resembled popular women's community welfare organizing under neoliberalism: they "pick[ed] up where the state left off" (Lind 2005, 93).

These accounts also indicate that Madres del Barrio hinged on an extant ideology of maternal altruism, which legitimated poor women's personal sacrifices and performance of unpaid labor for their communities in addition to their households, similar to CCTs in Nicaragua (Bradshaw 2008) and Argentina (Tabbush 2009). As Luccisano and Wall (2009) point out, CCTs interact with "local cultural understandings of gender and motherhood," which themselves are "moral regulatory processes" (200).

The accounts detailed above of the *madres'* community organizing and care work show that Madres del Barrio hinged on the intersection of such an extant maternalist ideology with Bolivarian state imaginations of women's unpaid labor and popular power within the revolution. In addition to promoting a model of a virtuous empowered woman willing to sacrifice herself and perform unpaid labor for her family and her community, the mission promoted a model of a virtuous mother sacrificing herself for the broader goals of the popular socialist revolution. Further, just as Bradshaw (2008) concludes in the case of Nicaragua's CCT, the Bolivarian state did not "problematize" the *madres'* maternal altruism for their homes, their communities, and the revolution, but rather promoted it as "the social norm" (201).

Challenges to Becoming "Productive" Protagonists When the State Externalized the *Madres'* Reproductive Labor

At the same time as Madres del Barrio Mission expected the *madres* to become mothers of their *barrios* by extending their reproductive work and giving their own social assistance money out to their communities, the mission also expected them to become independent of state assistance by joining together in economic associative units, receiving training in productive occupations, and launching and sustaining their own small businesses. According to Paula and Miriam, part of the *acta compromiso* consisted of the *madres* committing to form economic associative units and engage in socioproductive activities. For Paula, this was an integral part of the *madres'* commitment to *salir adelante*, "to get ahead." The mission expected the *madres* to *salir adelante* through intensifying their labor by performing both reproductive and productive labor, sometimes simultaneously. According to Aida and the Falcón EFOSIG director, the mission promoted the idea that the *madres* start their productive activities from home, so that they could attend to their households and their businesses at the same time.

Miriam, Aida, and both former municipal mission coordinators noted that the mission did not provide the *madres* with childcare services during periods of productive work or training for their productive occupations (or when they were participating in other mission activities).[22] Both Miriam and Aida also said that the "idea" of the mission was that they attend to their productive activities while their children were at school. Paradoxically, even though the government stated that the mission was born out of the constitution's recognition of unpaid housework, the mission treated the *madres'* unpaid reproductive labor as an externality when the *madres* aimed to fulfill the mission's productive work coresponsibility.

Indeed, the former Falcón municipal mission coordinator's words show that the mission itself appears not to have taken the *madres'* need for alternative care services into account; she said that she "imagined" the *madres* would either leave the people they cared for with family members or they would perform their productive labor while their children were at school (Second Interview with Adriana). Gioconda Mota, one of the mission's designers and the mission's president from 2006 to 2008, admitted that under her leadership the mission did not get around to addressing the issue of alternative care services for the *madres'* dependents.[23] And Miriam's, Aida's, and the two former municipal mission coordinators' responses indicate that after Mota left her post, the mission had still not addressed the issue of alternative care services.

Indeed, as Miriam's and Aida's stories show, they often brought their children with them to the site of their productive occupations and performed their productive and reproductive work simultaneously. In the absence of institutionalized public mechanisms to substitute these women's unpaid care work, the key to *saliendo adelante* and entering the paid market sphere rested on intensifying their labor and being able to perform not only a double shift[24] but also two jobs at once. Carolina, a national-level feminist public official problematized this scenario:

> The curious thing there is . . . because you fulfill nonmarket responsibilities, the mission selects you for that reason. When you enter to take part in the mission, the mission prepares you so that you form part of the market, and all the nonmarket work that you did that was previously recognized, is not taken up. . . . In other words, . . . they facilitate access to the market, and you can now be a "productive" person, but that does not resolve what was keeping you out of the market, which would be the situation of need or dependency that people in your family grouping have. That would require for example that there were care policies, day care policies, policies of attention. What appears to me to have happened . . . is that the mothers that have achieved their entrepreneurship have done so inside of their homes so that they can maintain simultaneity. And that . . . can represent a problem when you are not freed from the responsibility, when you are not socializing the care. The care is still the mothers' responsibility and furthermore they are asked to be active in the market. In other words, the double demand is clear, with some facilities, yes, but it remains. And the society or

the state does not share the care that kept you on the margins. (Interview with Carolina)

Thus, the mission's failure to provide structural alternatives to women's unpaid household care work and, by extension, its implicit assumption that *madres* would individually find alternatives and in many cases turn to other (female) family members' unpaid labor, belie Article 88. Starting out claiming to recognize poor women's unpaid care work, Madres del Barrio ended up reproducing the nonrecognition of that very same work.

Dividing the *Madres* Who "Get Ahead" from Those Who "Stay Behind"

The various popular women, state actors, and women's movement activists and analysts I talked with were not in agreement whether Madres del Barrio Mission fulfilled Article 88, but the former *madres* and state actors who had (direct) involvement with the Madres del Barrio I interviewed were all clear that the cash transfer was meant to be temporary and to assist the *madres* while they received training and started up their socio-productive projects. Aida stated: "The purpose is very clear . . .: it is temporary assistance where you can . . . train oneself as a woman, and do a socio-productive [activity] where you can later take care of yourself and you improve your quality of life. In other words, it's not that you stay there, but that you try to better yourself." According to Aida and Miriam, the *madres* who were originally incorporated into the mission were informed that the cash transfer would last for six months. Apparently the mission informed the *madres* that they should relinquish their temporary benefit in order to become independent of social assistance. According to Gioconda Mota, Aida, and Soraya, the mission also informed them that they should do this so that other women who were in need could take up their spaces in the mission. The mission implied that the *madres* were responsible for other poor homemakers' welfare, similar to how it framed their roles within their respective communities. In signaling that limited state social assistance was available, the mission set the expectation that the *madres* should fulfill their coresponsibilities to uplift themselves (and their families because of their roles as mothers) and also ensure that those limited resources would reach other poor women from their communities.

Yet, by 2012—six years into the mission's existence—all accounts I heard from both the former *madres* and state actors and authorities I interviewed indicated that few *madres* had left the mission and relinquished their cash transfers, in spite of all the economic associative units that had been formed among them[25] and all the public events where high-level state authorities up to President Chávez had granted them loans to launch their businesses. For example, Aida said that even though several hundred women from her *barrio* had been incorporated into Madres del Barrio, *madres* from her *barrio* had launched only three socio-productive projects, and Aida's cooperative was the only one that had made advancements. As Miriam expressed, the rest had *quedado en el camino*, "stayed behind." In contrast, the state had held up Miriam, Aida, and Soraya as the mission's poster women, because they had launched their cooperatives, relinquished their mission cash transfers, and ran their own shops. These three former *madres* had *salido para adelante*, as both they and state actors said. Aida relinquished her cash transfer a year after joining the mission, Miriam five years after joining the mission, and Soraya six years after joining. Why, in 2012, in spite of the mission's multidimensional conception of poverty and its corresponding professed provision of economic, social, and political assistance to the *madres*, had so few of them exited the mission? And why had it taken years for the few of them who had exited the mission to exit when the mission had purportedly originally envisioned that they would stay in it for only six months?

I posed these questions in my interviews with the former *madres* and all the state actors who had worked directly or indirectly with the *madres*. The majority responded that very few *madres* had left the mission because of their own (individual) behavior. However, several did provide different explanations that highlighted structural barriers with the mission and state more broadly. Soraya provided an example of the latter, responding that *madres* who had children with disabilities had not been able to exit the mission because no one else would assume their care, and these were the majority of the women who continued to receive the mission cash transfer. Soraya's remarks indicate a structural care deficit in regard to people with disabilities, yet she did not identify the state as potentially coresponsible for sharing this care burden with the *madres*. Alba Carosio[26] noted that many *madres* had not exited the mission because their care burdens had actually intensified: they were fulfilling their coresponsibility to carry out community work in addition to their household work, and they did not have time to successfully pursue paid work (Interview with Alba Carosio). In addition, Aida noted that the mission was no longer monitoring and supervising the *madres*; many of the new mission staff were not going to the *barrios*,[27] attending to the *madres* in them, and assisting them with getting their socio-productive projects off the ground. Adriana in Falcón also noted discontinuity in the *madres'* supervision—much of the previous mission staff who had developed close relationships with the *madres* in her municipality had been dismissed, and the new mission staff that replaced them did not regularly visit the *madres*. And Claudia, a municipal state gender institution worker in a different Falcón municipality where Madres del Barrio Mission was present, argued that the *madres* were not exiting the mission because the state was not adequately supervising them (Interview with Claudia).

Yet when asked about why so few *madres* had exited the mission, the majority of the people I interviewed (including the former *madres* themselves) tended not to identify structural barriers. Instead, they tended to turn their mirrors inward to the *barrios* to scrutinize the *madres* and their behavior and blame them for not *echando pa'lante*, not making an effort to get ahead. For example, Miriam explained to me that the other *madres* had not exited the mission "because they do not want to do the socio-productive [project], they don't want to do something, except nothing more than merely collect the money and that's it. You collected, you spent it, and that's it—there you go spending your time. And that's not the idea; the idea is to instruct yourself to undertake something." Here, Miriam attributed the *madres'* failure to undertake socio-productive projects to their lack of initiative. In so doing, she implied that these *madres* were doing nothing except continuing to collect and spend the money the state gave them. Miriam characterized them as nonproductive mothers—akin to the popular perception of the *vagas del barrio* (slackers of the *barrio*) that Falcón state gender institution worker Ana María described earlier in this chapter. Even though Aida had identified problems with the mission staff's supervision practices, she concurred with Miriam in blaming the *madres* who had "stayed behind" for remaining in the mission. Aida went further by explicitly asserting that, in not fulfilling the mission coresponsibilities and continuing to depend on the state, the *madres* were acting out of self-interest and doing nothing:

> The idea is that it had been for six months, but there are women that are there four years collecting and they have not arisen as persons; they remain there expecting nothing more than the benefit. . . . In other words, they don't have perspective. Sometimes I would like to get inside their heads to see how they can spend the whole day without doing anything, . . . They are accustomed to everything being given to them. Then, nothing is for free. Things have to be earned . . . they are always on the lookout for what is going to be given to them—interest first.

Miriam and Aida both argued that the *madres* who had "stayed behind" in the mission were not working. Here then were two popular women, who had "gotten ahead" with the assistance of a mission that explicitly claimed to recognize the value of women's unpaid housework, turning around and not recognizing that same work that their fellow *madres* were carrying out in their homes and communities.

These former *madres* were not alone in blaming the individual *madres* for not undertaking paid labor, exiting the mission, and "getting ahead." State women's and gender equality institution workers also did this. For example, Carla, a regional women's institution worker, stated:

> There are *madres* that have been benefiting from it for five, six years . . . and you have not gotten ahead? Because in some moment you have to survive because you don't have that assistance. But now what are you doing? It's as if you have a pension and you are an old lady. And you are not an old lady; you are someone who can do many things. (Interview with Carla)

Here, Carla echoed Miriam's and Aida's explanations in implying that the *madres* remaining in the mission were not working. She too overlooked the household work that they carried out, in addition to the community work they performed, where the state did not reach, and the political work they did supporting the revolution. Likewise, Yolimar, a national gender institution worker, ignored the value of the nonmarket activities that the *madres* were carrying out in support of their households, their communities, and the Bolivarian state. She cited the mission's coresponsibilities to justify her blaming the *madres* for not exiting it, arguing that the *madres'* continued dependence on the state violated the intention of the mission cash transfer as temporary social assistance:

> They have to leave the benefit . . . the mission was not made so that people were receiving a scholarship for their whole life; the mission was made as a process of transition toward the training and incorporation into productive work. . . . That is the fundamental condition and objective of the mission. In other words, it is finite. . . . But then so that the women understand, you have to tell them, not hand them over the money as if you deserve it. . . . They believe that they deserve it. "And because Chávez gave it to me and I earned it and that's it." No, it's not like that; you have to know why I am a candidate for this benefit, why they are giving it to me, in what I am contributing in the formation of a new model of a country of new men and women, why an activity has to do with the interests of the community to which I belong . . . they have to be made to understand, we have to understand the role that we play in our social space and that is important, most important. Because if not, the state has a bloodletting: all the money

lost . . . but no one remained at least ideologically trained. (Interview with
Yolimar)

In addition to blaming the *madres* remaining in the mission for violating the
mission's objectives, Yolimar also argued that they were violating the revolution's objectives by freeloading and bleeding the nation dry of resources
necessary to construct the new (socialist) social contract. For Yolimar, the
madres remaining in the mission had not assumed the participatory and
protagonistic character that the Bolivarian state and revolution expected of
them because they had not weaned themselves off state assistance and undertaken paid work. Similarly, Paula, the former municipal mission coordinator, contended that the *madres* who remained in the mission had not fulfilled their coresponsibilities set for them by the state.

In turning their mirrors inward to blame the *madres* for failing to fulfill their coresponsibilities and exit the mission, several state gender institution workers attributed these failures to what they saw as the *madres'*
entrenched culture of dependency. They argued that these *madres* were dependent mothers who had become accustomed to an ever-present "paternalistic" state. Paula, for instance, stated that in popular-sector communities,
"a culture of paternalism to which we are always accustomed" is "difficult
to leave behind" (Interview with Paula). Several other state gender institution workers asserted that the state's continued "giving" of the mission cash
transfer to the *madres* perpetuated such a culture of dependency. For example, Yolimar explained:

> Because if you keep giving a scholarship to a person . . . you are creat-
> ing a dependent person who is waiting for a scholarship in order to be able
> to live and who, even being of the age and having the strength and train-
> ing to incorporate herself in a productive activity or a productive job, she
> is not doing it because it is easier. Because I stay here in my house waiting
> for . . . what Madres del Barrio gives me, and I don't work. (Interview with
> Yolimar)

In other words, Yolimar believed that the cash transfer exacerbated the
madres' laziness and lack of productivity—a view that was shared by Adriana,
the former municipal mission coordinator, and apparently by the mission's
national leadership in 2012. Adriana repeatedly cited Nancy Pérez, then minister of woman's popular power and gender equality, who apparently had
stated that the mission "mutilates the *madres*."[28] Adriana explained that the
minister asserted this because

the *madres* get accustomed . . . there are many *madres* who do not progress inside of the mission because they think that always being in the same poverty, the state will never strip them of the benefit. Then when she says that it mutilates them, it's because it doesn't utilize them: the mother doesn't seek to fulfill other roles for the simple fact that the state is giving them economic support. (Second Interview with Adriana)

These state gender institution workers identified a paternalistic culture as a key barrier to *madres'* economic independence in the context of what they saw as a present (if not too benevolent) state actively assisting the *madres*, upon which the *madres* had become dependent. Yet their explanation appears not to have been informed by a bottom-up perspective in which *madres* themselves had identified the barriers they had encountered to exiting the mission.

Such an explanation blaming the bulk of *madres* who continued to depend on social assistance deflected the mirror away from Chávez, the magnanimous sorcerer who enacted Madres del Barrio, and the Bolivarian government, and averted reflection on how the government's structuring of the mission had enabled only a few women to "get ahead." In attributing the mission's failures to an entrenched culture of paternalism among the *madres* who "stayed behind," these former *madres* and state gender institution workers did not identify the *structural paternalism* in terms of the state's absences in care services, the state's implicit assumption that popular women would fill in such gaps and provide such care work for free, and thus how the state *depended* on them to fill in gaps in its social services. Nor did they identify men's absences in care work and household reproduction in the *barrios*. This in turn reinforced the privatization, individualization, and feminization of care, wherein the burden of care work was (once again) placed on individual popular women's shoulders. As Luccisano and Wall (2009) conclude, failure to fulfill CCT coresponsibilities "becomes both individualized and gendered, and mothers who do not take advantage of the opportunities" that CCTs provide "have no one but themselves to blame" (213). Such reinforcement of regulatory gender norms neglected to address how popular women's unpaid work constituted a significant obstacle to their ability to undertake paid socio-productive activities and economically support themselves and their children without state support.[29] CCTs depend on poor women's unpaid labor, yet they do not problematize it; they both deploy poor women's unpaid labor and "take it for granted" (Molyneux 2008a, 7). With Madres del Barrio Mission, the *madres'* unpaid community and political work was indispensable, yet its value remained invisible to the Bolivarian state. The *madres* in turn were blamed for not *echando pa'lante*, for not forming socio-productive activities, and for not exiting the mission—in essence, for continuing to depend on the state and "not work."

This antagonism toward the *madres* who "stayed behind" in the mission was exacerbated by the deployment of the image of the *madres* who had "gotten ahead" by getting off the mission cash transfer. The image of these success cases is one that former *madres* themselves used to set themselves apart from the *madres* who had not left the mission. For example, Miriam asserted:

> The idea is to . . . unite with other women . . . and form your socio-productive [project]. But there are many that don't want that, but only to collect the incentive and pass by unnoticed without doing anything. And that is not the idea; the idea is to capacitate yourself, do something—like we did, like we capacitated ourselves and we studied . . . they stayed behind . . . they only wanted to collect the money and continue doing nothing. . . . But us, we did, because the idea was to push forward and progress.

The former municipal mission coordinators also used these success cases as examples against which they judged the *madres* who stayed behind. For example, Paula mentioned former *madres* who had "gotten ahead" through launching their businesses and exiting the mission and compared them favorably to the "dependent" *madres* who remained in the mission (Interview with Paula). Adriana said that the mission staff held up the handful of *madres* who had studied, found work, and exited the mission in spite of their heavy care loads as examples for the other *madres* to follow. Once again, Madres del Barrio served as a dividing force among popular-sector women, both among the *madres* themselves and between the *madres* and the mission staff who judged them. Instead of serving as a vehicle for poor women to come together to interrogate how their unpaid work was positioned within the mission, the community, and the economy more broadly, the mission and popular discourses about it served as vehicles to set them against each other.

In making these comparisons, both the former mission participants and staff differentiated "independent" from "dependent" mothers, and in so doing reproduced a discursive dichotomy between good and bad mothers. Yet, building upon Molyneux's conclusion that the coresponsibilities that CCTs expect mothers to fulfill resignify conceptions of good and bad motherhood (Molyneux 2008a), I contend that these former mission participants and staff resignified a preexisting discursive dichotomy between good and bad mothers within the framework of the Bolivarian revolution. In the context of Madres del Barrio, they framed a good mother not just as a mother who would stay at home to care for her children and her household, but also as a mother who would form and sustain a small business in order to care for her children and sometimes would carry out both activities simultaneously, in addition to performing (unpaid) grassroots social and political work. For example, Miriam expressed that a good *madre* would start her own socio-productive project and get off state assistance because it "is something for your children and your family, for your own progress." A good mother would become an independent actor in paid activities and get ahead and progress for the sake of her family. Whereas a bad mother would act out of self-interest, continue to be involved in solely unpaid activities and depend on the state, and thus fail to embrace her participatory and protagonistic character necessary to construct the socialist homeland. In the worst of cases, a bad mother would use her cash transfer on something other than her family (and her community).[30] In popular discourse, a bad mother expected the state to "give to her" without working for her "scholarship."

So here Madres del Barrio completed a vicious about-face: *in starting out claiming to recognize the socioeconomic value of poor women's unpaid labor, the mission ended up reproducing nonrecognition of such work, even as the mission intensified it.* The deployment of this resignified good mother/bad mother dichotomy enabled the mission's failures to be attributed to the *madres* instead of attributing them to the structure of the mission, (the lack of) state care services, and the economy more broadly. In addition, persistent gender roles that charged women with household care burdens, especially in the absence of the fathers of the *barrios*, enabled the mission's failures to be attributed to the *madres* as individual women. Instead of creating solidarity, or sisterhood among popular-sector women, the deployment of this discursive dichotomy reproduced and resignified divisions among them.

But if one looks to the example of the living and working conditions of the good mother produced through this mission—a mother such as Aida or Miriam—a woman who worked nonstop both inside and outside the home, simultaneously fulfilling productive and reproductive responsibilities alongside community and political responsibilities, a woman who was no longer dependent on the welfare state but now dependent on the bank and without a stable and guaranteed income—why would a *madre* reasonably have chosen to become a "good mother" if she did not have to? These few examples of good Madres del Barrio were exalted—they were interviewed, highlighted in the press, some of them even got to meet the president. But, at the end of the day, their lives and incomes often remained precarious, state assistance to support their socio-productive projects was often thin at best, and they were exhausted.

In addition, Miriam, Aida, and Soraya all possessed years of experience with community organizing and leadership before their incorporation into the mission. Aida and Soraya also possessed years of experience in the paid labor force prior to joining the mission. They drew on such previously acquired skills and experience once they were in the mission to take advantage of the opportunities that the mission offered them. However, Madres del Barrio beneficiaries were supposed to be extremely poor, previously excluded homemakers in a "state of need." All the *madres* probably did not possess similar levels of skills and experiences to Miriam, Aida, and Soraya, which would enable them to *salir adelante* and form their own businesses with the mission's support.

Why would a *madre* who remained in the mission, who may have had less organizing, leadership, and paid labor experience than Miriam, Aida, and Soraya, who continued to receive 80 percent of a minimum wage, and whose labor already had been intensified, choose to intensify her labor further if she were to become indebted and have no guaranteed income? The mission appears not to have been asking this question in evaluating its design, performance, and achievement of its stated objectives. Yet the *madres* who "stayed behind" appear to have been answering it by making a strategic choice for both themselves and their families in remaining in the mission. They chose to continue receiving their cash transfers in spite of the stigma they faced so long as the state and the economy could not offer extremely poor women viable alternatives to income precarity and care for their dependents.

Conclusion

Because Madres del Barrio Mission had not reached all extremely poor homemakers in Venezuela, questions arose concerning the transparency of whom the mission had reached and how it had come to reach them. At the same time, the mission appears to have served as a vehicle for improving the welfare of the limited numbers of poor homemakers that it did reach. Through receiving the monthly cash transfer of 80 percent of the minimum wage, the women who had been incorporated into the mission had gained some income security—if only temporarily. The former *madres* and former mission coordinators indicated that the *madres* had both been expected to and used their benefits for their dependents' welfare. The mission cash transfer and related benefits from the state (such as access to discounted household appliances) had helped them to fulfill their roles as mothers, similar to CCT program benefits and services targeting women in Mexico

(Molyneux 2006, 2008a), Nicaragua (Bradshaw 2008), and Argentina (Tabbush 2009). For women such as Miriam who had male partners, the mission benefits may have also given them a newfound control over resources and household expenditure. In such cases, the mission may also have contributed to *madres'* household bargaining power and independence, as appears to have happened with Miriam, who separated from her partner while in the mission. As Miriam herself stated, the *madres* now were not going to be "cheated, manipulated . . . treated badly by any man, because there are men all over who want to minimize women. Then, listen, that has now ended." Both former mission coordinators also spoke of *madres* who had been able to leave or transform situations of domestic violence because of their involvement in the mission.

Although Madres del Barrio contributed to improving the *madres'* and their families' welfare, the mission appears largely not to have contributed to changes in gender roles and the gendered division of labor, similar to CCTs in Argentina (Tabbush 2009), Mexico (Molyneux 2008a), and Nicaragua (Bradshaw 2008). Poor women were incorporated into the mission through their role as mothers. Participating in the mission, their reproductive function and labor were intensified by extending their care work from their households to their communities. In so doing, these women became the mothers of their *barrios*. Yet the mission did not target the fathers of the *barrios* and aim to enhance their roles in household and community reproduction in a context in which many of the program beneficiaries were single mothers heading households. The mission had not involved or sought to make the fathers of Aida's and Soraya's children responsible for their maintenance. And as Miriam's story shows, her former partner did not assume any more household responsibilities because of her involvement in the mission and her cooperative. If and when the mission reached and involved the fathers of the *barrios* in its activities, it appears to have been incidental and not by design. Even as the Bolivarian state had reached more poor, vulnerable, and excluded members of the *barrios* through its new social policy measures, it had turned to the *madres* to organize and contribute their time, labor, and even their own money to make up for the shortfalls in its social policies. In the absence of increased support from men and the state in care provisioning and with the expectation that they care not just for their own dependents but also for vulnerable members of their communities, the *madres'* maternal gender role and reproductive labor appear to have been intensified and the gendered division of labor appears to have been deepened.

At the same time, organizing as mothers in their communities provided the Madres del Barrio with new spaces for sharing their knowledge and experiences, building their self-confidence, developing their community leadership skills, and training for productive occupations. Miriam, Aida, Soraya, the state gender institution workers who had worked with the *madres* and the *madres* I observed participating in an EFOSIG workshop all spoke of the *madres'* increased self-esteem and social and political participation. Stories such as Aida's and Soraya's indicate that their increased social and political participation vis-à-vis the mission had enabled them to become community leaders or further their leadership positions where they were already exercising them. Where this had occurred, the *madres* appear to have enhanced their status in their communities by extending their maternal roles to caring for their communities.

Yet, as this chapter has shown, though Madres del Barrio Mission served as a vehicle for the social inclusion of some poor women, the mission simultaneously served as a vehicle for the social exclusion of poor women both within and outside the mission. With the unfulfilled expectations it raised, its targeted and nontransparent selection mechanisms, and its reliance on local popular power organizations to select beneficiaries, the mission divided popular-sector women between those touched and those not touched by it. The mission also served to divide women touched by it into independent (i.e., good) mothers and dependent (i.e., bad) mothers through their fulfillment or nonfulfillment of the coresponsibilities it had established for them to carry out. The mission, in its presences, its absences, its everyday institutional practices and discourses, and the state–society relations that it promoted and fostered, constituted both a unifying force and a dividing force in the *barrios*.

Madres del Barrio was able both to unify and divide popular-sector women and popular sentiment in general because it rested on motherhood as its central basis for incorporation. In other words, poor women were incorporated into the mission through their role as mothers—a socially valued yet circumscribed traditional role for women, which if fulfilled as per the state's, the community's, and popular expectations, served as a basis for gaining status and respect. However, if they did not fulfill these maternalist expectations, they became the subject of stigma from state actors and other popular-sector women. In this sense, the mission served as a vehicle to reproduce popular regulations of motherhood. Yet, it not only reproduced such gender regulations; it also resignified them by introducing the expectations that mothers incorporate themselves into socio-productive activities, which fit the larger Bolivarian state framework for the national socialist revolution, and become independent of social assistance, which was treated not as a right but as an executive gift. These expectations were not merely determined by the state and one-sided. Rather, they filtered down and were internalized by the *madres* themselves, because they drew on popular conceptions of maternal responsibilities, of ties between President Chávez and the popular sectors, and of popular participation and protagonism in the revolution.

Dividing the good mothers from the bad by judging the *madres'* performance of their roles as mothers in their households, their communities, the market, and the Bolivarian process in turn deflected scrutiny away from the state and how its structuring of the mission may have largely prevented women from exiting it and becoming independent of social assistance. Blaming the *madres* as lazy, unproductive individuals for the mission's failures in turn helped to uphold the magical revolutionary Bolivarian state narrative, by not faulting the state for its attention (or lack thereof) to the range of poor homemakers' needs. Paradoxically, even though Chávez stated that Madres del Barrio Mission was in accordance with Article 88 of the 1999 Constitution—with the rights to recognition of housework's socioeconomic value and social security for homemakers—in both its design and its everyday institutional discourses and practices, the mission treated the *madres'* reproductive labor as an externality. The mission assumed that extremely poor homemakers' poverty was largely due to a deficit of participation in the productive sphere, but it did not address some of the key underlying causes of their lack of productive participation. Because it was a requirement to join the mission, most Madres del Barrio probably had heavy household care burdens. Indeed, as Miriam's, Aida's, and Soraya's stories show, they withdrew from the paid labor force and experienced income precarity because of their family care burdens and the lack of family members and/or institutions that could assume these burdens so that they could reenter the paid labor force. Just as the CCTs in Argentina and Mexico that neither provided care services for program participants' dependents nor took their need for such services into account (Molyneux 2008a; Tabbush 2009), Madres del Barrio Mission did not notice or address the structural care deficit that kept the *madres* from paid labor force participation. As Molyneux (2008a) concludes, such poverty relief programming is "abstracted from the social relations that produce women's poverty" (61). Rather, the mission expected the *madres* to join the productive sphere by starting their own small businesses with other *madres*, but it did not provide them with substitute care services to free up their time and labor power so that they could. Nor did it provide them with substitute care services when they conducted their community organizing and political work, which they were expected to carry out as per mission guidelines, often on short notice. CCTs create added time burdens for women, yet they do not take into account how such responsibilities may potentially overburden them (Luccisano and Wall 2009; Molyneux 2008a; Tabbush 2009). To meet all the Madres del Barrio Mission coresponsibilities in the absence of family members who could assume their care burdens, the *madres* would have had to intensify their labor, make their labor flexible, and be able to perform their reproductive and productive work simultaneously.

Few *madres* were like Miriam, Aida, and Soraya and able to accomplish this feat, even with the mission's economic assistance. And even for the *madres* such as Miriam and Aida who had, they had not achieved income security, and it had come at costs of personal exhaustion and anxiety about paying off debts, making ends meet, and organizing care for family members.[31] Yet the majority of *madres* were judged to be lazy and unproductive when they did not follow the examples of independent *madres* set by women such as Miriam, Aida, and Soraya who were publicly exalted by the state, because they had not fulfilled their coresponsibilities.

Thus, the Madres del Barrio—the same popular-sector women state authorities and actors discursively invoked as key participants and protagonists in sustaining the Bolivarian revolution—were held responsible and blamed for state failures in designing, rolling out, monitoring, and evaluating the mission. The mission turned its back on Article 88 by demanding and intensifying the unpaid work the Madres del Barrio performed for their households, their communities, and the state, yet disregarding the value of this work. Far from the spirit of Article 88, the mission appears to have entrenched popular gendered conceptions of unpaid reproductive labor as not constituting work.

CHAPTER 5

In the Shadows of the Magical Revolutionary State: Popular Women's Work Where the State Did Not Reach

During Chávez's presidency, more popular women in Venezuela who were potentially eligible for Madres del Barrio Mission were not incorporated into the mission than were incorporated into it. Blocked myself from directly engaging with Madres del Barrio, I set out to learn about the experiences of popular women in Falcón state who were potentially eligible for the mission but had not been reached by it, in order to understand what constitutional recognition of housework meant for their work, welfare, gender relations within their families and their communities, and social and political participation. I wanted to understand their relations to the Bolivarian state, their experiences of (non)incorporation into other state programs, and the meanings that they attributed to their experiences with the state.

This chapter illustrates that, just as popular-sector organizations proliferated during the revolution, the state's lack of articulation with popular-sector communities and lack of collective popular organization also characterized the Bolivarian process. Most empirical studies of state–society relations between the Bolivarian state and Venezuelan popular sectors during Chávez's tenure examine growing, active social movements and organizations and their varying articulations with the state as part of Venezuela's post-neoliberal turn (Bruce 2008; Ciccariello-Maher 2013b; Fernandes 2007, 2010; Hawkins 2010b; Motta 2009, 2010, 2012; Schiller 2011; Valencia 2015).[1] Few, if any, studies focus on the absence of social movements and collective organization in popular-sector communities and what such absence meant for the Bolivarian state's reach and capacity to promote popular welfare and power.

Following the Bolivarian state's revolutionary narrative of its promotion of popular women's power, I moved to Coro,[2] Falcón, to conduct my field research on relations between popular women and the state. State women's and gender equality institution workers from both Falcón and national offices had presented Falcón to me as a special case of regional-level state promotion and advancement of women's issues. The governor, Stella Lugo de Montilla, was one of only two female governors in the country at that time and one of the few women to be elected governor in Venezuelan history. She had previously led state-based women's organizing initiatives in Falcón when she was its first lady. Once she assumed the governorship, she increased funding and resources for the Falcón state gender institutions. And Lugo de Montilla was the first governor in Venezuela to grant cabinet-level status to regional gender institutions. The Falcón government's commitment to women's and gender issues and the Falcón gender institutions' work with popular-sector women, I was told, were advanced compared to the regional governments and gender institutions in other states. The fact that they had the largest state-organized women's front in the country, in spite of being a rural state with a relatively small population, in addition to multiple programs organizing, assisting, and educating popular women, was testimony to the articulation between state gender institutions and popular women in Falcón. Falcón state gender institution authorities and workers granted me access to multiple sites in which they engaged with popular women; yet, they could not grant me access to Madres del Barrio Mission in Falcón.

Underlying the appearance of rapid and massive social inclusion associated with the magical revolutionary Bolivarian state were *barrio* women's everyday experiences of nonincorporation and/or patchy and slow incorporation into Bolivarian state programs. Focusing on women's experiences of nonincorporation into state programs and waiting for incorporation, I draw from Javier Auyero's (2012) theoretical contributions developed in *Patients of the State* on the experiences and meanings of poor people's waiting for the state to act on behalf of their welfare. As Auyero does, I explain what happens to popular-sector women in one Falcón *barrio* "when nothing apparently happens" (19). These popular women's everyday experiences illuminate the temporal disjuncture between the rapid, radical transformations in state rhetoric, policy, and presences and the uncertain and extended time some popular women spent waiting to be reached by them. Their experiences reveal the "everyday political domination" (Auyero 2012, 19) that constituted the fabric of these women's relationships to the Bolivarian state during Chávez's presidency.

Patients of the State analyzes the everyday relations and interactions between the urban poor and the Argentine state during the "post-neoliberal" era as routinely producing and reproducing an order of political domination. To do this, Auyero (2102) uses what he terms a "tempography of domination:

Figure 5.1. Government sign of Falcón state governor Stella Lugo de Montilla embracing a child, Coro, Falcón, 2012 (photo by author)

a thick description of how the dominated perceive temporality and waiting, how they act or fail to act on these perceptions, and how these perceptions and these (in)actions serve to challenge or perpetuate their domination" (4). This hermeneutical focus on poor people's experiences of waiting for the state to act on behalf of their welfare reveals the temporal dimensions of political domination. Examining poor people's experiences of waiting across multiple sites of engagement with the Argentine state, Auyero shows how the state uses multiple means—veiling its operations, delaying or rushing service delivery, and giving confusing messages—that force the poor to wait in "zones of uncertainty and arbitrariness" (73–74). Auyero is careful to note that such diffuse subtle tactics are part of a "strategy of domination without a strategist" (Bourdieu and Wacquant 1992, cited in Auyero 2012, 61) because they are not part of an explicit state "master plan" (61) for its dealings with the poor. Yet he contends the state's forcing poor people to wait does constitute "an insidious but banal exercise of power" (80). For it obliges the poor to surrender their power and time to others, and it reveals that the poor do not control processes of state welfare distribution.

At the same time, Auyero asserts that this form of state power is not merely repressive; it is also productive. Drawing from Foucault and Bourdieu, especially the latter's notion of doxa, or "accumulated shared understandings," he argues that state power over welfare produces and reproduces a commonsense understanding, for state actors and poor alike, of how welfare resources are to be distributed. He finds that this form of state power also routinely produces patiently compliant subjects—whom he terms "patients of the state," or subjects who understand that they must act according to this established doxa and acquiesce to the state's directives in order to receive necessary welfare services (Auyero 2012, 9). In turn, on a daily basis, the Argentine state produces and reproduces an order of political domination of the poor in place of their incorporation as full, active citizens in Argentine society.

Patients of the State focuses on the urban poor in general, but Auyero begins to show how the constant production and reproduction of this order of political domination in Argentina particularly entrenches female dependence. He notes that the patients of the Argentine state are primarily women because welfare policies and institutions are structured around gender divisions. By making welfare services inefficient and unreliable, the Argentine state "implicitly coerces women to attach themselves to male breadwinners" (Auyero 2012, 126), who can provide them with material security that the state does not.

Barrio women's experiences of waiting in the shadows of the magical revolutionary Bolivarian state for incorporation into welfare programs further illuminate the gendered implications of waiting for the state. The experiences described in this chapter of *barrio* women's waiting for state welfare services in Falcón interacted with their experiences of community disorganization and disintegration, everyday violence, and persistent gender roles to produce a negative feedback loop of nonsubstantive recognition of their unpaid labor. These women's stories reveal how, in the absence of social and political organization to channel their interests, the Bolivarian state's presences and absences and actions and inactions upheld relations of gender and class domination in this popular-sector *barrio*.

Ten *Falconiana Barrio* Women

In a popular-sector *barrio* of Coro, I conducted interviews with ten popular women,[3] ranging in age from their twenties to their sixties with differing care burdens and family structures.[4] Some of these women dedicated themselves exclusively to unpaid housework, while others combined unpaid housework with paid informal work that they carried out mostly in their homes, but they all were responsible for caring for others in their households. They all had either no income or their income was below minimum wage. All of these women therefore potentially met the criteria for Madres del Barrio Mission, but none had not been incorporated into it.

Diana was in her fifties and cared for her male partner, with whom she lived, and her two adult male children, one of whom lived with her. Diana had worked as a waitress in a bar, and she withdrew from paid work ten years before because she did not like her work and her partner wanted her to leave it. She had no income of her own, and she lived off what money her partner and her eldest son gave her. Since her son who lived with her had recently started employment, his contributions to her and their household had enabled her to become less dependent on her partner. She had never contributed to social insurance.

Joana was in her forties. She withdrew from her paid work as a domestic worker when her elderly parents became ill and needed extensive care. Her father had recently died. She was now caring for all of the family members with whom she lived: her blind and infirm mother, her four nieces and nephews, and her granddaughter. She had made all her necessary contributions to social insurance but was unable to collect her pension because she was not yet of retirement age. Her mother did not receive a pension either because she had not contributed to social insurance, and she was waiting to receive one from Amor Mayor Mission. Joana had no income and lived off what money her daughter gave her.

Sara was in her sixties and had always worked as a homemaker. Her adult child lived apart from her. So Sara now cared for her husband and her pets. She had no income or pension of her own and she lived off what money her husband gave her.

Daniela, Sara's daughter, was in her forties. She previously worked in the retail sector, but currently worked solely as a homemaker, caring for her husband, her three children, and her one grandchild. She had never contributed to social insurance, and she lived off what money her husband gave her.

Jenny was in her twenties and a mother of two young children. She dropped out of high school when she became pregnant with her first child. She used to live off what money her children's father gave her, but they had recently separated. Since the separation, she had started a business with her friend, and from the house that they shared, they sold clothes that they bought in bulk. She was also studying for her high school equivalency through Ribas Mission. She had never contributed to social insurance.

Hilda was in her thirties. She lived part of the month in a city in a different state, where she cared for her preschool-age son. The other part of the month she lived in this Falcón *barrio* where she cared for her two other children and her sick, elderly mother, in addition to her preschool-age son. She used to live off what money her children's father gave her, but they had separated. After their separation, Hilda worked for a year in an informal baking business, but she had to leave this work to care for her mother when her mother became ill. Hilda now lived off the rent of a room in her house to a tenant. She had never contributed to social insurance.

Carol was in her thirties. She previously worked in a pharmacy, but she had to leave this work when her newborn baby accidentally incurred a developmental disability and subsequently needed extensive care. Carol had studied for her university degree through Sucre Mission, but she had to drop out following her baby's accident. She now stayed home caring for her husband and their five children. Even though her disabled child was now seven years old, she still required regular intensive care. This persistent need for care prevented Carol from continuing her studies and reincorporating into the paid workforce, as she would have liked. She had never contributed to social insurance and she lived off what money her husband gave her and occasionally from selling clothing (bought in bulk) from her house.

Irene was in her sixties. She worked as a kitchen assistant for six years before starting her family and dedicating herself to unpaid housework. She now cared for her husband and her sick, elderly mother, who lived in another *barrio* of Coro. She never contributed to social insurance and she did not receive a pension even though she was of retirement age.

Inés was in her forties. She cared for her son, her adult nephew, and her aunt. She did piecework sewing from her house to maintain herself and her son, but she earned less than minimum wage. Because she had been sewing for a living since she was a teenager, she had developed an occupationally acquired disability with her hands. This disability in turn limited the amount and kind of sewing she could do and how much money she could make. Her aunt did help her with household expenses. Inés previously worked as a seamstress in a factory. While she worked there, she contributed to social insurance, but she had not paid all the contributions necessary to benefit from a state pension once she reached retirement age.

Veronica was in her thirties. She cared for her two preschool-age children and her elderly mother, who was in an advanced stage of Alzheimer's and required round-the-clock care. Her mother did not receive a pension. Veronica received some monetary assistance from her second child's father. To supplement that child support and pay her own and her other child's expenses, she took in piecework laundry when she could, but she earned less than minimum wage. She had recently worked as a shop attendant, but she had to withdraw from that work when her mother became very ill. Prior to her mother's illness, she dropped out of high school when her father became terminally ill, and then she began to work as a nanny. She had never contributed to social insurance.

This group of women was not representative of popular-sector homemakers in Venezuela, in Falcón, or in Coro, but it was constitutive of the fabric of popular women's ties with the Bolivarian state: their experiences show how the state's practices penetrated their everyday worlds (Smith 1987). Their experiences shed light on state (non)recognition of unpaid housework and popular-sector women's engagement with their rights and the state.

I used the interview summary review process as an opportunity to conduct short follow-up interviews with most of them, especially in regard to their experiences of (non)incorporation into state social programs since the initial interviews. These follow-up interviews illuminated the centrality of waiting for most of these women's engagements with the Bolivarian state. I conducted more extensive follow-ups with two of the women when I attempted to use my contacts within the state to link them to state programs and services because of their particular situations of vulnerability. These experiences provided additional insight into the often slow and nontransparent process of state incorporation and the uncertainty that this produced among them, which seemed to characterize the process of state incorporation for many popular-sector homemakers.

Understandings of Work Disarticulated from Rights

None of the women I interviewed in this *barrio* expressed awareness of the 1999 National Constituent Assembly, and only one was aware that the 1999 Constitution entitled her to social security as a homemaker. When I asked them what constitutional rights they had as women, three of them were able to name a right—to live free from violence—and one of these women also named the right to receive state social assistance for her dependents.

Even as they were not aware of the 1999 Constitution's recognition of their unpaid labor, nine out of the ten women expressed awareness of their unpaid household labor as work. Several of them referenced the replacement cost of unpaid housework to explain how their housework was work. Moreover, four of the women explicitly spoke of how they were workers who received no salary, placing them in disempowering positions. For example, Carol concluded that housework was not rewarded:

Yeah, chances are that your children and your husband give thanks that the house is cared for . . . but who recognizes us now? Nobody, nobody recognizes us. Then, goodness! Sometimes I prefer to go out onto the street[5] to be less stressed, clean less, wash less, iron less. And in the street at least you have your middle of the month and your end of the month payment and your schedule.

Similarly, Joana noted that now that she worked taking care of her own household—as opposed to when she took care of another family's house as a domestic worker—she worked for free, her workload was greater, and her work hours were longer. Further, Sara's insight into her status as an unpaid worker and her economic dependence on her husband sheds light on how the nonrecognition of her labor gave her little household bargaining power: "At least they give me every day for food, and that is not for my salary—that is to eat. Then, I don't have a salary. And if one were to at least charge, the husband would leave the house because he wasn't going to pay what one has to pay."

What accounts for this disarticulation between these women, almost all of whom recognized their unpaid labor as work, and their constitutional right to state recognition of their unpaid housework? Furthermore, what accounts for this disarticulation among popular women in a state that had been heralded by the Bolivarian government for being particularly progressive on gender equality and organizing popular women? With so much presence of women's issues within the Falcón state government, why was there such absence of rights awareness among popular-sector women in the very capital of Falcón?

The answers to these questions lie in a contextual analysis of the mutual imbrications of much longer processes of state disarticulation, absence, and patchy service delivery; community disorganization and disintegration; and persistent gender roles that charged women with the bulk of unpaid care work and relegated them to the private sphere of the household. My interviews with these women provided snapshots of those longer intersecting processes and were embedded within them.

When I spoke to these ten *barrio* women about their knowledge of the 1999 Constitution and their constitutional rights as women and specifically as homemakers, three of them responded that these issues did not interest them. These three explained that their rights were situated within a broader context of state disarticulation, wherein the state failed every day to reach women, enforce women's rights, and promote and defend women's welfare. For example, Sara said to me: "It doesn't interest me. Or rather, if I am going to know a thing which I am not going to benefit anything from, why am I going to be interested and apply my mind to that thing? It's neither here nor there, let's leave it like that." Her daughter, Daniela, explained further why the Constitution and their rights did not interest her mother and her: "What happens is that they do it, they set it out, and it stays in the air. For example, they tell you that they are going to do something and they don't do it. Then, what are we doing with burying ourselves in that?" For these homemakers, they understood that even though their rights may have existed on paper, they were irrelevant to their everyday lives because they were supposed to be enforced by a state that they had not seen deliver on its promises to women citizens. Their words show that they understood that, as popular women, they did not control processes of state service delivery to them. They viewed engaging with and waiting for state social assistance as futile, and they turned instead to their male partners to help make ends meet.

For many of the women I interviewed in this Coro *barrio*, and not just the three mentioned above, state nondelivery and/or patchy or insufficient service delivery and rights enforcement appeared to characterize much of their relationships with the Bolivarian state. The majority of the women did use Barrio Adentro Mission and Integral Diagnostic Centers—two free public health programs established by the Bolivarian government—and they spoke favorably of these programs, noting their accessibility. At the same time, these positive experiences with new state welfare services did not extend to their experiences with other popular Bolivarian programs. For example, both Diana and Veronica had studied in Ribas Mission for their high school equivalencies. Diana said she quit after a few weeks because the teacher did not come to class, and the substitute teacher only showed videos and did not explain anything. Veronica said she successfully completed all the coursework, but the mission never granted her degree or the scholarship it had promised her.

Half of the women I interviewed chose not to use Mercal Mission, even though they could have stood to benefit from purchasing subsidized foodstuffs, because they said they did not have the time to wait in line at Mercal—waits that the women interviewed spoke of lasting anywhere from three to eight hours.[6] This group of women not using Mercal included Inés—a single mother running a business from her home—and Joana and Carol, whose extensive care burdens of dependents with disabilities demanded they spend almost all of their time at home. Daniela also said she did not use Mercal because of violent incidents that had broken out in those long waiting lines.[7] The women who did use Mercal used it because their poor economic circumstances left them with no other choice, even though using this public service could add considerably to their workdays and create problems with providing care for their dependents while they were away so long from their homes.

Carol pointed out the political subordination of the poor in her *barrio* that the Bolivarian state produced by forcing them to wait in line for food for many hours under the hot sun. She noted that poor elderly women would wait in those lines, while the governor and the governor's mother would not because they could afford to shop at private supermarkets. Carol pointed out a contradiction between state rhetoric and practice of welfare delivery: "Then, where is the government if they [the poor elderly women] are the priority?"

Waiting for the Magical Revolutionary State

At the end of 2011, Chávez announced that the executive was taking further measures to prioritize the elderly poor's and extremely poor children's welfare by enacting two new "great missions"—Misión en Amor Mayor[8] (Great Mission in Elderly Love) and Misión Hijos de Venezuela[9] (Children of Venezuela Great Mission)—in which the state would transfer cash to them. Upon decreeing these great missions, Chávez declared that they constituted social justice measures contributing to the broader national revolutionary process of constructing socialism.

The Bolivarian government aligned the rollout of Amor Mayor and Hijos de Venezuela with its decentralization governance framework, in which state policies of popular-sector social inclusion were accomplished in large part by delivering services to them in the communities where they lived. The primary means by which the executive designed the official registration of the elderly poor and extremely poor children in these great missions was through community visits by local multidisciplinary teams called "quartets"[10] in a house-by-house census process.[11] In the case of Hijos de Venezuela, potential recipients were supposed to go through a further layer of screening after being surveyed and registered by the quartets, wherein popular power organizations from their communities would conduct "validation assemblies" to verify that potential recipients were really in need of public assistance (Gran Misión Hijos de Venezuela 2012). Thus, rather than making potential recipients visit state welfare offices, an articulation between the state and popular power organizations would conduct outreach throughout popular-sector communities to screen and register potential recipients for these missions.

Many of the elderly and child dependents of the women I interviewed in this *barrio* were potentially eligible for these great missions, and many of these women registered their dependents for them. The Amor Mayor pension and the Hijos de Venezuela cash transfer were targeted at the interview participants' dependents, so their dependents' incorporation was of immediate interest to these women because they were the ones who cared for them. State assistance to their dependents could therefore alleviate some of their own care burdens. As I interviewed these women several times over 2012, I could follow part of their dependents' incorporation processes into these missions. Auyero (2012) notes that waiting for the state is "stratified," because different people do not experience it equitably (27); these *barrio Falconianas* experiences and understandings of waiting illustrate this point. They each waited different times for these great missions, the state treated them differently, and they diverged in how they chose to engage with the state and how they understood their waiting processes.

Irene was the only one of the seven women whose dependent had received a benefit from a great mission for which she had registered. Irene's elderly mother, who lived in another *barrio* of Coro, had recently begun to receive her Amor Mayor pension. Irene described the pension's arrival as a relief for her mother and for herself because her mother was previously surviving on whatever monetary and nonmonetary assistance Irene could give her. Now with this pension money, Irene was able to buy her mother medicines and a refrigerator. Irene concluded that Amor Mayor was both "well done" and an "act of justice."

But for most of 2012, Irene's case of her mother's incorporation into a great mission was unique in the group of women from the same *barrio* I interviewed. For all but Irene, the women who had registered their dependents for the great missions spent most of 2012 waiting for such assistance to arrive, not knowing if and/or when it would arrive. As with Madres del Barrio Mission, these popular women's experiences of waiting for Amor Mayor and Hijos de Venezuela and not knowing if and when their dependents would be incorporated into them shows that these new Bolivarian state presences concomitantly generated new state absences in welfare delivery to the popular sectors.

The decentralized great mission incorporation process made state power over incorporation into them particularly diffuse and opaque for the women I interviewed who attempted to register their dependents in them. Auyero (2012) contends that, by ensnaring the poor in often arbitrary and shifting processes that confuse them while forcing them to wait, the state mystifies its power over them. He concludes that mystification of state power plays a key role in the acquiescence of the poor to state dictates (34). In the case of the Bolivarian great missions, the state further mystified its power by designing these missions according to its framework of decentralization and popular power. This design masked who had decision-making authority over access to and distribution of benefits and, in turn, shrouded followup and recourse procedures. All but one of the women I interviewed said that the quartets visited them at their respective homes and officially registered their dependents for the great missions. Yet they spoke of not knowing what the quartets did with their dependents' information once they left. They said the quartets did not return to visit them again and no validation assemblies occurred. Nor did they know with whom or how to follow up on their dependents' registrations. What they did know was that they had to wait for the state to incorporate their dependents, though they did not know for how long.

The women I interviewed who attempted to follow up on their dependents' registrations in the great missions spoke of a long, nontransparent, and confusing process of engagement with the Bolivarian state bureaucracy.

For example, after waiting five years for public assistance from the National Institute for Social Services (INASS) for her elderly mother, Veronica registered her mother for an Amor Mayor pension at a great mission registration table.[12] When I first interviewed Veronica in May 2012, her mother had not received assistance from either state agency, nor had a quartet visited their house. Veronica had gone to INASS to inquire on the status of her mother's pension application, and, according to her, "then they tell me to wait, to wait in the other list [Amor Mayor]. I go to the other list, I don't appear on it, they tell me the other list [INASS]." Veronica's story illustrates the confusing and delaying processes Auyero (2012) explicates—processes by which the state ensnares the poor—as Veronica was given "contradictory and puzzling messages" and "kicked around" (73–74) from one state service to the other, leaving her still waiting and uncertain.

Visiting Veronica at her home—her workplace—I found her situation of vulnerability to be particularly acute compared to the other women I interviewed in this *barrio*. She had two preschool-age children running around, a demented mother who constantly relieved herself all over the house, and she had to do all the household laundry by hand (including her mother's constantly soiled clothes and sheets). She found herself in regular conflict with her extended family over her mother's care. These care burdens left Veronica with very little time to work for an income. I offered to bring her mother's and her children's social assistance needs to the attention of the state gender institution authorities, given my research relationship with them. I wrote a brief report about Veronica's dependents and submitted it to the head of the regional gender institutions, who informed me that she would request a social worker to visit them at home. When I inquired more than a month later about the state's follow-through on Veronica's family's case, the authority responded to me that she had not yet addressed it because she had been very busy working out of the office in communities around the state. Much of this was political work in the run-up to the presidential election. When I visited Veronica at her home again in July 2012, neither her mother nor her children had been incorporated into the great missions. Yet, she had managed to find out that they had not been officially registered for these missions, so she was trying to find out how to register her dependents for them again.

At the other side of the *barrio*, the Bolivarian state at first appeared to be more attentive to Joana's dependent's incorporation into a great mission, yet the state later made Joana wait in suspension. In April 2012, a great mission quartet informed Joana that her mother had appeared on the Amor Mayor[13] beneficiary list and that Joana should go to the bank to collect her mother's pension. Joana did go to the bank, only to find out that her mother's pension had not yet arrived there. When I visited Joana again in September 2012, the pension had still not been deposited in the bank, and Joana had received no news as to when it would come.[14]

Such incidents when state cash transfers were not deposited in bank accounts are examples of the Bolivarian state's "veiling" of power over the poor, because "human actions responsible for the extensive wait time are masked behind the operation of nonhuman operations" and "no individual is presented as responsible for it" (Auyero 2012, 73). The veiling of the human forces behind Joana's mother's absent bank deposit made the error appear technical. Yet Joana and her mother were left to wait further, not knowing when the bank deposit would be made. Such veiling incidents "freeze with indifference the circulation" that the state "sets in motion" (Secor 2007, 42). In Joana's case, the Bolivarian state first promoted her disabled elderly mother's claim for a pension and later suspended it. And the state literally set Joana in motion over this claim—between first registering her mother for the mission at a registration table and later traveling back and forth to the bank, only to be turned back without assistance to wait further in a "zone of uncertainty."

Other women I interviewed who had registered their dependents for the great missions chose to wait to receive news about the social assistance. At the same time, several of these women did not express confidence that the assistance would arrive, and they had not received follow-up communication from the state or popular power organizations as to the status of their dependents' registrations. The state's lack of follow-up made them doubt whether their registrations were being processed. For these women who expressed doubts, the great missions seemed like they could amount to another instance of state disarticulation and failure to follow through and deliver on its promises to their *barrio*.

When a couple of women who chose to wait did express hope that social assistance would arrive, they spoke of appearing on the beneficiary list as a "question of luck."[15] For example, when I first interviewed Hilda in June 2012, she told me that the night before she had watched Chávez announce on national television that no grandparent in the country would go without a pension. Hilda, in turn, told her mother "to have hope, because that is the last thing to be lost." Hilda's words reflected belief in Chávez's promise that the Bolivarian state's new magnanimous welfare programs would reach her family. She was in a magical state, receptive to Chávez's spell. Yet, in this same year, on television Chávez also repeatedly admonished the Venezuelan people to exercise "patience, patience, and more patience" in their expectations for the Bolivarian state's revolutionary transformations to reach them. When I visited Hilda again in October 2012, her mother had still not received her pension, and they did not know when it would arrive. Nonetheless, their expression of hope that they would be "lucky" enough to receive social assistance for their dependents was disarticulated from an understanding of social assistance as a right that pertained to them and their dependents as Venezuelan citizens.[16] Rather, their hope was based on their faith in Chávez's word and the potential fruitfulness of waiting for his word to be made good.

Carol was undergoing the same experience in 2012 of waiting without information as to when her disabled daughter would be incorporated into Hijos de Venezuela. She contended that waiting without information and follow-through from the Bolivarian state was common to the missions' functioning in Falcón. For example, Carol had previously signed up for Madres del Barrio Mission, but she had never received a response from the state as to whether and when she would be incorporated into it. She noted that when and where she had been able to receive public assistance for her disabled daughter, she had achieved it not through waiting, as she had been told to do, but only through persistent struggle, circumvention of regional authorities, and direct appeal to national authorities in Caracas. For example, even though Carol volunteered for six years at the Falcón state children's institution that Governor Lugo de Montilla previously headed when she was Falcón's first lady, Carol never received assistance from Falcón state institutions with her request for a subsidized housing mortgage. She received state credit to purchase her house only when she traveled to Caracas pregnant and stormed the presidential palace security gates, where she demanded to speak directly to Chávez. Chávez and his advisors then received her. Carol said that within three days she received the credit to purchase her house in the *barrio*. Carol's story of contention with the state reveals that the order of everyday political domination of popular women in this *barrio* was not total but contingent. Though the Bolivarian state was largely opaque, it was porous enough in some areas for her to be able to make certain authorities hear and fulfill her demand. Key to making the state honor her demand was her refusal to acquiesce to the state's instructions to wait and be patient.

Yet the majority of women I interviewed from this *barrio* did not take Carol's combative, frontal approach to demanding resources and assistance from the state. In the absence of making such demands either individually or collectively, they remained waiting in "zones of uncertainty" for answers from a largely noncommunicative, nontransparent state apparatus.

Their waiting in silence, without protest, for state social assistance that they and their families were supposedly due reveals a doxa of state assistance for poor women in Bolivarian Venezuela. My interactions with Inés, in particular, illuminate this doxa—a normal and normative arrangement between state actors and poor women on the way state resources were distributed. When I first met Inés, she was waiting for her child to be incorporated into Hijos de Venezuela. I witnessed her struggle to make ends meet for her child and herself through her sewing piecework, which was compounded by her occupational disability. I informed her then about the Woman's Development Bank (BanMujer)[17] so that she could potentially access discounted credit from the state to purchase better equipment to undertake her work. After I discussed the bank with her, Inés's communication showed me that she would approach the bank for assistance only if I directly connected her to it.

Given my connections with and knowledge of state authorities, Inés appeared to see me as a *palanca*, literally, a "lever," and a term that is popularly used in Venezuela to connote someone who has leverage or influence with state authorities. So I approached the bank on Inés's behalf, and after some persistence, I managed to secure a bank fieldworker's visit to her house. The fieldworker registered Inés for incorporation into the bank. The fieldworker also treated me as Inés's *palanca*, noting that I had basically done the pre-screening for Inés's incorporation into the bank because the fieldworker trusted me. She told Inés that her credit application would be sent to the bank's national office in Caracas, where it would be reviewed and decided upon. She informed Inés that this process would take some time, but she did not give her a precise time frame for how long she should expect to wait. After waiting just more than a month without any news, Inés contacted me to inquire about her application status. I responded that I did not know anything about it since I was not a state authority, but I could give her the fieldworker's contact details, in case she had lost them, or she could go to the bank offices in Coro to inquire. Inés replied to me that she did not want to "bother" the fieldworker or the bank; she would just wait.[18] As her *palanca*, then, I voiced her needs to the state; without my assistance, she would remain silent—a patient of the state. Yet this mode of communication with the state was so normal, so assumed that it went without explanation. My intervention, the fieldworker's words and actions, and Inés's response shed light on this doxa—a set of "accumulated shared understandings" (Auyero 2012, 62) on the fundamentals of state assistance—which shaped her interactions with the Bolivarian state. Inés understood that access to state assistance was contingent on *palanca*, on possessing influential contacts within the state. Inés knew she must not be passive and just wait for assistance; she must act strategically and use her *palanca* for her request to be heard. At the same time, she understood that she must pull the lever and then silently wait for it to act on her behalf. Inés, as did the patients of the state in Argentina, knew that, as poor people, to "obtain the much needed 'aid' . . . they have to show that they are worthy of it by dutifully waiting. They know they have to avoid making trouble" (Auyero 2012, 9). Ines's knowledge and actions thus reveal an entrenched doxa of the importance of both cronyism and waiting patiently for the distribution of state resources in a historical context of patchy state incorporation of the popular sectors.

Gendered Implications of Community Disorganization and Disintegration

One of the reasons why these women were waiting for the state and not making demands for social assistance was because they were not collectively organized. Community organization is not necessarily always a vehicle for women to raise their awareness about their rights and to formulate demands around them, but it can potentially serve as such.[19] None of the women I interviewed belonged to the Frente de Mujeres Josefa Camejo or the Puntos de Encuentro, in which the Falcón state women's and gender equality institutions organized popular women territorially as women.[20] Further, none of the women I interviewed belonged to a communal council. Only one woman had participated in a community or political organization.

A chief reason why many of these women were not participating in organizational life that could potentially assist them in making demands of the state to meet their needs was their communities' lack of integration. In a national context in which popular community organization had been not only heralded but also legislated as a legally binding form of public administration to meet community members' needs,[21] many of these women found themselves embedded in a local context in which their communities failed to unify, organize, and become legal state entities. In turn, their communities, as potential alternative forms of government, did not receive resources from the state. Rather, they described their communities as lacking social cohesion.

For example, Carol, Inés, and Sara were are all from the same sector of the *barrio*, where a few community members had made several attempts at organizing the sector into a communal council. Yet none of these attempts proved successful. Carol explained that their sector had not formed a communal council because of conflict within the community about why the organization should exist and for whom it should exist:

> The people . . . do not want a communal council to be formed because they say it is more of the same . . . the people do not work, but they get nominated. . . . Then there is that rivalry and that question that "no, the communal council didn't give to me." Then I say that we also have to change our way of thinking: we can't say all the time that the government has to give to us or that the communal council has to give to us; we have to change ourselves to support the community or support the government in something in order to be able to receive.

Carol viewed the struggle to form a communal council in her sector as a theater for the playing out of local power relations. According to her, certain community members would use the legalized communal government space to serve their own interests rather than the broader community interests and the particular interests of the most vulnerable.

Sara noted that community relations were not always like this in this sector—in the time of the *juntas de vecinos*,[22] she said that "the mothers who did not have a house, obtained a plot here in [the *barrio*] and help and a block for the house was asked of the neighbors and their houses were made. Now, no. . . . Right now there is no union; before there was." Inés also noted how community cohesion had diminished over time, and she added that now in their sector, neighbors were shut into their individual houses all the time and they were resistant to coming out and meeting with each other.

This reticence to leave their individual houses and meet and engage as a community could have been due at least in part to the increased levels of violence in their sector. These women spoke of increasing violence in their community, some of them in detail and with great trepidation as they asserted that the state did not guarantee their safety but rather treated their community in general as perpetrators of violence. For example, Sara's daughter, Daniela, noted that "here the police pass by once in a while, when they agree to. Or when a police officer is robbed in his house . . . or when they hold up a bank, the first that they [the police] invade is [this *barrio*]. And that happens when they rob over there [in another section of the city]: they come to look for the things here in [this *barrio*] because this is the red zone now." What Daniela described appears to be a historical continuity with the neoliberal era when the Venezuelan state increasingly entered the *barrios* as a repressive force, with security forces carrying out raids against *barrio* residents (Fernandes 2010). Her words also support Petras and Veltmeyer's (2009) contention that the police in Bolivarian Venezuela tended to view poorer *barrios* as "criminal breeding grounds" (176). Since the Bolivarian government had assumed power, proclaimed its anti-neoliberal stance, and created more state policies, programs, and institutions aimed at popular-sector social inclusion, the national homicide rate had increased by more than 150 percent from 2000 to 2012 (OAS Hemispheric Security Observatory, n.d.). At the time of my research, Venezuela had the highest homicide rate in South America and it ranked among the countries in the world with the highest homicide rates (United Nations Office on Drugs and Crime 2013). Coro and its *barrios*, though located far from the country's most dangerous centers, were not immune from these high and increasing rates of violence and homicide. In Falcón, the number of homicides—arguably the most severe form of violence—had increased by 170 percent from 1999 to 2011 (Ministerio de Salud y Desarrollo Social 2000; Ministerio del Poder Popular para la Salud 2014).[23]

Both Sara and Daniela said that the increasing violence in their community bore down especially hard on the women within it. For example, Sara told the story of a woman who was nearly raped outside Sara's house, but the woman's assailants ceased attacking her when Sara began screaming. Now Sara was waking up two or three times in the middle of the night to keep watch over her house. During the time period I was conducting interviews with these women, Diana was attacked and robbed right outside of her house, and my research assistant heard of several women attacked on the same street where Sara, Carol, and Inés lived. These experiences of everyday violence in this *barrio*, lack of state protection from it, and their impediment to community integration and organization therefore lend credence to Petras and Veltmeyer's (2009) claim that "'popular power' will only become meaningful" to the popular classes when they feel safe enough both to enter and use public spaces and stay in their own homes (177).

In addition to high levels of violence, the intensity of several of the women's unpaid work also restricted them from participating in community organizations. For example, community members had successfully organized and formed a communal council in Veronica's sector. Veronica would have liked to participate in it, but she could not because she did not have time to because of her heavy household care burden. Veronica's case illustrates how the gendered division of labor shaped social and political participation in popular power organizations—women's primary responsibility for reproductive labor can serve to constrain their access to political processes (Lister 2001; Orloff 1993).

Several of the women I interviewed also indicated that their individual care burdens constituted a barrier to gaining awareness about their rights. For example, two women spoke of not knowing how the 1999 Constitution recognized them as homemakers and their work's value precisely because of the nature of the work that they carried out every day. Joana and Carol had very long workdays and especially heavy care burdens; they each cared for a disabled family member in addition to other family members. They spoke of not having the time or space to read about their rights and become knowledgeable in them. Joana explained:

> There I have my nephew's Constitution stored away. Not even do I have the time to open it and read it because there is no time. . . . Now at least, I don't know anything about that. Right now I don't read the news or the newspaper, nothing. At least here, I am paying attention to this [the house]. I am not paying attention to the TV, nor anything. And I turn on the radio, and that is like I don't even hear it.

Ironically, the very work for which the 1999 Constitution specifically interpellated these women as bearers of rights restricted them in the first instance from becoming aware that they had such rights. As with the Madres del Barrio, the value of these popular women's unpaid reproductive labor went unrecognized.

Persistent gender roles and gendered divisions of labor that charged these women with the bulk of household care work, if not all of such work, in turn limited the time that they could potentially be involved in community and political activities and organizations. Three of the women interviewed said they did not receive any help from family members in carrying out their reproductive labor, while seven said they received varying degrees of help from family members. When women did report receiving help from family members with their work, it was more often than not from female family members. Four of these women also did receive state support in the form of day care and education for the preschool-age children for whom they cared where these children also received meals. Yet, for three of these four women, while their children's attendance at public preschool did lighten their work burdens, it did not necessarily free up their time because they were also caring for elderly, sick, or disabled family members who did not have access to state care services. Where the women identified changes in their care work, they noted technological and infrastructural changes that lightened the burden of their work, such as running water, electricity, refrigerators, and washing machines. They did not identify changes in gender roles within their households.

Reading Popular Women's Acquiescence to Everyday Social and Political Domination

The women I interviewed tended to talk about housework as implicitly women's responsibility, with four of them explicitly stating that they did not discuss responsibility for housework with the fathers of their children and/ or the men in their households. Three of them noted that they chose not to broach household responsibilities with the men in their lives in order to avoid conflict with them; they knew they would not win, and such conflict would only complicate things for them. For example, Diana and I discussed how it was decided who was responsible for the work in her household:

Rachel: You have told me about your daily activities inside the home. Can you describe to me the daily activities of the other members of your home, of your partner and your son? What daily activities do they do?
Diana: What do they do? Sleep, eat, and go to the bathroom. . . . Inside the home . . . they do not do anything.
R: And how is it decided who carries out which activity in the home? How was it decided that you are going to do everything—the cooking, cleaning, washing, ironing—and they are going to sleep and eat and go to the bathroom?
D: Myself.
R: You decided that?
D: Yes, myself.
R: And why did you decide to do all that work?
D: Because if one orders someone to help, then they don't take notice. Then what one does is become angry, irritated, and to say bad words, fight with them, growl at them, and they don't do anything. Then it is better to do it alone and not to say anything to anyone in order not to be arguing. Because you are the one who is going to get angry. . . . I get angry and no one pays attention. And in all cases, I have to do my work, because even if I become crazy and fight and scream, no one is going to take notice. It's like that in the majority of homes here in Venezuela.
R: So that there is peace inside the home?
D: Yes. And then no one orders anyone. One does their own things, and everyone is happy.
R: And the men do not want to participate?
D: No! For nothing. In my case, I live with two males, three males. And I don't know why; maybe that it will strip them of their manliness if they are going to wash a plate, if they use a broom or if they wash clothes.

Women such as Diana spoke of "choosing" to do all or almost all the housework. Yet Diana's own words illustrate how such a "choice" was often not made freely but rather was profoundly shaped by gendered assumptions and gender inequalities that played out in these women's everyday lives.

Several of the women spoke of not wanting to bother or disturb (*molestar*) the state to assist them with their reproductive burdens in addition to not wanting to bother or disturb the men in their lives to assume responsibility for housework. The majority of these women's reluctance to demand or even ask assistance from men and the state in sharing their burdens constitute "acts of recognition of the established political order" (Auyero 2012, 9) of everyday gender and class domination. Yet their acquiescence to their subordination was not necessarily freely willed; they were well aware of the tensions that this created within them. These women talked as if this was their fate, which would only be exhausting and futile to challenge. In the absence of collective organization to support potential claims for recognition of their unpaid work and support in carrying it out, their chances of successfully challenging their fate indeed seemed slim.

Yet this does not signify that these women were merely passive subjects. As Auyero (2012) asserts: "The overall lack of contention over what is for us as observers a rather grievous process should not be seen as passivity on the part of the welfare recipients and applicants. . . . Poor people are actively seeking solutions to their problems and strategize accordingly" (121). In not raising their voices for changes in social services, these *barrio* women therefore avoided conflicts where they knew the odds were stacked against them. They understood that processes of state welfare delivery were outside their control. Even though the Bolivarian state produced differences in these women's understandings of their ties to it, it was a state upon which these women knew they largely could not depend. So whether or not they decided to wait for the state to reach them, they looked elsewhere for immediate and everyday solutions to their and their dependents' welfare needs. Their acquiescence to their subordinate positions vis-à-vis men and the state was conflictual, but these were measured and rational choices given the history of patchy and nontransparent state service delivery in their community, their lack of control over state practices, the failure of their community to organize, and the limited resources that they had at their disposal.

Conclusion

These popular women's stories illustrate that what was taking place in this *barrio* of Coro was not the unfolding of an empowering participatory process for popular-sector homemakers triggered by the National Constituent Assembly and the broader Bolivarian revolution. Rather, these women experienced a negative feedback loop of nonsubstantive recognition of their unpaid labor that tended to reinforce their vulnerability. They did not participate in community organizations because they did not have time to, they felt unsafe, and/or they did not see the point of doing so in a context of community disintegration and slow and/or unresponsive state services. This in turn created a gap in collective women's and community organization, which could have potentially challenged their conditions of vulnerability vis-à-vis the state and the men in their lives. And in the absence of strong welfare state and community organization (that was now supposed to act as a local government), these women and their families in this *barrio* were left to their own devices for survival. Thus, as individual families, they continued to fill in the gaps in social reproduction where the Bolivarian state did not reach. Some women, in turn, depended economically on the men in their lives, and if not on men, then on female family members. Where women did not have men or family members to depend on, they struggled to make ends meet for themselves and the people they cared for by doing home-based work and piecework, which they combined with and often performed at the same time as their unpaid housework. Not only did some women speak of not having time to participate in community organizations that could potentially address some of their own and their families' welfare needs, but some also noted that widespread violence in their community hindered such organization. Indeed, the violence and the state's failure to prevent and arrest it served to reinforce both women's place within the home and individual family mechanisms of survival (instead of community mechanisms), because women either remained or retreated to working behind household gates and fences. These women's stories therefore tell of a process of reinforcement of gender roles, the gendered division of labor, and the state of ruling relations—the everyday order of gender and class domination—in this popular-sector *barrio* lying in the shadows of the magical revolutionary state.

CHAPTER 6

Mobilized yet Contained within *Chavista* Populism: Popular Women's Organizing around the 2012 Organic Labor Law

This chapter focuses on how popular women, their organizations, and their democratic demands for labor rights were positioned within the *Chavista* populist dynamic. I analyze women's rights activists' last effort to legislate Article 88 during Hugo Chávez's presidency, when Chávez broke through the impasse on labor law reform and enacted the Organic Law of Work and Workers by executive decree in 2012. Popular women's organizations linked with the populist chain supporting Chávez, his government, and his labor law initiative, yet popular women's participation and inclusion in this executive legislative process were contested. Within *Chavismo*, the dialectical relationship between forces from above and below intersected with tensions in popular women's gendered positioning in the revolution, undercutting popular women's organizing to advance their labor rights and Article 88 in particular.

Examining differences in Bolivarian-aligned popular women's organizing and their relation to the state during the organic labor law drafting process, I contrast radical, participatory, bottom-up popular women's organizing driven by social movements with vertical, top-down popular women's organizing directed by the state.[1] I explore tensions between these two forms of popular women's organizing and show how these divergent cases were connected through and shaped by their containment within a *Chavista* populist dynamic. This dynamic was heightened by the national political conjuncture in which the labor law was drafted and enacted: President Chávez was ill, often absent from the country because of his illness, and up for reelection later that year. Popular women's organizations' containment within this populist dynamic both opened up and closed down opportunities for mobilizing for their gender interests in the 2012 organic labor law. Their convergence as popular women in defense of state authorities' vision of Bolivarianism's broader interests reveals the type of popular women's participation and inclusion that the Bolivarian state was promoting. That is, the state held popular women's organization and mobilization as central to the revolution's continuation. Yet it attempted to limit their autonomy and marginalize the advancement of their particular interests within the Bolivarian process.

Populist Linkages

With populist phenomena, the range of subjects making popular-democratic demands comes to constitute the "people"—an empty signifier that can represent, contain, and synthesize the heterogeneous and divergent demands within this assemblage opposing the dominant political-institutional system (Laclau 2005). This coherence as the "people" against the dominant bloc is at once unifying and divisive. For, as Laclau (2005) explains, the "people" in populist phenomena are not all subjects in that political community, but rather a "partial component" that aims to be seen "as the only legitimate totality" of that community (81).

Since the basis of populism is the "people," it conceives of popular participation and direct popular "involvement in political decision-making as an absolute good" (Hawkins 2010a, 172). Populism, therefore, can generate openings for popular organizing (Olcott 2010), especially of sectors previously excluded by the dominant power bloc, such as popular women.

At the same time, as Laclau (2005) explains, what gives counterhegemonic strength to particular democratic demands, such as popular women's demands for expanded labor rights, is their linkage within the chain of popular-democratic demands that together constitutes the "people." However, such particular demands can be compromised or sacrificed within the larger chain of popular-democratic demands of a populist movement (Laclau 2005). A populist leader's will and control can also compromise particular demands within movements (Hawkins 2010a)—populist linkages between state and society tend to be top-down (Cameron 2009) and mediating organizations tend to have low levels of control independent of populist leaders (Hawkins 2003). Top-down state–society linkages and low levels of organizational intermediation can render particular demands vulnerable to state leaders' disregard or instrumentalization of them.

Populism, then, is a double movement between the empty signifier's homogenization and the heterogeneous particular demands it represents (Laclau 2005). A populist leader—an empty signifier—must represent the particular demands for them to coalesce and cohere around him or her; he or she cannot act completely autonomously of them. Yet a populist leader is more than the sum of the particular demands she represents; she transcends them. She *"constitutes* that totality, adding a qualitatively new dimension" (Laclau 2005, 162) that necessarily imposes order on and subordinates particular demands to that totality. Populism is at once both a unifying articulation and a tense linkage among particular popular demands and between such demands and the leader that represents them. It is an inherently dialectical political phenomenon, contingent on a balance between opposing forces of particular demands and their homogenization.

In directly expressing popular antagonisms against dominant power blocs and generating strong affect for and between the "people" and their leaders, populist politics, as Karen Kampwirth (2010) points out, is "passionate politics." Because populist politics entails passion and charisma and the expression of passion and charisma is mediated by gender, populist politics involves performances of gender (Kampwirth 2010). Populist politics is also about the articulation of gender, gender differences, and gender divisions within an assemblage of popular demands and linkages between state leaders and the subjects they represent.

Gender and Populist State–Society Relations under *Chavismo*

As the Bolivarian revolution progressed and oil prices rose, enhancing state capacity to finance public goods and services for the popular sectors, and political polarization persisted in Venezuela, Chávez, the empty signifier originally uniting and leading a heterogeneous ensemble of popular forces, became increasingly imbued with definite radical content (Ciccariello-Maher 2013b). *Chavismo*, the movement encompassing the dialectical relations between Bolivarian government forces and popular forces/movements aligned with Chávez and the government, also became increasingly radical. Chávez radicalized his government in part by bypassing entrenched bureaucratic structures and modes of interest mediation and by promoting, institutionalizing, and granting decision-making authority to local popular power organizations.

Although Chávez and the Bolivarian government moved toward popularizing and decentralizing power under the twenty-first-century socialist framework, and popular social movements and organizations grew, *Chavismo* also retained top-down state–society linkages. Scholars of Bolivarian popular social movements and organizations have observed internal differentiation among them, especially in their relation to the state, and they have found them to be located on a spectrum between autonomy and dependency (Azzellini 2010; Fernandes 2010; Schiller 2011; Valencia 2015). Ciccariello-Maher (2013b) and Fernandes (2010) note increasing self-organization and autonomy among Bolivarian social movements over time as the revolution radicalized. Yet, as Fernandes (2010) points out, with Bolivarian state promotion and support for popular power organizations came their dependency on the state. This dependency in turn rendered them vulnerable to control and manipulation by state authorities, as seen with the Madres del Barrio. A concurrent centralization of power among Bolivarian state and party authorities transpired, following what Sara Motta (cited in Spronk and Webber 2011, 251) calls a "state logic" of "power over" popular organizations, which undercut participatory decision-making and organization-building processes. Both Motta (cited in Spronk and Webber 2011) and Ciccariello-Maher (2013a) refer to this as an encroaching state strategy of governance toward popular organizations and movements.

Thus, Bolivarian state and party authorities both promoted popular-sector political organization and mobilization and attempted to delimit their radicalization and autonomy. Or as Motta (cited in Spronk and Webber 2011, 251) puts it: the Bolivarian state reinforced a political "division of labor in which there are . . . leaders and followers." Fernandes (2010, 237) concludes that this resulted in popular movements' successful organization around defending Chávez and the Bolivarian revolution, yet they encountered "difficulty in sustaining a common agenda to represent their own interests before the state."

This tension between social movement radicalization and governability within *Chavismo* shaped the ways in which popular democratic demands for labor rights were made and contested. A key persistent and unfulfilled popular democratic demand among leftist forces within *Chavismo* was the crafting of legislation and institutions to steer labor relations toward socialism. And popular women's demands for enhanced labor rights that recognized their gender interests, including Article 88's implementation, fit within this chain of radical popular demands for a socialist labor law.

Throughout his tenure, Chávez's populist appeal to include previously excluded sectors of society created openings for popular women's increased political activism (Kampwirth 2010). Autonomous and state-led popular women's organizing proliferated, and the Bolivarian state increasingly recognized popular women's centrality to the revolution and incorporated a discourse framing feminism as essential to the revolution. In bypassing the legislature by announcing that he would decree a new labor law in 2012, Chávez created a particular gendered political opportunity for popular women to organize to advance their labor rights. Yet, in multiple instances during the labor law drafting process, organizing and mobilizing for Chávez's reelection overshadowed popular women's gender interests. The *Chavista* populist division of labor between leaders and followers intersected with the gendered division of labor. This chapter therefore shows how gender differences shape, and are in turn shaped by, organizing and the compromising of particular popular-democratic demands within populist phenomena. That is, the hierarchical nature of populist linkages can intersect with gender and class hierarchies to limit popular women's power and recognition of their gender interests.

My analysis of how popular women did and did not organize for the advancement of their rights in the 2012 labor law illuminates how Bolivarian state and party authorities attempted to control a multitude of popular women for what officials saw as the revolution's broader interests. Bolivarian officials promoted and expected popular women's political mobilization at the same time as they acted to constrain popular women's organizations' political autonomy. Shedding light on popular women's containment within this populist dynamic throws into question central issues about their organizing—such as for whom they were organizing, who controlled their organizing, and the instrumentalization of their organization. Ultimately, then, this chapter examines what Motta conceives as the tense relationship between forces from above and below within Bolivarianism over the shape of popular democracy (Motta 2010) and popular women's position and participation within it.

Bolivarian Social and Women's Movement Struggles to Reform the *Puntofijista* Organic Labor Law

Even though the 1999 Constitution mandated the National Assembly to reform the *Puntofijista* Organic Labor Law within the Bolivarian regime's first year, it failed to fulfill this duty (including during the second legislative term from 2006 to 2011, when the *Chavistas* held a complete majority and later an overwhelming qualified majority). From 1999 on, though, many social, political, and workers' organizations formulated and submitted proposals to the National Assembly for labor law reform.

Women's and feminist organizations counted among them, with La Araña Feminista (The Feminist Spider) spearheading such initiatives during the second legislative term. La Araña Feminista, or the Araña, was a self-

Figure 6.1. Araña Feminista logo (*source*: Araña Feminista)

defined network "of revolutionary socialist feminist collectives and individuals" (La Araña Feminista 2012)—which included organizations of popular women, peasant women, academic women, Afro-Venezuelan women, and lesbian, gay, bisexual, and transgender activists—from different regions of Venezuela who identified with Bolivarianism but who chose to "remain on the margins of the state apparatus" (Angeleri 2012). The Araña practiced a form of "engaged autonomy," wherein it "negotiated with [and] participated in" the Bolivarian movement and "dominant . . . political institutions, while maintaining a critical and *feminist* stance" (Alvarez et al. 2003, 543; emphasis in original). Just as the CONG (which networked women's rights activists and organizations in 1980s and 1990s), the Araña networked across different spheres of feminist activism, included several key academic feminists and the Popular Women's Circles, and worked with state institutions to advance women's gender interests. Yet, most of the Araña's member organizations emerged and developed during the Bolivarian regime and identified not as NGOs but as collectives and movements.

In 2010, the Araña Feminista discussed and organized a set of proposals for labor law reform with the Frente Bicentenario de Mujeres (the Bicentenary Women's Front)—the national popular women's front organized by the Bolivarian state and led by María León (the longtime feminist and communist activist-leader who was minister for woman's popular power and gender equality at the time). In order to advance women's labor rights, they formed a strategic alliance between women's groups aligned with Bolivarianism. The Araña—a network that defined itself as not controlled by the state—led this initiative. The Araña/Frente proposals contained a standalone chapter on "housework," which laid out that unpaid homemakers' social security would be financed by state contributions and would cover the contingencies of maternity, the nursing period, incapacity, disability, and old age (La Araña Feminista 2010).

The Araña's and the Frente's intent with their 2010 labor law proposal was to incorporate some of the spirit of the Social Protection for Homemakers Bill, which the National Assembly had previously failed to pass into law (Interview with Alba Carosio). This was part of the Araña's and the Frente's broader attempt to have all workers (including unpaid workers) recognized as workers and protected by the social security system. The Araña and the Frente also proposed recognition and sharing of care duties, which included social security–covered paternity leave and paid leave for women and men workers to care for sick, disabled, and elderly family members (La Araña Feminista 2010).

The Araña and the Frente publicly submitted their proposals to the National Assembly commission charged with labor law reform. Yet the assembly made no advances in reforming the law before the new legislative period began in 2011, in which the opposition gained a sizable minority of seats within the assembly. Pressure from Bolivarian-aligned popular movements and organizations on the assembly to reform the labor law then mounted. Throughout 2011, multiple social movements and unions staged marches with thousands of workers to the National Assembly and organized petitions to demand a new labor law. Popular women's and feminist organizations formed part of this mounting chain of popular-democratic labor demands on the Bolivarian state. In March 2011, using the platform of International Women's Day (IWD), the Araña once again marched with the Frente and allied organizations to the National Assembly to submit their labor law proposals. In their communiqué for this event, they drew particular attention to unpaid homemakers' lack of social protection and demanded Article 88's implementation (La Araña Feminista y otros colectivos 2011).

Chávez's Populist Initiative to Enact
a New Labor Law by Executive Decree

Chávez, and not the National Assembly, responded to these demands from outside the state yet within *Chavismo* to advance labor legislation. In November 2011, less than a year before the 2012 presidential election, Chávez exercised his magnanimous sorcerer capacities when he announced that he would use his enabling powers[2] to decree a new organic labor law by May Day 2012, just before his legislative powers expired. He stated that he would decree a new labor law, rather than reform the existing law, in order to "pay the debt that the revolution has with Venezuelan workers" (Rodríguez 2011). From the outset, Chávez framed the new law he would enact as a revolutionary rupture with past labor legislation, depicting it as redressing the needs of the working class.

Reaction was mixed among popular-sector Bolivarian forces to Chávez's announcement of his sudden unfreezing of suspended claims for advancing workers' rights. Some workers' organizations that had pressed Chávez to decree a new labor law hailed his announcement as a "historic victory" and staged public actions in support of his initiative. However, several prominent Bolivarian-aligned national workers' organizations publicly critiqued the centralized process by which the new law would come into effect, and they viewed widespread public debate, input, and decision-making as essential to the law's development (Boothroyd 2011).

Chávez appointed a commission to draft the new labor law and gather proposals for it.[3] Only one of the commission's members was a woman, and none of these commission members were directly involved in women's and feminist movement organizing. Neither Chávez nor the presidential commission announced or published formal procedures for gathering proposals and for popular-sector consultation and decision-making on the law's content. From its inception, then, the labor law drafting process was opaque and bypassed traditional modes of legislating and interest mediation.

A Gendered Political Opening for Popular Women
to Advance Their Labor Rights

However, many Bolivarian-aligned social movements, unions, and workers' organizations took Chávez's populist labor law initiative as an opportunity to organize across Venezuela to generate popular proposals for the law that advanced workers' interests within the *Chavista* populist framework. These organizations employed the term "working people" (*pueblo trabajador*) to articulate their subject positions, their organizing, and the assemblage of their demands.

The Araña Feminista in particular took Chávez's decision as an opportunity to organize, develop its proposal further, and gather support for it with a broader range of organizations and movements across Venezuela. Both Alba Carosio, an Araña member and former advisor to the National Assembly on legislating Article 88, and Gioconda Mota, an Araña national coordinating team member, interpreted Chávez's decision as a gendered political opening for their proposal's advancement. They viewed the National Assembly deputies as barriers to advancing women's movement labor demands and passing the law (Interview with Alba Carosio; Second Interview with Gioconda Mota), but they thought that, as Carosio stated, "the president has shown much sensibility toward women's causes" (Interview with Alba Carosio).

The Araña responded immediately to Chávez's announcement by holding meetings and debates with its member organizations and with other Bolivarian-aligned women's and feminist organizations and allied workers', peasants', health, and student organizations from different regions of Venezuela that valued a gender focus in the new labor law. Separately, the Ana Soto Women's Movement, a self-defined anticapitalist, anti-imperialist women's organization based in Lara state (Carajo 2010), drafted its own proposal with unions organizing in the state telecommunications (CANTV) and electricity sectors. The Araña met with these organizations and agreed on the core ideas for a combined proposal. Representatives from the Araña, the Ana Soto Women's Movement, CANTV, the Socialist Movement for Quality of Life and Health, the peasant movement, and the Frente then drafted the "Proposal from Revolutionary Women for a New Labor Law with Gender Equity" (Interview with Alba Carosio). Thirty-two organizations signed onto this proposal under the umbrella of La Araña Feminista,[4] and twenty-three allied organizations outside the Araña,[5] including the National Union of Workers, several other workers' organizations representing a range of occupations, educational organizations and movements, and disability and LGBTTI organizations, signed onto it, forming what Gioconda Mota called "a popular women's movement" proposal (Second Interview with Gioconda Mota).

The final "Proposal from Revolutionary Women for a New Labor Law with Gender Equity" built on the 2010 Araña/Frente proposal, yet it reflected an ontological shift toward a socialist feminist conceptualization of the way work and workers should be understood within Venezuela. Appropriating and engendering the Bolivarian twenty-first-century socialism framework in their proposal, the self-described "revolutionary women" placed care work at the center of their vision of a socialist society. Carosio, one of the proposal's drafters, explained why they centered unpaid and paid care work: "Understanding a more human society as socialist, it has to be a society that takes care more into account, because care is . . . the basis of life. Then it is necessary that it be recognized, that it be included as work, but that it is also made visible" (Interview with Alba Carosio). They aimed to render visible the workers who carried out such socially necessary work. In their proposal focusing on the intersection of gender and class issues, the "revolutionary women" argued that mechanisms to eradicate gender subordination in addition to exploitation were necessary for engendering socialist work and society (Mujeres Revolucionarias 2012). They further contended that legislating a socialist labor law with a gender perspective meant focusing on the intersection of ethnicity with gender and class, in order to "defend the interests of the working majorities who are those people who contribute their labor power and time to produce wealth for our society" (Mujeres Revolucionarias 2012, 2).

Going beyond defining work as human activity for the production of exchange value, the "revolutionary women's" proposal conceptualized work as "human activity that produces values in the form of things, services and care of persons, to satisfy social, material and non-material needs, with the goal of exchange and/or family/community consumption that gives rise to the strengthening of social relations and the maintenance of life" (Mujeres Revolucionarias 2012, 3). Mota explained that their intention was to extract the definition of work "from the logic of employment"—from the logic of a dependent relationship between employer and employee utilized in the existing labor legislation (Second Interview with Gioconda Mota). Instead, they aimed to give it a much broader meaning that would enable the working conditions of independence,[6] precarity, insecurity, and lack of protection of the majority of women workers to be made visible and protected against through legislation (Second Interview with Gioconda Mota). The "revolutionary women" included a range of employed, dependent, independent, autonomous, self-employed, cooperative, family, paid, unpaid, residential, home-based, peasant, fishing, artisan, and indigenous workers in their definition of workers with full rights (Mujeres Revolucionarias 2012). For Sandra Angeleri, an Araña national coordinating team member, these underlying conceptualizations of "work" and "workers" grounded the proposal in a shift "from a law of *work* to a law of *workers*," wherein the focus changed from work for profit-making to the people who labored (Interview with Sandra Angeleri; my emphasis).

The "revolutionary women" proposed a new institutional framework to protect previously excluded work and workers, which included a social protection workfund for nondependent workers—including people who carried out unpaid care work—to cover the contingencies of pregnancy, nursing, illness, disability, and old age, financed with contributions from the state, public- and private-sector employers, and workers themselves. They also proposed outlawing employment discrimination of people who carried out unpaid care work of infants, toddlers, the sick, the disabled, and the elderly. In addition, for paid employees, they proposed recognition and protection of their unpaid care work through an extension of paid postnatal maternity leave to six months; paid paternity leave of one month; a reduction of the working day by two hours for parents of children younger than three years who did not receive day care at their parents' workplace; and a maximum of six months paid leave for workers who needed to care for sick or temporarily disabled children or elders (Mujeres Revolucionarias 2012).

For activists who developed the "revolutionary women's" proposal, the process by which they generated it was historically significant, engendering both a sense that they had a right to and were able to shape legislation—they were a "legislating people" (*pueblo legislador*). At a public forum in which the "revolutionary women" discussed their proposal, for example, one activist spoke of the alliance seizing their right to participate politically in order to focus particularly on women's realities. Carosio saw the "revolutionary women's" organizing for the new labor law as part of the larger "explosion of participation" taking place in Venezuela under Bolivarianism, wherein different popular subjects from different geographical places and organizations and movements previously excluded under *Puntofijismo* were now included in legislative debates (Interview with Alba Carosio).

The "revolutionary women" also expressed that, through exercising their participatory democratic rights, they accomplished a sense of unity across leftist organizations throughout Venezuela committed to women's labor rights. Mota spoke of a "great political achievement" reached when different participating organizations worked together to formulate a single proposal for gender equity in the 2012 labor law (Second Interview with Gioconda Mota). She described this not as the mark of a "unified women's movement" (because that had yet to be achieved, and women's rights activists not aligned with Bolivarianism did not participate in this coalition-building for the new law), but as a conjunctural unity in diversity among women's and allied organizations on the left (Second Interview with Gioconda Mota).

The incorporation of women's and feminist organizations committed to socialism and popular organizations whose primary focus was not gender issues into this conjunctural coalition signaled a popularization and mainstreaming of women's movement demands within allied Bolivarian popular organizations.

Part of the "revolutionary women's" strategy to build unity and pressure for their proposal consisted of utilizing alliances with Bolivarian government leaders to lobby the presidential commission to consider it. This included drawing on articulations with old feminist allies within the state, such as Nora Castañeda and María León, and cultivating new alliances, such as with certain receptive national ministers. In addition, the Araña formed a working alliance with Jesús Rivero Workers' University, whose coordinator served on the presidential commission drafting the new labor law, and with National Assembly deputy Braulio Álvarez, who was a peasant movement spokesperson and also served on the presidential commission. With the Workers' University, the Araña and allied organizations found that both groups shared a deeper vision of labor, and they agreed to engage in a process of mutual articulation of their respective proposals.

The Araña also used the institutional footholds it had previously gained within state print and TV media to regularly publicize and discuss the "revolutionary women's" labor law proposal during the months preceding the law's enactment. This included weekly articles in the national state newspaper, *Correo del Orinoco*, and the Caracas state newspaper, *Ciudad CCS*. And *Entrompe de Falopio*, an Araña-aligned television program airing regularly on state television, produced several weeks of programming addressing women and paid and unpaid work. The constant use of available media spaces was part of the "revolutionary women's" larger strategy of generating popular awareness of and support for their proposal and publicly persisting with their demands.

The Araña's and their allies' organizing strategy for gender equity within the 2012 organic labor law appears similar to the "conjunctural coalition-building" organizing strategy used by women's movement activists to mobilize and defend their interests in the *Puntofijista* years and for the 1990 Organic Labor Law reform in particular. As discussed in chapter 1, this model of organizing rejected clientelist forms of interest mediation and incorporated women within and outside the state who worked "in concert in particular times around particular issues without demanding organizational or ideological coherence" (Friedman 2000b, 284).

Yet political divisions within Venezuela strongly shaped the "revolutionary women's" conjunctural coalition-building for advancing women's gender interests in the 2012 labor law. The "revolutionary women's" organizing was limited to organizations and activists within *Chavismo*. Broader political polarization within the country affected women's movement organizing for the new labor law. Women's movement activists and organizations not aligned with Bolivarianism did not participate in this coalition-building for the law. Nor did they draft and/or submit any proposals of their own to the presidential commission. Further, the backdrop of broader political polarization interacted with the political conjuncture of the election year in which Chávez was ill and often absent from the country to constrain women's labor rights conjunctural coalition-building within *Chavismo*.

Conflicting Modes of Women's Organizing within *Chavismo* and Their Convergence in Defense of Chávez and the Revolution

The "revolutionary women" activists noted popular women's broadening and deepening participation in the labor law process, yet popular women's organizing around the law in 2011 and 2012 was also marked by political tensions and disarticulations within *Chavismo*. These internal fault lines ran between women who were derogatorily termed *gobierneras* (women who were perceived as servile and obedient to the government) and women who claimed they were not *gobierneras* (women who supported the Bolivarian government and simultaneously defended their space to critique and be independent of it) (Interview with Sandra Angeleri). Both types of groupings of organized women were contained within *Chavismo*, yet what differentiated them was how they participated in the Bolivarian process and the degrees of their organizational autonomy and control in relation to the Bolivarian state. The first type of grouping constituted what Molyneux (2001, 150) conceptualizes as "directed organizations": the state sometimes created their organizations (such as the Frente and Madres del Barrio) and they were "subject to [the] higher (institutional) authority" of the state and under its control and direction. Their linkages with the state tended to be top-down. In contrast, the second type of grouping, such as the Araña, tended to use more horizontal, participatory, bottom-up methods. This form of women's organization engaged in "associational" linkages with the Bolivarian state, forming alliances with state and party organizations around certain issues, but it was "not directed by a superior power, as women members "set [their own] agenda" (Molyneux 2001, 148–149). Fernandes (2010, 28) explains that such Bolivarian-aligned organizations identified "as part of the state in order to highlight the new forms of access and inclusion" but exercised their power by "maintain[ing] a sense of their autonomy to be able to put pressure on the state where necessary." Such associational linkages can potentially successfully lobby for state reforms, yet they "run the risk of cooptation resulting in the women's organization losing its capacity for agenda setting" (Molyneux 2001, 149).

I witnessed such tensions between organized women within *Chavismo* as I traveled back and forth between urban centers of Venezuela and the rural state of Falcón to attend women's events in the months running up to the labor law's enactment in 2012. The Araña and allied organizations taking part in the "revolutionary women's" proposal process consistently invoked their participatory democratic rights and discussed their specific demands and their implications for transforming Venezuela toward a caring and socialist society. While in Falcón, I talked with several women working within municipal and regional levels of state gender institutions about their participation in the women's labor rights organizing process. Three of them said they had not participated in this process and did not know of any forum in which they could, and two noted that they had participated in drafting the previous proposal a few years before when women were organizing for the law's reform. Four workers told me they had never seen the 2012 "revolutionary women's" proposal, but one worker said she saw it when it arrived by fax to the regional gender institutions' central office a few days before it was to be submitted to the labor law presidential commission. This worker said that the proposals were formulated at the national level of state-led women's organizations and not through scaling up a participatory process with state-led women's organizations across Venezuela. The Falcón state gender institutions' management[7] seemed to have never heard of La Araña Feminista, yet they understood that some groups were working with María León (the Frente head) on drafting proposals. Yet these regional state gender institutions' management were responsible for organizing the Frente's regional front in Falcón. These workers and managers formed part of the state-led women's front that was organizing with the Araña. However, their accounts show that the Frente did not incorporate them and Falcón Frente members generally in a bottom-up participatory manner in the labor law proposal generation, organizing, dissemination, and lobbying process, if it incorporated them at all in this process.

Rather, much of the Falcón state gender institutions' work in the months while the "revolutionary women" were debating, drafting, and disseminating their proposal appeared to be focused on organizing popular women from across the state for the International Women's Day (IWD) parade in Coro, Falcón's capital, in March 2012. This parade featured floats and groups of women organized territorially, politically, or by work sector within *Chavismo* and from throughout the state, symbolically displaying *Falconianas'* broad range of participation in society. Yet popular women's participation in this parade was limited to organizing their floats and the ways they marched in it, chanting slogans about Chávez and the revolution while marching in military step, listening to state officials speak, and dancing and celebrating at the end. The keynote speaker, Lizeta Hernández—the PSUV governor of Delta Amacuro state—spoke about the centuries-long history of women's struggles internationally, regionally in Latin America, and nationally in Venezuela. She asserted that the women in the crowd were part of those epic struggles for independence, rights, and inclusion. However, she did not link those historic struggles to Venezuelan's women's current struggles to advance their rights in the 2012 labor law. Rather, Hernandez linked the "protagonistic participation" of the women in the crowd to their historic "mission" to reelect Chávez later that year. Thus, the 2012 state-led IWD parade in Falcón largely served as a demonstration of popular women's support for Chávez and a presidential campaign rally for him. The hundreds of popular *Falconianas* present in the crowd lost a potential mass educational and organizational opportunity to become aware of and build the movement around current women's labor rights demands.

Tensions between the "revolutionary women" and the Bolivarian government came to the national fore with the organization of the 2012 IWD march and rally in Caracas. Less than a week before IWD, the Araña Feminista published an article calling on popular movements to join the march

Figure 6.2. International Women's Day parade, Coro, Falcón, 2012 (photo by author)

Figure 6.3. International Women's Day parade, Coro, Falcón, 2012 (photo by author)

that it was organizing (Mota Gutiérrez 2012). The Araña and allied organizations were planning to march separately from the state- and PSUV-led (*oficialista*, or official) women's march, but meet up with it in the same plaza at the end in order to submit their labor law proposal to state officials in attendance. Yet, a few weeks before IWD, Chávez announced the reappearance of a tumor—after his treatment in Cuba for a cancerous tumor the year before—and he returned to Cuba to have it removed. Just before IWD, MinMujer and PSUV representatives asked the Araña and allied organizations to march with the official march to demonstrate unity while Chávez was out of the country. Alba Carosio explained that this was in order to counter ideas circulating that internal conflicts existed within *Chavismo* and that the unification of the different social groups contained within it hinged on Chávez (Interview with Alba Carosio). The Araña and allied movements agreed to the *oficialista* request, and decided to march as a bloc of social movements within the official march. As Sandra Angeleri, from the Araña, explained, this decision was also guided by the Araña's understanding that public critiques of the government could be "appropriated" by the opposition for its own ends (Interview with Sandra Angeleri). Thus, the national political conjuncture of the president's illness and absence and the approaching presidential election placed the Araña, as a network that

Figure 6.4. Nancy Pérez (holding microphone), minister for woman's popular power and gender equality, on the 2012 International Women's Day rally stage, Caracas, 2012

defined itself as supporting the Bolivarian government but not servile to it, in a position that Ciccariello-Maher (2013b) and Martinez, Fox, and Farrell (2010) have described as walking a tight-rope between defending the government from potential opposition threats while pressing the government to accede to its demands.

Yet, in this national show of popular women's unity with the Bolivarian government in this particular political conjuncture in which IWD 2012 transpired, women's campaigning for Chávez's reelection overshadowed women's campaigning to advance their own rights as workers. This conclusion is not to deny the legitimacy of popular women's organizing for Chávez's reelection, given the social, political, and economic inclusion many experienced during Chávez's presidency. Rather, it is to draw attention to how the Bolivarian state's instrumentalization of popular women's organizing deflected a unique opportunity to forward their movement and campaign for labor rights, in the face of uncertainty generated by Chávez's illness, absence from Venezuela, and bid for reelection.

Thousands of women and their male allies from across Venezuela were bused into Caracas (many, if not most, at state expense), marched, and rallied together in the center of the capital on March 8. On this day sanctioned to honor working women, little of the official discourse emanating from the stage mentioned women's labor rights, how they had specifically advanced under Bolivarianism, and where struggles for their further ad-

Figure 6.5. International Women's Day rally, Caracas, 2012 (photo by author)

vancement still lay. Praise for Chávez and the ways his presidency had improved popular women's welfare and participation dominated the *oficialista*-directed rally, which developed into chanting, singing, dancing, stomping, and praying for Chávez's health and his victory in the upcoming election. From the main stage, the rally emcees interpellated the women present as "Chávez's women"[8]—the women who "loved," supported, and prayed for their "commander," and who would bring him to "triumph" through their campaigning on his behalf. And Nancy Pérez, MinMujer minister, insisted that as *Chavista* women, those present should "follow Chávez's lines." Pérez asserted that their most important mission then was the "October 7th Mission"—the mission to reelect Chávez on that date. From the crowd, many women responded jubilantly to such *oficialista* gendered interpellations.

Only several hours after the rally began were women's proposals for the 2012 labor law mentioned, but this occurred as many women were already filtering out of the plaza. However, after Araña Feminista representatives struggled with state authorities to ascend the stage, they handed over their proposal to three women in influential positions of national power—one of whom was the only woman serving on the presidential commission drafting the labor law.

The differing forces of organized women within *Chavismo* agreed not to publicly show their fault lines on IWD 2012, yet a unique opportunity for broad-based articulation between popular women and women in political power to build the movement supporting women's demands for the 2012 labor law was lost in this effort to show unity for Chávez and the broader revolution on the day specifically dedicated to women's labor and struggles. The 2012 Venezuelan national march and rally commemorating IWD illustrates a "debilitated inclusion" (Motta 2009, 81) of popular-sector women. By limiting popular women's participation mostly to support of Chávez and the Bolivarian government, state and party authorities acted to undercut popular women's autonomy and an exceptional chance for a scaling up and across of their labor demands.

Lack of Transparency and Questions of Popular-Sector Inclusion in the Labor Law Drafting Process

In the last two months before Chávez decreed the labor law, while the "revolutionary women" continued publicly advocating for their proposal and the Falcón state gender institutions and state-led popular women's organizations did not participate in this process, uncertainties and tensions mounted within *Chavismo* more broadly around how the law was being drafted and how popular-sector demands would be included within it. Such concerns arose because of the hasty and nontransparent process of the law's drafting. In mid-March 2012, a month and a half before the new law was to be decreed, the presidential commission held an "enabling street parliament" in the center of Caracas, where it received proposals for the law. The commission stated it would review them and then draft the bill, which it would open for public consultation in several weeks (Martínez Rodríguez 2012). Approximately a week later, Chancellor Nicolás Maduro, a presidential commission member, indicated that the commission had reviewed all the proposals it had received (M. Martínez 2012). Yet, given that the presidential commission had received around 19,000 proposals, questions and concerns arose both within *Chavismo* and among the opposition as to how the commission could possibly systematize and consider all those proposals and decide which demands to include into a draft bill within a few weeks. And as the weeks progressed toward May Day, even as Chávez and the presidential commission invoked notions of "street parliamentarism" and popular debate to characterize the bill's drafting, they withheld the bill from the public sphere, leaving the nation waiting in suspense.

Several prominent Bolivarian-aligned organizations called for the bill to be released for public comment and consultation (Aretuo 2012; *Últimas Noticias* 2012), pointing out the need for genuine working-class participation beyond presenting proposals for the law's drafting (Marea Socialista Press

2012). Because the drafting process remained opaque to the public, critique grew within *Chavismo* regarding how the executive was actually including the working class in determining the law's content. Such critique pointed toward broader questions of the Bolivarian government's respect for popular protagonism and participatory democratic rights and the extent to which *el pueblo trabajador* (the working people) had control over crafting the legislation that would govern their working conditions.

Chávez insisted that the law had "been made by the workers, not by the bourgeoisie" and in "consultation with the grassroots" (Hernández Toledo 2012). Yet, he did not release the bill for public consultation among workers, their organizations, and the grassroots more broadly. Instead, as rumors circulated within Venezuela about the bill and Chávez's health and absence, Chávez suddenly and unexpectedly returned to Venezuela to sign into law the Organic Law of Work and Workers—a spectacular move that broke the national suspense—just before May Day and less than six months before the 2012 presidential election.

Women's Gender Interests in the 2012 Organic Law of Work and Workers

The 2012 Organic Law of Work and Workers did specifically recognize workers outside of employment relationships both as workers and as subjects of social security rights and responsibilities. Yet the new law merely repeated Article 88 of the 1999 Constitution—it did not actually guarantee that poor homemakers and all workers who were not employees would enjoy social security benefits. At the same time, the new law specifically advanced women's labor rights and the struggle to spread out responsibility for care work. It did so by outlawing sexual harassment and workplace discrimination based on sex, sexual orientation, and pregnancy. In addition, the new law extended the period of protection for mothers from being fired without due cause during and after childbirth (*inamovalidad*) from the initiation of pregnancy to two years after birth (rather than the *Puntofijista*-era stipulation of one year). Provision for pre- and postnatal leave was enhanced from a previous total of eighteen weeks to a total of twenty-six weeks. It also granted fathers two-week paternity leave and *inamovalidad* for two years after their child's birth. In addition, the new law granted permanent *inamovalidad* to both mothers and fathers of children with disabilities. Further, it expanded the concept of work to a "social process" that had the objective of producing goods and services that "satisfy human needs through the just distribution of wealth" (Chávez Frías 2012, Art. 25). Yet, unlike the "revolutionary women's" definition of work, this legal definition centered the family, stipulating that another primary objective of work was to "create the material, social and spiritual conditions that allow the family to be the fundamental space for the integral development of persons" (Chávez Frías 2012, Art. 25). At the same time, the new law rhetorically centered workers through its title, Organic Law of Work and Workers, and employed gender-sensitive language in the title and throughout the text, discursively rendering women workers visible and central within the document.

The presidential commission appears to have taken some of the "revolutionary women's" demands into account when it drafted the 2012 labor law, but it did not publicize its deliberations and debates around their proposal. In keeping the drafting process from the public sphere, the state veiled its considerations of women's demands within this process. To paraphrase Coronil (n.d.), the real power of decision-making forces in this executive legislative process remained unseen. This populist mode of legislating means that questions about the "revolutionary women's" organizations' degree of influence on Chávez and the presidential commission to legislate and implement Article 88 cannot be definitively answered.

State Promotion of the 2012 Organic Law of Work and Workers and Women's Rights within It

Although the Organic Law of Work and Workers drafting process raised concerns within *Chavismo* about nontransparent decision-making and top-down state–society articulations, state officials quickly moved to publicize the new labor law's content. The presidential commission held a nationally televised conference explaining what it saw as the law's most salient provisions and advances. And in Falcón state, Gov. Stella Lugo de Montilla invited National Assembly deputy Gladys Requena (who did not serve on the presidential commission drafting the law) to speak in Coro on the new labor law and its benefits for women.

Less than a month after the new law's enactment, Deputy Requena spoke in Coro to a crowded room of mostly women, many of whom came from around Falcón and were transported to and from the event at state expense. Requena focused on the new law's articles particularly relevant to women workers as part of a broader shift from a capitalist conception of work to a conception of work for a Bolivarian, socialist society. She began her talk by discussing the process by which the law was drafted so as to counter what she claimed was "the opposition's disqualification" of the law. Requena argued that Chávez addressed the "workers' request" by enacting the new law (but she did not note how labor law reform was mandated by the 1999 Constitution). She asserted that there had been "a broad debate with the presidential commission," and this commission, the National Assembly, and workers accompanied Chávez in drafting the law, such that the drafting was a "collective effort." Requena spoke to audience members as "subjects" who were constructing this new society, and she encouraged them to discuss the new law, continue the conversation with state institutions that she was initiating that night, and ensure that the institutions responsible for fulfilling the new law "really functioned."

Deputy Requena discussed women's ongoing responsibility for unpaid housework, women's double shift, and how unpaid care duties hindered their abilities to participate socially and politically outside the home equally to men. Even though she highlighted the need to democratize participation in unpaid housework, Requena did not address the state's role in sharing reproductive labor burdens in a socialist society. She specifically did not mention the article in the 2012 Organic Law of Work and Workers that repeated Article 88 of the 1999 Constitution, nor did she touch issues of informal-sector workers (who were disproportionately women) and how the new law recognized them. Requena neglected questions of state protection of the most vulnerable women workers that popular women's organizations within *Chavismo* had raised during the law's drafting process. She also neglected the long-held demand by feminist activists to fulfill the constitutional promise of Article 88. That demand, which originally stemmed from the actions of organized women across the political spectrum, seems to have been disappeared by state authorities seeking to have Chávez receive the credit for granting "his women" what they needed in the new labor law. The public neglect of this demand therefore helped to uphold the magical revolutionary state narrative, because the state "selective[ly] present[ed] . . . elements that create[d] the illusion" (Coronil 1997, 3) of gender justice.

Conclusion

In the context of a presidential election year and the Bolivarian state's lack of transparency, Chávez's populist style of legislating combined with his illness and absence from Venezuela to cloud the compressed organic labor law drafting process with uncertainty. This opaque process raised questions about not only the law's content but also how the popular sectors were included in shaping the law and ultimately about their power and control in the process. By using his magical enabling powers, Chávez responded to and suddenly unfroze suspended claims by popular organizations, including women's organizations, for labor law reform. Chávez's populist initiative galvanized popular movements and organizations to draft proposals and mobilize for their inclusion in the new law. Yet, in the end, the labor law drafting process was controlled from above: decision-making about the law remained outside the public sphere, and the president and his commission kept popular organizations and the nation more broadly in suspense. As Burawoy (1998) notes, "institutions reveal much about themselves when under stress . . ., when they face the unexpected" (14). During the labor law drafting process, when facing the unexpected stress produced by the uncertainty around Chávez's illness, absence, and thus the revolution's future, Bolivarian state and party authorities revealed the top-down nature of popular women's political participation that they were promoting. The *oficialista* demand for popular unity during Chávez's illness and absence from Venezuela and in the run-up to the presidential election undermined autonomous popular mobilization and pressure on the Bolivarian state to include them and their demands in the drafting process, and popular women's organizations and demands in particular.

Women's organizing around the 2012 labor law sheds light on the dialectic between the Bolivarian state and conflicting forms of popular women's organizations within the Bolivarian process (between radical social movement participation and state-directed participation) and the implications of these state–society relations for the struggle to advance women's labor rights. Even though these forms of organization diverged in how they incorporated popular women and how they envisioned popular power, both were contained within *Chavismo* and constitutive of *Chavismo*. They both acceded to *oficialista* requests to converge in defense of Chávez and Bolivarianism in the midst of the labor law drafting process and on the day sanctioned to honor their specific labor struggles.

Where these two forms of organization converged, the Bolivarian state interpellated them as "Chávez's women," thus revealing how the state imagined their political participation and inclusion within this national political conjuncture. The state expected them to be both mobilized and contained for what it saw as the broader interests of the Bolivarian revolution. Ultimately, their containment within this populist dynamic limited the autonomy of both these forms of popular women's organizations and opportunities to build a movement together and put pressure on the state to advance their labor rights and gender interests. In the tensions between the struggle to build women's power and advance women's rights from below and the Bolivarian state's efforts to control inclusion from above, women's rights activists' efforts to advance the promise of Article 88 were quieted down once again.

Imagining a More Dignified Map for Popular Women's Unpaid Labor and Power

I wish to have a map that would ask us to proceed with caution . . . but that would recognize the marks of human daring, a map that would dare our imagination, that would show new vistas and make us desire to mold the existing order into a different, dignified landscape for humankind.

FERNANDO CORONIL (2001, 129)

As I conclude *Engendering Revolution,* I turn back now to the Venezuelan anthropologist Fernando Coronil, whose cultural materialist perspective highlights the role that the magical revolutionary narrative took in shaping the Bolivarian process during Hugo Chávez's presidency. He argues that Chávez's epic narrative of collective popular-sector integration conjured a magical state that merged words "with world, confusing the boundaries between representations and the real" (Coronil, n.d., 22). Following Coronil, I have aimed to render visible facets of the artifice of the Bolivarian state's production of its extraordinary radical inversion of history by illuminating boundaries between representations of gender justice and real gender justice. In the preceding chapters, I have gone behind the discourse of this national popular revolution with a "woman's face" to reveal the ordinary, lived realities of multiple popular-sector women and contestations over their unpaid labor during Chávez's presidency. This analysis has shown that popular women, their unpaid labor, and discourses about them were central to building the revolution and sustaining the Bolivarian state, yet many popular women remained socially, economically, and politically vulnerable. It has therefore illustrated that the Bolivarian revolution cannot be understood without understanding the gendered nature of state–society relations contained and fostered within it. Indeed, it has been necessary to gender not only the revolution but also twenty-first-century socialism, post-neoliberalism, and the concept of popular power. In so doing, my work has upset notions of the Bolivarian state's promotion of popular power and post-neoliberal achievements in the revolutionary process.

This critique of the Bolivarian state's narrative is *not* an argument against popular power and state promotion of popular power. Nor is it an argument against the imagination's crucial role in the necessary transformation of the state and state–society relations away from neoliberalism toward the construction of socially equitable alternatives. Rather, as Ann Oakley (1984, 191) asserts: "All writing is an invitation to the imagination." My critique is an invitation *for* a much fuller and more nuanced conception of popular power and women's positioning within it than the one the Bolivarian state was promoting and fostering.

I am arguing for a conception of popular power based on awareness of the social contexts in which it is imagined and practiced—a conception informed by the everyday realities of popular women's labor, organization, and interactions with the state such as those I have brought to light. What this book shows is that these are social contexts very much marked by structural and symbolic gender and class inequalities and the intersections between them. The state can reproduce and reconfigure such inequalities through its actions and inactions. Popular power should be understood as mediated by gender and class divisions, and as in turn (re)shaping such divisions. Thus, imaginations of an alternative social order in which popular power is meaningful to all members of the popular classes need to proceed with caution and be grounded in a recognition of how gendered divisions of labor profoundly condition actually existing practices of popular power and who benefits and does not benefit from them.

Such imaginations also need to entail envisioning the state's role in relation to popular power. As a gendered institution, the state enables and/or constrains people's public participation and exercise of power based on the way it intervenes in the gendered division of labor. If such imaginations are to include state support of meaningful popular power and gender justice, they need to involve envisioning how the state can promote self-governing organization from below, led by women, rather than controlling popular women's organization from above and overburdening them.

Applying this feminist cultural materialist perspective in examining the Bolivarian Republic's foundations has shown that women's organizing for state recognition of unpaid housework's socioeconomic value, homemakers' social security, and the constitutional enshrinement of these claims as rights, though necessary measures, are not sufficient for transforming the gendered division of labor and achieving gender justice. Rather, these rights need to be enforced and enforced universally for their target population in order for their transformative potential to be realized. Although the Bolivarian populist rupture with the old established political system enabled Article 88's constitutional enshrinement, *Chavista* populist governance did not enable the creation of policies, laws, and institutions that guaranteed Article 88's implementation. Populist governance tends to bypass bureaucracy and institution-building, yet stable state institutions with the capacity and (nonpartisan) commitment to implement rights universally are precisely necessary if all homemakers are to enjoy social security. Article 88's implementation also failed because no mass movement demanding these rights existed and popular women lacked substantive representation in governance to compel the enforcement of these rights. The legislative contestations for the implementation of these rights detailed in this book point to the limits of populist governance and the need for an enabling political opportunity structure in order for these rights to be meaningful to popular-sector women. This would include ongoing substantive representation and the political will to advance women's gender interests within the state, sustained pressure from society on the state, accessible political education for popular women about their rights, and strong state institutions, in addition to substantial economic resources.

In the context of Bolivarian Venezuela during Chávez's presidency, Article 88 meant both everything and nothing. It meant everything, because it was testament to the revolutionary potential of the Bolivarian process and what women's organizing could achieve within it. Article 88 provided a platform to legitimate ongoing claims for recognition of homemakers and redistribution of wealth to them. For women's rights activists, it signified the culmination of decades of feminist demands for state recognition of unpaid labor's socioeconomic value and homemakers' entitlement to social security. For state actors, this article evinced the Bolivarian process's revolutionary character—they were often quick to hail it publicly as representing the country's radical transcendence, especially in relation to popular women's gender interests.

At the same time, Article 88 meant nothing in many poor homemakers' everyday lives, work, and interactions with the state. Many popular-sector homemakers were unaware of the very existence of this article that specifically interpellated them as bearers of social rights. This lack of awareness occurred within a national context in which the 1999 Constitution was written because of and ratified by popular vote, available for sale on street corners, and incessantly cited by state authorities. Rather than a legal tool to achieve gender equity, Article 88 often served as a rhetorical device that confused the boundaries between representations of gender justice and real gender justice. Bolivarian state agents invoked it constantly, while its effect on the lives of the homemakers it was meant to reach was unclear and patchy at best. Article 88 thus meant everything and nothing because it was a foundational promise by a state that was everywhere and nowhere at once for popular women.

Because this magical revolutionary state was both everywhere and nowhere at once, including some popular women and their claims for justice while simultaneously excluding and/or suspending others, it held popular women and its recognition of their labor in an uncertain state. From the relation of Madres del Barrio Mission to Article 88, to the times some women waited to be reached by Madres del Barrio, Hijos de Venezuela, and Amor Mayor missions, to the suspension that former Madres del Barrio were held in waiting for state support of their microenterprises, to the unclear conditions and duration of economic benefits for the remaining Madres del Barrio, to the backstage deliberations on women's rights in the 2012 labor law—all these Bolivarian state interventions were pervaded by uncertainty with regard to state recognition of popular women's labor. These "zones of uncertainty" in which the state made popular women wait for substantive recognition and redistribution show, as Auyero (2012) has stated elsewhere, that popular women did not control state actions. In other words, they could not be certain that the state would recognize their labor and redistribute wealth to them because they did not enjoy substantive representation: they did not have the power to steer the state and its actions.

Woven together, the multiple stories detailed within these chapters illustrate the deeply gendered nature of Venezuela's attempt to construct twenty-first-century socialism. Unlike the Cuban revolution before the "Special Period," which prioritized the development and expansion of production, the Bolivarian state, in spite of its socialist aspirations, did not meaningfully and sustainably diversify and expand Venezuela's productive forces during Chávez's presidency. Bolivarian Venezuela remained a petrostate heavily dependent on non-labor-intensive oil extraction and importation of essential goods, such as food, medicine, and clothing. Rather, the revolution's development and continuation pivoted on sowing the nation's oil wealth to restructure social reproduction relations, particularly with the popular sectors. The Bolivarian revolution's legitimacy rested in large part on what Ruth Pearson (1997) has termed elsewhere[1] as "a reproductive bargain, a bargain which ensured the continuity of social as well as aspects of human reproduction in the county" (680). Such a reproductive bargain is political, in that the population offers the regime political support as long as the government continues to offer and/or improve upon a basic standard of living (680). The Bolivarian revolution's legitimacy also rested on reconfiguring representation. As part of its pursuit of twenty-first-century socialism, the Bolivarian state accepted and promoted active popular-sector social and political participation. Restructuring the relations of reproduction in tandem with fomenting popular participation in the public sphere were key to Bolivarian Venezuela's construction of a new social contract between the state and society.

In this new social contract that privileged popular participation in community service delivery and political mobilization, popular women, their labor, and their organization became central to the Bolivarian process because of women's primary responsibility for reproduction. This gendered responsibility was reconfigured and resignified in support of the revolution. Popular women became the backbone of the revolutionary process because of their maternal gender role, their positioning within the gendered division of labor, and their ties to their households and communities.[2] Their social and political labor sustained the revolutionary Bolivarian state. Venezuela's developmental model remained *extractivist*, dependent on both natural resource extraction *and* the extraction of popular women's unpaid and underpaid labor. Similar to other "post-neoliberal" Pink Tide governments in Latin America (Friedman and Tabbush 2018), the Bolivarian government relied on both the extractive industries and poor women's labor to implement pro-poor redistributive policies and reduce poverty. Yet the Bolivarian government's ongoing dependence on this extractivist development model and failure to transform productive and reproductive relations left the revolution tenuous.

Indeed, the Bolivarian regime promoted the feminization of social and political participation. Molyneux (1985, 245) observes that revolutionary governments often incorporate women into social and political organizations in order to expand their power bases. With the Bolivarian regime, the government incorporated popular women socially and politically not only to expand its power base but also as *its central power base*. The male Madres del Barrio Mission coordinator cited at the beginning of this book illustrates this point in recognizing that women participated more politically and "sustain[ed] the revolution."

The centrality of popular women and their labor to the Bolivarian revolution points to shifting strategies of socialist governance in the wake of decades of neoliberal restructuring of states, economies, and societies. Organized labor, traditionally considered the locus for progressive social change, has been splintered and weakened in Latin America (Levitsky and Roberts

2011a, 415) and in Venezuela (Roberts 2003) in particular. Both in Venezuela and Latin America more broadly, where many established political parties became increasingly distant from the masses, grassroots and neighborhood organizations and protest movements emerged to meet popular needs and voice their interests (Craske 1999; Roberts 2003) in response to neoliberal policies. Popular women often were central to such grassroots organization and mobilization. By cutting back welfare states and threatening human survival and access to the most basic means necessary for human subsistence and reproduction, neoliberalism has served to politicize the domain of women's everyday work and struggles. Before neoliberalism, women's reproductive labor was often viewed on the left to be prepolitical. But such women-driven organization around social reproduction issues under neoliberalism represents an epistemic break with old leftist conceptions of organizing. And with the weakening of traditional (male-dominated) trade unions and national industrial development projects, the informal sector has grown correspondingly. A feminization of the labor force has occurred, and women have been increasingly viewed as active subjects of development by states and multilateral organizations. In addition, the rise of neoliberalism coincided with the rise in second-wave feminism (Fraser 2009), and feminist movements across the globe experienced gains in compelling states and social movements to mainstream gender. Now gender-sensitive state policies and practices tend to be viewed both domestically and internationally as a measure of a state's commitment to modernity,[3] and "gender and sexual rights advances are seen as key to 'modernizing' . . . revolutionary nation[s]" (Lind 2012b, 538). In neoliberalism's wake, socialist and/or post-neoliberal projects aiming for pro-poor redistribution and social and political inclusion must address popular women's roles in politics, society, and the economy not merely as a footnote.

Yet the case of Bolivarian Venezuela shows that pro-poor "post-neoliberal" policy and practices can also "institutionalize women's struggles for survival" (Lind 2005) similarly to neoliberalism, if they are not committed to socially redistributing reproductive labor. When lacking a gender analysis of and political will to substantively address the everyday realities in which poor women work and interact with men and the state, such social policies can redistribute wealth while not redistributing the gendered burden of material and time poverty. Indeed, this book's gender analysis illuminates some of the Bolivarian revolution's key continuities with neoliberalism, similar to twenty-first-century Ecuador's citizen revolution's primary focus on class redistribution (Lind 2012a, 2012b). Such analysis shows a "contradictory mix of legal/policy strategies and cultural interventions" around social reproduction at the heart of "post-neoliberal" national development frameworks (Lind 2012b, 539).

Such a contradictory policy mix occurred in the Bolivarian government's intervention in the economy to promote popular women's productive roles by providing interest-free and low-interest microcredit to them during Chávez's tenure, through programs such as Madres del Barrio and Ban-Mujer. The Bolivarian government encouraged poor women's entrepreneurship and use of microcredit just as many neoliberal governments did,[4] but unlike neoliberal governments, it subsidized poor women's productive participation. Yet, unlike the revolutionary Cuban government, it did not pursue policies of full employment and expanded formal-sector employment for women. Rather, the Bolivarian government supported the intensification and flexibilization of popular women's labor through homework and simultaneity, similar to neoliberalism. Yet, unlike neoliberal governments, the Bolivarian government did not retreat but intervened directly with economic and social resources for popular women to provide backing and incentives for the intensification and flexibilization of their labor. However, similar to neoliberalism, such Bolivarian policies "rel[ied] on the assumption that women have endless amounts of time to participate, do not require high (if any) salaries, and do not mind extending their traditional reproductive roles to the realm of community management" (Lind 2005, 146). This flexibility of popular women's labor and their ties to their households and communities enabled them to be more readily available to organize socially and politically in support of the revolution.

Indeed, because of the Bolivarian government's revolutionary maternalist approach toward popular women, a general gendered redistribution of productive and reproductive labor did not occur under *Chavismo*. Rather, Venezuela experienced gendered continuities with neoliberalism in spite of the government's rhetoric promoting feminist socialism. As in the neoliberal era, women in Venezuela increasingly entered the paid workforce (Á. Martínez 2010, 26). Yet, their incorporation was more into the informal sector of the economy (Á. Martínez 2010; Richter 2007), where they tended to occupy the lowest-paid and most precarious positions (Richter 2007). Women generally earned lower wages, experienced poorer working conditions, and suffered higher rates of unemployment than men (Richter 2007). And women's experiences with state-promoted cooperatives were largely unsuccessful (Centro de Estudios de la Mujer de la Universidad Central de Venezuela 2011, 31) and generally did not provide women with sustainable occupations: BanMujer, for example, had extremely high loan-default rates (Rakowski and Espina 2011, 190). At the same time, women in Venezuela remained largely responsible for unpaid housework. During the latter portion of Chávez's presidency, for example, approximately 57 percent of working-age women remained outside of the paid labor force because of household and caring duties (ECLAC

2013, 37). Many women with preschool-age children remained outside the paid labor force because of lack of childcare alternatives.[5] Further, the proportion of female-headed households increased from approximately 29 to 39 percent of all Venezuelan households during Chávez's presidency (Instituto Nacional de Estadística 2014b, 25). Poverty and extreme poverty rates decreased quite substantially,[6] yet female-headed households disproportionately experienced poverty (Paredes 2011)[7] and extreme poverty (Instituto Nacional de Estadística 2007). Thus, during Chávez's tenure, even as poverty decreased dramatically (unlike under neoliberalism), the gendered division of household labor and the burden of poverty on women did not change (as under neoliberalism).

The stories detailed within this book therefore show that rendering popular-sector women and their unpaid labor visible in a revolutionary "post-neoliberal" process does not necessarily entail granting them power. To socially and politically include popular women and interpellate them as key protagonists in state transformation does not necessarily mean that they control this process. In the Bolivarian revolution, the utilization and discursive invocation of popular women's unpaid labor did not necessarily serve to transform gender power relations.

Rather, unequal gender power relations and divisions of labor fueled the Bolivarian government and revolution, just as oil did. Popular-sector women performed for little or no pay much of the everyday socially and politically necessary labor to build and sustain the revolution. In this way, the conclusion that the Bolivarian revolution had "a woman's face" was both fitting and illusory; as part of the magical revolutionary narrative, it revealed the revolution's gender dynamics even as it concealed them. Popular women carried out the grinding, repetitive, necessary work that undergirded much of the magic of the revolutionary state. Their unpaid labor rolled out many new Bolivarian social programs *and* filled in the gaps when these programs did not reach portions of the popular sectors. Popular women also constituted the bulk of community-based political foot soldiers who carried out unpaid electoral organizing work for Chávez and *Chavista* candidates and mobilized in mass defense of the revolution. As the Red Popular de los Altos Mirandinos stated in the opening to this book: they, the "women home-makers home-workers . . . are those that are carrying out the actual work that carries this revolution forward." Just as Chávez asserted that there was no socialism without feminism, this book shows that there was no Bolivarian state without popular women and their unpaid labor. When Chávez and his government constantly asserted that the Bolivarian revolution had "a woman's face," as President Correa also asserted about Ecuador's citizen revolution, he was "impl[ying] that women as mothers and caretakers would be the political and reproductive foundation of the new socialist nation" (Lind 2012a, 255–256). Yet such a proclamation was "not insinuating that women [we]re autonomous subjects"; rather, it framed women "as the 'subjects of others'" (Lind 2012b, 542). In Venezuela, this meant that they were "Chavez's women."

To be made visible in the Bolivarian revolution, then, meant that state and party authorities recognized that popular women and their labor were crucial to upholding the revolution, yet these authorities often did not view their specific gender interests as central to this process. Once again, María León, the former national minister of woman's popular power and gender equality and leader of the state-led national popular women's front, speaks precisely to this point in reference to the 2012 presidential campaign year: "I'm not saying that women renounce their struggles; however, we can't place them as a central theme of politics." Resembling the Sandinista revolution in Nicaragua (Molyneux 1985), Bolivarian authorities expected the subordination of women's specific gender interests to the revolution's broader goals. Popular-sector women, their unpaid labor, and their social and political participation were needed, promoted, and celebrated in some instances, but many of them remained vulnerable.

The type of popular power that much of the Bolivarian state apparatus was promoting and fostering among popular women was one in which they were socially and politically mobilized yet contained in line with state and party directives—they were *gobierneras*, governed and obedient, their power controlled from above. For instance, Sandra Angeleri, an Araña Feminista member, gave the following example: "In all the communal councils, the women are the majority, but they (. . . the political [institutional] sphere) want our work, but they don't want our power" (Interview with Sandra Angeleri). When state and party authorities reached down to popular women to control their social and political participation, this created tensions with some women and their organizations, as shown by the Araña Feminista's self-defined stance defending its autonomy in relation to the state. Yet these tensions within *Chavismo* were often glossed over and not substantively addressed when conflicting actors and forces acted or felt they must act unified in defense of Chávez, his government, and the revolution in a broader context of ongoing and profound political polarization. The Araña's decision to cede to state and party authority requests to march with women organized by the state, whom they saw as *gobierneras*, on International Women's Day illustrates this dynamic.

Popular women's organizations' alliances with the Bolivarian state and support for the broader revolution created opportunities for organizing for substantive recognition of their unpaid labor and the legitimation of such organizing, but it also closed down such opportunities. Similar to state promotion of mass women's organizations in the Cuban and Nicaraguan revolutions (Friedman 2009; Molyneux 1985; Smith and Padula 1996), state-promoted women's organizations in Bolivarian Venezuela achieved important gains for popular women, but the state's primary goal with such organizations was to mobilize popular women to support and defend the revolution. The strategic positioning of popular women's organizations in alliance with the Bolivarian state—their linkage in the *Chavista* populist chain—could be productive for their struggles, but it could also be dangerous to them. It could serve as a means for popular women's organizations to act in power with the state, but it could also serve as a means for the state to exercise its power over them. This potential for endangerment was heightened because popular women did not control the state, which rendered their organization vulnerable to co-optation by the state and/or to silencing by the state.

Moreover, this book also points to the danger to women's mobilization posed by the blurring of state and party lines in a national context in which the state was actively promoting popular-sector social and political organization, and popular women's organization in particular. Precisely because popular women did not control the Bolivarian state, their organization and mobilization then became vulnerable to co-optation by the state for partisan ends. For example, in the May 2012 *Chavista* presidential campaign event in Falcón mentioned in my introduction, state–party propaganda on the centrality of women's role in the revolution formed the backdrop of the stage. State gender institution workers advertised this event to popular women community leaders throughout the state as a "meeting with the governor." Many of the approximately 300 women who arrived to Falcón's capital came ready to discuss their community work and needs, only to find that the female governor and several other female state and party leaders drew them there to dictate to them how to organize their communities for Chávez's re-election. These state and party authorities convened these popular women community leaders to the state's capital because of their vital roles in household and community organization, thus bringing them in physical proximity to political power. Yet these same authorities facilitated the event so as to contain the women in the crowd in order to mobilize them to support the revolution according to *oficialista* directives.

Popular women were uniquely vulnerable to such state direction, appropriation, and manipulation of their organization because of their gender role and their positioning in the gendered division of labor. Because they were the ones who cared—materially and discursively—and because they were more often tied to their households performing flexible labor, their labor and organization could more easily be extended to caring for and serving their communities, Chávez, and the revolution. This book also suggests that popular women were more vulnerable to political manipulation when they depended on the state for resources, such as cash transfers, because the state could more easily control them, their organization, and their mobilization, as seen with the state's positioning of the Madres del Barrio as uncertain clients who were expected to mobilize as "Chávez's women."

Although the Bolivarian state appropriated popular-sector women's unpaid labor and organizing, this does not mean that it incorporated all popular women in the same way or without resistance. Indeed, this book has illustrated that popular women's relation to the Bolivarian state was not uniform, since the Bolivarian state under Chávez's tenure was contradictory and uneven. Further, many popular women did exercise their agency individually and collectively and use their counterhegemonic critical and imaginative capacities within the real constraints they faced in the Bolivarian process. For example, the opening quote from the Red Popular de los Altos Mirandinos is testimony to the agency of organized popular-sector women, who directed their scathing critique of the state bureaucracy's exploitation of their labor to the head of the Bolivarian state. This quote is also testimony to their imaginative capacities, reflecting their desire for an alternative revolutionary order in which their work would be recognized and they would have power. Some state actors also shared this desire and promoted popular women's self-governing organization and leadership and substantive recognition of their labor. Yet these state agents' convictions and actions did not become hegemonic within the Bolivarian state apparatus. However, this counterhegemonic resistance did mean that the appropriation of popular-sector women's unpaid labor and organization created tensions between some popular women and the state, and contradictions between the radical magical narrative of (feminist) socialist revolution and the lived daily realities of many popular women.

This disjunctiveness between a state and a society conjoined in a popular revolutionary process also entailed a dynamic in which new welfare state presences to support the popular sectors generated new state absences for the subjects promised these new pro-poor policies, goods, and services. From its failed regulation and implementation of the promulgated 2005 Law of Social Services, to its exclusion of many poor homemakers from Madres del Barrio, to making many popular women wait in uncertainty for their dependents to be incorporated into Hijos de Venezuela and Amor Mayor missions, the Bolivarian state during Chávez's presidency was a state that raised many popular women's expectations of social inclusion, only to leave them unfulfilled. Woven together, these stories of simultaneous inclusion and exclusion of popular women and their dependents in Bolivarian Venezuela tell the story of largely fragmented and incomplete social policy, unlike the general policy thrust of universal social protection in revolutionary Cuba. They tell of a state that was contradictory and uneven—a state, once again, that was everywhere and nowhere at once for popular women.

This disjunctiveness in social service delivery occurred not only in the Bolivarian state's penetration of its territory and popular-sector communities within it but also in the state's handling of time. For here was a state that was ever-changing, a state that often acted suddenly, surprisingly, without notice and transparency—magically, as it seemed to possess powers that came from itself—a state that operated at a dizzyingly fast pace in its institutional expansion and its decisive discursive incorporation of popular-sector subjects, organizations, needs, and claims for justice. At the same time, this was a state that, in its everyday practices of public administration, operated frustratingly slowly and opaquely, holding so many popular-sector subjects and claims in suspension, making them wait—often without regard for *their* time—for these revolutionary transformations and promises to reach them. Similar to Secor's (2007) characterization of the Turkish state, the Bolivarian state was at once coherent in the circulations of justice that it set in motion and fractured spatially and temporally in its treatment of these same circulations.

My examination of the Bolivarian process during Chávez's presidency from popular-sector women's standpoints illuminates that this was very much a revolution about time and its disjunctures. The ways poor people experience time are "political artifacts" (Auyero 2012, 155): their temporal experiences are historically produced marks of political processes, actions, and inactions. Feminist economics has also placed emphasis on time as a resource that is mediated by gender in terms of its use and availability. Drawing from these insights, this book has shown that the Bolivarian revolution was also about the time popular women spent performing unpaid labor and how such time use constrained their social, political, and economic participation and their ability to benefit from the revolution. If we return to Veronica's home in the Falcón *barrio* (described in chapter 5), for example, and we take note of the time she spent cleaning up after her demented and incontinent elderly mother, while she was also caring for two preschool-age children, trying to take in piecework laundry to make ends meet, and waiting for the state to intervene on her elderly and minor dependents' behalf, we see a political artifact of the Bolivarian revolution. The unreliability of the Bolivarian state—the magical, revolutionary state that was everywhere and nowhere at once—to substantively recognize popular women's unpaid labor reproduced many popular women's vulnerability and time poverty. This uncertain, unreliable state reinforced gender differences and the gendered division of labor in the time that it made popular women wait for its social assistance.

This revolution that penetrated space and time with its presences and absences, its actions and inactions, also penetrated the moral orders, and in particular gendered moral orders, of the subjects whom it interpellated. Linked with its institutional restructuring, the Bolivarian revolution during Chávez's presidency was also a normative process that resignified understandings of work and workers, power, popular participation and activism, and popular women's gender role and unpaid labor in particular. As William Carroll (2011, 152) states: "Often the new reworks the old, with radical effects. Viewed dialectically, the new preserves yet transforms extant reality." This book has shown that the Bolivarian state drew on the extant hegemonic maternal gender role for popular women and transformed it in service of the revolution to ordain the extension of their unpaid labor from their households to their communities and political organizing. Similar to the Nicaraguan revolution in which the meaning of the socially conventional role of motherhood was appropriated and politicized in support of the revolution (Molyneux 1985), Bolivarian Venezuela resignified popular-sector mothers as revolutionary subjects. The moral order conditioning their care work was also resignified as a revolutionary maternalism. Popular women's political participation sometimes "provided the power to refashion gender subjectivity into an important asset . . . to grassroots organizing" (Valencia 2015, 93). Yet this process of moral transformation preserved the normative underpinning of maternal altruism that popular women, as mothers, should sacrifice themselves to care for others—a norm that has long underpinned capitalist and neoliberal capitalist development frameworks (Lind 2012b). This normative underpinning was also resignified such that popular women were expected to sacrifice themselves for their communities, the revolution, and its commander, in addition to sacrificing themselves for their families. Such revolutionary maternalism is seen in the Madres del Barrio, who were expected by the state and expected themselves as "socialists" to use their monthly cash transfers (of less than minimum wage) not only to meet their families' needs but also to meet vulnerable members' of their communities welfare needs that the Bolivarian state did not meet. Here, in "post-neoliberal" Venezuela, the "curious alliance between communitarianism and neoliberalism" (Molyneux 2001, 148) underpinning postadjustment women-led poverty relief programs had transformed into a curious alliance between communitarianism, (neo)liberal individualism, and revolutionary maternalism, which helped to uphold the purported socialist revolution and its lack of wealth redistribution from the rich to the poor. This emergent moral order supported the gendered division of labor, the deepening of this division, and popular-sector women's double and triple shifts—all gendered outcomes that carried on from the neoliberal era.

This book has shown that such gendered normative resignification within the revolution was also a regulatory device that served to refashion popular understandings of good and bad motherhood, with the effect of exacerbating existing social divisions between popular-sector women and generating new forms of social divisions between them. Similar to Lind's (2005, 2012a) observations of both neoliberal and post-neoliberal Ecuador, in Bolivarian Venezuela, "caring labor continue[d] to sustain the national economy," while being "imbued in a stratified logic of 'deserving' and 'undeserving' mothers of . . . the nation" (Lind 2012a, 256). Further, as in the Cuban (Smith and Padula 1996) and Nicaraguan revolutions (Molyneux 1985), Bolivarian revolutionary moral discourse on gender issues contained expectations of women to change their role and behavior, with few expectations of men to change their behavior and role in reproduction. What remained the same in Bolivarian Venezuela was the blaming of popular-sector women as individuals for their own and their children's socioeconomic conditions and the moral—and practical—exoneration of fathers and the state from sharing responsibility in care work. The revolutionary process therefore preserved a structural and discursive paternalism toward popular-sector mothers that overlooked and undervalued their unpaid labor.

In pressing forward for a nuanced conception of popular power, I close by turning back to Article 88—to this foundational promise that triggered my imagination and study of Bolivarian Venezuela—and to the struggle for recognition of unpaid labor that women's rights activists in Venezuela and beyond have been fighting for over many decades. Article 88 can serve as a starting point for a fuller and more nuanced envisioning of popular power, for a more dignified map that asks us to proceed with caution while daring our imaginations, as Coronil writes. For if popular power is to be meaningful to the women who carry out the bulk of reproductive labor, the value of their labor for their households, their communities, and broader society must be substantively recognized, and affirmative action measures must be taken to protect them and provide them with a universal minimum social floor. Recognition of unpaid reproductive labor and redistribution of re-

sources to the poor and working-class women who carry it out are necessary but not sufficient measures for achieving gender justice. Substantive
representation and meaningful, bottom-up democratic participation of the
women who perform such work are also necessary. A more dignified map
of popular power, then, should show us the importance of popular women's
control of the terms under which they and their labor are recognized. Such
a map should also show us the need for both state support for and autonomy
from the state in the movements, organizations, and demands that popular
women form.

Autonomy must be essential to mapping popular power, whether under
left-wing or right-wing governance. The question of autonomy, as the Bolivarian case has shown, can become tricky terrain for popular organizations to navigate under the Left. What they need to untangle is how they
can support and act with the state, when necessary, while maintaining their
independence and power to pressure the state to steer toward gender justice and serve them, instead of becoming subordinate to the state. Indeed,
as this book has illustrated and other research has concluded, "the Latin
American Left does not promote gender equality simply by virtue of being leftist" (Blofield, Ewig, and Piscopo 2017, 347). Rather (in addition to
other determinants), it "*reacts* to" feminist organization and mobilization
(Blofield, Ewig, and Piscopo 2017); and this is why sustained autonomous
popular feminist mobilization is essential. With right-wing governance,
popular autonomy can appear simpler because of the oppositional nature of
the Right to popular-sector class interests. Yet, decades of experience under
neoliberalism has shown that the Right can also co-opt popular women's
organizing, especially around social reproduction issues and when people's
basic subsistence is threatened. Popular power needs to be reimagined in
ways that do not double down on popular women's maternal gender role
and unpaid labor as essential to household and community survival, especially now that Venezuela has experienced long-term crisis after Chávez and
much of Latin America shifts back to the right and retrenches public welfare programs. Without progressive redistribution of reproductive labor,
popular women are left vulnerable to shouldering the worst burdens of neoliberal policies and crises. Mapping the way forward and way out of development frameworks underpinned by maternalism and women's unpaid labor appears to lie in transformations of *both* the state *and* popular power
that hold redistribution of reproductive labor central.

The Venezuelan socialist feminist Alba Carosio (2010, 11) concludes: "To
emphasize women's presence and their contribution to . . . well-being . . .
without a parallel search for the transformation of unequal structures of

work organization, recognition, valuation and protection leads to an instrumentalization of women and perpetuates the inherent exploitation in the sexual division of labor." Thus, I suggest Article 88 serves merely as a starting point for a fuller imagining of popular power and gender justice. Such a map would entail imagining a redistribution with men and the state of the socially necessary reproductive labor popular women perform so that they can participate equally in instances of popular power.

Notes

Introduction

1. State institutions that make and administer policy on gender-related issues.

2. A widely used term in Latin America referring to people from the poor and working classes. I use this term because, as Elisabeth Jelin (1990b, 10–11) notes, informality and precariousness characterizes their living and working conditions, and "working class" therefore does not accurately define their socioeconomic positions. Throughout this book, I use English translations of both terms: popular-sector women (*mujeres de los sectores populares*) and popular women (*mujeres populares*).

3. In this statement, the Red Popular uses the popular colloquial term *amas de casa*, which is commonly translated into English as "housewives" even though that is not the literal translation of the Spanish term. Throughout this book, I use the term "homemaker" instead of "housewife" to reflect the fact that the people who engage in unpaid reproductive labor are not passive but actively working in taking care of others and themselves.

4. This is a political term referring to ranging lighter variations of the color red, traditionally associated with the Left.

5. This includes Argentina, Bolivia, Brazil, Chile, Costa Rica, Dominican Republic, Ecuador, El Salvador, Guatemala, Honduras, Nicaragua, Paraguay, Peru, and Uruguay, in addition to Venezuela.

6. Populism is not an ideology or principle (Laclau 1977, 2005), nor is it an economic phenomenon—a mode of wealth distribution and redistribution (Weyland 2001). This political definition explains why populism emerges on the right and on the left.

7. Some analysts (Leiva 2008; Macdonald and Ruckert 2009; Petras and Veltmeyer 2009; Razavi 2009; M. Taylor 2009) argue that although PT governments expanded the social role of their states and decreased poverty, they left neoliberal macroeconomic structures that produced poverty and inequality in place. They contend that PT governments attempted to manage neoliberalism's internal contradictions rather than transform them. Levitsky and Roberts (2011b, 23) counter that none of the PT governments should be considered neoliberal because they all "used state power to implement progressive redistributive policies" to varying degrees. Fo-

cusing on state–society relations under PT governance, other analysts (Beasley-Murray, Cameron, and Hershberg 2009; Velasco 2015) argue that such governments' rise to power signified a struggle over the form of democracy: they represented a popular rejection of liberal democratic regimes that historically failed to incorporate popular-sector interests and advance their welfare. And Brand and Sekler (2009) claim that neoliberalism was delegitimated in Latin America, enabling a field of post-neoliberal discursive and institutional possibilities to arise, where ruling forces and progressive social movements existed in dynamic tension with each other.

8. The country did indeed "decide" this; the Venezuelan electorate voted in a national referendum whether to ratify the 1999 Constitution. This does not mean that the electorate read and debated Article 88 prior to the referendum; they had a choice to vote "yes" or "no" to the entire draft constitution and not to this article alone. The following chapters discuss how the general lack of public debate about Article 88 in the constituent process shaped the ways in which it was (not) claimed and (not) contested by the Venezuelan state and society during Chávez's presidency.

9. A diversity of gender identities exists within a country's gender order, because they take on class- and race-specific forms. Yet, even as people's individual lives may depart from a given gender order, such as a male breadwinner/dependent housewife order, the gender order is the hegemonic mode of shaping the ways labor is divided, organized, and recognized.

10. As Molyneux (2001, 171) points out, the meaning of motherhood varies according to age, ethnicity, and class position.

11. I use the concept of "interpellation" in an Althusserian (Althusser 1971) sense to describe how discourses and institutions hail individuals as subjects. In their recognition of such hailings, individuals are transformed—they become subject(s) to the discourses and institutions that hail them. Interpellation, then, is a dialogical process between forces that identify individuals and those individuals who respond to, are subject to, and shaped by such hailings.

12. This is not to suggest that extralocal interests and forces did not play roles in shaping institutions, ideologies, practices, and identities within Bolivarian Venezuela. During Chávez's presidency, the Bolivarian state continued to be thoroughly embedded in and dependent on networks of transnational capital and international trade because of its ongoing reliance on the extractive industries. Indeed, the Bolivarian state and its trajectory can be adequately understood only in relation to global capital and to the state's opposition—both internal and external and the dialectical interaction between these forces.

13. The Venezuelan state was originally characterized as a "magnanimous sorcerer" by the playwright and scriptwriter José Antonio Cabrujas.

14. This term refers to the elite power-sharing agreements that set the framework for democratic interaction from 1958 to 1998.

15. This break is marked discursively in the public imaginary—both state and society actors refer to the *Puntofijista* era as the Fourth Republic and the Bolivarian era as the Fifth Republic.

16. Women's gender interests refer to historically, socially, and culturally produced interests that women "may develop by virtue of their social positioning through gender attributes" (Molyneux 1985, 232).

17. For example, Rafael Caldera appointed two women to head ministries dur-

ing his presidency (1994–99), while Chávez appointed nine women to head ministries during the first five years of his presidency (1999–2004) (García and Valdivieso 2009, 140).

18. I have not seen gender-disaggregated statistics on communal council membership. However, state gender institution authorities and workers constantly stated that women constituted the majority of communal council members. Thomas Purcell also notes from his research with cooperatives in Bolivarian Venezuela that women were the central participants (cited in Spronk and Webber 2011), while Gioconda Espina and Cathy Rakowski (2010) state that most volunteers running Bolivarian social welfare programs were women.

19. 30 May 2012. Josefa Camejo Women's Front, Carabobo Campaign. Coro, Falcón state.

20. "Autonomous" perhaps is not the most fitting qualifier for the relationship between many popular women's organizations and the state under Chávez. Rather, women's organizations allied with Bolivarianism supported the government, and they might even have used state resources to carry out their work, but some saw themselves as simultaneously independent of the government and able to critique it.

21. In addition, Chávez issued two separate decrees in 2007 granting pensions to 150,000 elderly people in total, with the second decree granting pensions to 50,000 poor elderly women in particular, some of whom were homemakers. The 2001 census states there were 1,952,406 elderly people in total in Venezuela, and 1,204,708 elderly women (my own calculation) (Instituto Nacional de Estadística, n.d.).

22. Barrio Adentro, and the public health system more broadly, and Mercal became universally available.

23. As women are differentially positioned in societies because of the intersection of their gender with other social attributes, such as class, race, and ethnicity, a general unity of interests among women cannot be assumed to exist (Molyneux, 1985).

24. The popular women with whom I conducted my research came from different racial backgrounds, ranging from white to *mestiza* to black, as well as from racially mixed communities. They experienced racial differences, but I focused on their experiences of gender and class, and not specifically on their different racial experiences.

25. This methodology extends from different women's experiences to explore how broader social and political relations shape them (Smith 1987, 10) and how social complexes are organized (Smith 1999).

26. As Burawoy (1998, 14) explains: "In the view of reflexive science, intervention is not only an unavoidable part of social research but a virtue to be exploited. It is by mutual reaction that we discover the properties of the social order. Interventions create perturbations that are not noise to be expurgated but music to be appreciated, transmitting the hidden secrets of the participant's world. Institutions reveal much about themselves when under stress or in crisis, when they face the unexpected as well as the routine."

27. A popular term meaning "the squalid ones," used by some *Chavistas* to label the opposition.

28. A popular term, loosely translated as "the real reds," used by some *Chavistas* to label whom they saw as real *Chavistas*.

29. *Chavista*, or *Chavismo*, refers to the movement encompassing the Bolivarian government and popular forces, organizations, and movements aligned with Hugo Chávez.

30. I drew from Javier Auyero's and Débora Swistun's (2009) approach in *Flammable* to the rumors about the state's and polluters' (in)actions that circulated among residents of the contaminated Argentine shantytown.

Chapter 1: Out of the Margins

1. It draws from archival analysis of the 1999 ANC and document analysis (of books and popular articles) covering the ANC and related processes preceding it, and in-depth interviews with key women's rights protagonists involved in historical processes leading to Article 88's inclusion in the 1999 Constitution.

2. Corporatism refers to regimes of class-based interest mediation between workers' unions, employers, and the state that generally preceded neoliberal regimes in Latin America.

3. Coronil (1997) uses this term to explain the development of twentieth-century Venezuelan national identity and citizenship, which came to be understood not only as participation in formal politics but also as entitlement to the nation's oil wealth. Struggles for democracy thus were linked to struggles for "collective ownership of the common subsoil."

4. The Democratic Republican Union party also formed part of the Punto Fijo power-sharing agreement, but never enjoyed the substantial power that AD and COPEI did under *Puntofijismo*.

5. Clientelist forms of interest mediation refer to people's (clients') lending of political support to patrons in exchange for material rewards that meet their practical needs. Patrons need clients' political support and clients can manipulate this to meet their specific needs, but the negotiation between them remains hierarchical in that clients' access to resources is conditional on subordination to the patron (Fox 1997; Taylor 2004). Patron–client interactions are not mediated by formal and generalized laws and procedures, but by personal ties and social customs (Taylor 2004).

6. Women from leftist organizations joined the guerrilla struggle. Four decades later, some of them came to occupy prominent positions within the Bolivarian regime (Ciccariello-Maher 2013b).

7. Edgardo Lander (2005, 22) notes, for example, that income distribution was not substantially altered during *Puntofijismo*'s height.

8. With the FEVA, Yolanda Poleo de Baez was instrumental in later advancing women's rights in the 1982 Civil Code reform and the 1990 labor law reform. In both her roles as judge and legislative activist, Poleo de Baez worked within and from outside the state to advance women's gender interests. She carried forward the demand for state recognition of unpaid housework in her organizing for the Civil Code reform (Poleo de Baez 1977) and later in her organizing for the 1990 labor law reform (see discussion below in this chapter's discussion on the reform organizing process).

9. In *Martín Hilario Toledo vs. Companía Transporte Colectivo del Tuy C.A.*, Judge Poleo de Baez (1975) found that the bus company with which the plaintiff's wife was

traveling and whose driver caused an accident that resulted in her death was responsible not only for moral damages to the plaintiff and his children but also for material damages compensating for the replacement cost of her lost unpaid housework as a full-time homemaker. In her judgment, Poleo de Baez (1975, 18) stated that "in the Venezuelan family, the wife who does not undertake a paid activity outside of the home, fulfills her obligations in the maintenance of the home, the children and the husband with the multiple labors that she executes 'full-time' in the home and that generate goods and services. On the subject of labor and particularly in the working class, it is judged that such goods and services, product of this 'disguised' or 'invisible' work increases the salary produced by the husband and improves the family's level of life, a salary that would not be enough if the family had to invest in paying for such goods and services."

10. Elisabeth Jay Friedman (2000b, 145) explains that their history of exclusion in the democratic transition revealed to women's rights advocates "the need for an agency that would promote women's issues within the powerful executive branch. Because Venezuelan political life was to a great extent carried out through semi-corporatist bargaining, women recognized that they had little chance at promoting substantial gender-based legal or social reform without such a resource."

11. Women's rights activists successfully organized for congressional discussion of Civil Code reform by being the first social or political group ever to take advantage of the 1961 Constitution's popular initiative article, which stipulated that a bill could be directly introduced to Congress through a proposal signed by 20,000 citizens. Women's rights activists collected more than 35,000 signatures in support of their reform initiative (Friedman 2000b).

12. The CONG was a politically autonomous network incorporating "feminist, professional, popular, labor, political solidarity . . . party-linked, religious, and health groups" (CONG [1988], as cited in Friedman 2000b, 203). At its peak, around thirty organizations were active members in the CONG (Gioconda Espina, as cited in Rakowski 2003).

13. The study used both the replacement and opportunity costs of women's unpaid household labor in cases of then current gender wage gaps and in the ideal case of gender wage equity to calculate these figures.

14. The contribution of men to unpaid household labor in 87 percent of the representative sample of Venezuelan households was found to be "marginal" or "insignificant" (Banco Central de Venezuela 1983, 71).

15. The study in its entirety was never published, but a shorter, academic version of the study was written by Lourdes Urdaneta and first published by the BCV in 1986 as *Participación económica de la mujer y distribución del ingreso*.

16. Founded in the 1970s, the CFP grew nationally to become the largest politically autonomous women's organization during *Puntofijismo* (Friedman 2000b). The circles organized popular-sector women using popular education and non-hierarchical methods and focused on their immediate needs and representing their political interests.

17. Red Todas Juntas was a network of popular-sector women and popular women's organizations from Caracas and inland Venezuela, established to explicitly articulate popular-sector women's needs. According to one of the Todas Juntas co-founders, the network was founded because CONG members were predominantly

middle-class women. One of Todas Juntas's central organizing focuses was domestic workers. The network also worked with popular homemakers and on conscientizing them about the value of their unpaid labor (Interview with Red Todas Juntas Cofounder).

18. This package included the elimination of subsidies for basic goods—including the doubling of petrol prices—the elimination of price controls, unification of exchange rates, fluctuation of the currency, tariff decreases, interest rate deregulation, government services price increases (Coronil and Skurski 2006), and the introduction of a value-added tax (Grindle 2000).

19. The structural adjustment program was indeed a great turnaround, as Pérez had campaigned for the presidency on an antiausterity platform and assumed the presidency only two weeks before he announced this orthodox neoliberal program. It was also a "great turnaround" in a historic sense: Pérez had introduced the concept of a "Great Venezuela" under his first presidency (1974–79) with his oil-boom-financed import substitution industrialization, modernization, and social investment policies.

20. Estimates of deaths of civilians in the *Caracazo* range from several hundred to several thousand, in addition to several thousand wounded civilians.

21. It reoriented social policies from universal to targeted measures in order to cushion the costs of structural adjustment for the poorest sectors of society (Gómez Calcaño 1998). Although the government increased its social policy expenditures in the early 1990s, these post-*Caracazo* measures were incapable of compensating for income losses resulting from the rise in unemployment, decreases in real wages, the elimination of subsidies, and rising inflation (Gómez Calcaño 1998; López Maya, Lander, and Ungar 2002).

22. Both Sanjuán (2002) and Fernandes (2010) note that the state increased its repressive force in the *barrios* in the 1990s as it retreated from its interventionist and social welfare roles, and gangs and the drug trade grew to fill this vacuum. As Elisabeth Jay Friedman (personal communication) concludes, the Venezuelan state replaced its magic wand with a baton.

23. For example, later in 1989, the government enacted political decentralization reforms, which enabled voters to elect their political leaders at local and state levels for the first time.

24. Whereas the *Caracazo* signaled a fundamental break between large sectors of society and the state, the 1992 MBR coup attempt signaled a fundamental break between significant (lower and middle) sectors of the military and the state. The relationship between the *Caracazo* and the 1992 coup attempt was dialectical—the MBR noted that they resented the state calling on the military during the *Caracazo* to repress the popular sectors, from which many of them came and with whom they identified.

25. Five years before the 1998 presidential elections that brought Hugo Chávez to power, the Venezuelan electorate already signaled its desire for an antiestablishment alternative to AD and COPEI by electing Rafael Caldera of the new *Convergencia* electoral coalition to the presidency.

26. These authors show that gender wage gaps persisted and women tended to congregate at the bottom of occupational hierarchies and experience higher rates

of unemployment under neoliberalism. In addition, they note high rates of female-headed households, which characterized around half of poor households in Venezuela.

27. Friedman (2000b) points out two disparate tendencies in civil society women's organizing during the 1990s: increasing organization among popular-sector women and decreasing cross-class organization among women, especially through the CONG. In this sense, the mutually reinforcing crises constituted both threats to and opportunities for women's organizing, thereby showing how central context effects and class can be on women's organization as an interest group.

28. This group included professional, academic, union, and popular-sector women—an example of a reignited women's conjunctural coalition under a new but yet-to-be-defined political regime.

29. The 1993 Law of Equal Opportunities stipulated that the state must found a permanent national state agency for women's rights. Implementing this statute would ensure that the agency's fate no longer depended on the president's will and priorities, and thus be "subject to the vagaries of state expansion and reduction" and "constant structural reorganization" that had marked its trajectory since its founding in the 1970s (Friedman 2000a, 73–74).

30. The first few months of Chávez's presidency were marked by several Supreme Court challenges over the constitutionality of Chávez's decree of a national consultative referendum on the ANC's convocation. One of the legal challenges centered on the ANC's procedures; prior to his assumption of power, Chávez had appointed and convened a Constituent Assembly Presidential Commission, which drafted the procedures for electing representatives to the assembly (Combellas 2005). The Supreme Court ruled that Chávez could not alone decide the ANC's procedures, but it allowed him to ask the electorate in the national consultative referendum if it would authorize him to set the procedures for the ANC that were partially modified by the National Electoral Council.

31. Both questions received more than 80 percent approval from voters, but 62 percent of the electorate abstained from voting in the referendum (García-Guadilla and Hurtado 2000, 19). The passage of this referendum also included authorization for Chávez's proposed procedures for electing ANC representatives, which entailed a simple majority system in which candidates would run as individuals and not as political party representatives.

32. The ratio of candidates opposing *Chavismo* to candidates aligned with the *Chavista* Patriotic Pole averaged approximately 8.5 to 1 (my own calculation based on statistics provided by García-Guadilla and Hurtado 2000, 21–22).

33. The Patriotic Pole did not officially run candidates, but Chávez promoted unofficial lists of candidates (Segura and Bejarano 2013).

34. Patriotic Pole–aligned candidates gained 94.5 percent of the seats in the ANC, even though they won only 62 percent of the popular vote (García-Guadilla and Hurtado 2000).

35. This is not to imply that there was not ideological divergence within the Patriotic Pole ANC delegates. Indeed, at this time, the Patriotic Pole was a pluralistic coalition of actors, organizations, and parties. This pluralism was reflected in some ANC debates around substantive issues. Yet all of them generally identified with Chávez's platform for regime change from neoliberalism toward instituting a so-

cial and participatory democracy. At this same time, the Patriotic Pole's programmatic convergence did not entail consensus on the need for gender mainstreaming throughout the constitutional text and also specific recognition of unpaid housework and homemakers.

36. This result, in turn, would assist the ANC in drafting the constitution within the six-month time period it was legally allotted to do so by the popular referendum.

37. Debates around the ANC's interpretation of its own powers and its conflicts with the extant constituted powers—namely, the judiciary and the Congress—occupied the bulk of the first month of the assembly's deliberations, thus detracting delegates' time and attention from popular consultation and constitutional drafting. These conflicts were able to emerge because of the ambiguous language contained within the April referendum's polling bases (Abbott 2011). Before the referendum, the Supreme Court had ruled that the 1961 Constitution would remain in force until the new constitution was ratified, but the National Electoral Council maintained in one of the referendum polling bases that the ANC was an "originary power that gathers together popular sovereignty" (*Gaceta Oficial No. 36.669,* 25 March 1999). The majority of ANC delegates chose to recognize the ANC itself as possessing supraconstitutional powers granted to it by the sovereign people in the April referendum. This interpretation entailed conceptualizing the ANC's powers as prior to and above the constituted powers, thus enabling it to modify and transform the existing constitutional order before popular approval and enactment of the new constitution. Using this interpretation, the majority of ANC delegates voted in August 1999 to pass statutes and decrees declaring the subordination of all public powers to it, the reorganization of institutions of public power, a state of emergency for the judicial power and its subsequent reorganization, and limitations to the legislative power at national, state, and municipal levels. A bloc of congressional representatives opposing *Chavismo* decided to challenge the ANC's assumption of powers in the Supreme Court. The ensuing conflict over the ANC's powers culminated in a violent confrontation between progovernment and opposition forces outside the legislative palace in Caracas at the end of August 1999.

38. They did this by first conducting one round of discussion of every draft article and then swiftly concluding deliberation on the next constitutional draft by discussing and voting on blocks of chapters instead of each individual article within them.

39. For the women's rights activists organizing around the ANC, mainstreaming a gender perspective entailed not only an awareness of how all proposals for the new constitution would affect women and gender relations but also a recognition of the female gender alongside the male gender throughout the constitutional text, because all subjects are gendered in the Spanish language.

40. For example, this strategy was tactfully employed by both the CONG and CONAMU in their promotion of women's rights proposals and conjunctural coalition-building for the ANC. The CONG entitled its published proposals that included but went far beyond women's rights to contain a popular perspective of necessary rights, duties, and institutions in the new republic: "Las Mujeres Discuten un Nuevo País: Su Aporte a la Constituyente"—translated as "Women Discuss a New Country: Their Contribution to the Constituent Process." CONAMU entitled its forums and published proposals supported by civil and political women's or-

ganizations, "Una Visión de País con Ojos de Mujer"—loosely translated as "A Vision of the Country from a Woman's Perspective."

41. Women Together For Venezuela; the CONG; Venezuelan Association for Sexual Education; Center for Social Research, Training, and Women's Studies; Central University of Venezuela's Center for Women's Studies; Popular Women's Circles; Population and Sustainable Development Network; and the Permanent Forum for Gender Equity.

42. Women's rights activists had been developing their political agenda since preparing for the 1995 United Nations World Conference on Women (Interview with Nora Castañeda).

43. The UN also supported some of these events.

44. The coalition included: CONG; Bicameral Commission for Women's Rights; Caroní Municipality Mayor's office; Women's Studies University Network; Venezuelan Network against Domestic Violence; Legal Assistance Services Network; Woman and Environment Network; Peasant Woman and Indigenous Woman Network; Network of Women Labor Leaders; Women Leaders United; Network of Women's Popular Education; Venezuelan Prevention of Premature Pregnancy Network; Central University of Venezuela's Center for Women's Studies; Popular Women's Circles; the Permanent Forum for Gender Equity; and CONAMU.

45. The demand they made was for "social security" for homemakers, but their fundamental objective was actually narrower: a pension for retirement-age homemakers (First Interview with Gioconda Espina; Interview with Inocencia Orellana; Second Interview with Marelis Pérez Marcano), since the social security system covered a range of contingencies, including but not limited to old age.

46. Interestingly, even though Chávez's proposal was thinner than the women's movement's proposals on gender-based rights, he proposed extending the discrimination ban to grounds of sexual orientation—a demand that some women's rights activists did raise, but on which the conjunctural coalition had not reached consensus for their ANC proposal.

47. Even though the Patriotic Pole did not propose social security for homemakers, the Patriotic Pole of Women did (Polo Patriótico de Mujeres 1999).

48. Debate did emerge within the ANC plenary around this draft article, but not on whether it should be included. The issue raised with this article by a male delegate, supported by other delegates, was that the proposed article discriminated against men and therefore should be expanded to include men—in his words, the "home owners" (Asamblea Nacional Constituyente 1999b, 71).

Accounts from Portocarrero (2000), Pérez Marcano (Second Interview with Marelis Pérez Marcano), and Morelba Jiménez (Interview with Morelba Jiménez), a member of the women's rights technical assistance team, indicate that Portocarrero lobbied her fellow ANC delegates in the Constitutional Commission hard for this article's inclusion in the draft constitution. Apparently an interpretation existed in the Constitutional Commission that this article was not necessary because they had already agreed to include a different article that would enshrine social security as universal. Portocarrero and Pérez Marcano insisted that the article recognizing homemakers in particular should be maintained as a means to justify affirmative action social security policies for homemakers in the new regime (Second Interview with Marelis Pérez Marcano). However, by 2011, when I began my research, no publicly available records of these debates existed within the ANC archives, and Portocarrero had passed away.

Chapter 2: Between Fruitless Legislative Initiatives and Executive Magic

1. I conducted archival and document analysis of post-ANC legislative, policy, and women's rights organizing processes related to Article 88 and in-depth interviews with key actors involved in these processes.

2. These polling victories include elections for representatives at national, regional, and municipal levels as well as popular referenda. This is not to imply that *Chavismo* won all elections for representatives at all levels (except when the opposition boycotted the 2005 elections for the National Assembly and *Chavismo* did gain complete legislative control). Rather, *Chavismo* consistently won the majority of representative positions at national, regional, and municipal levels.

3. Julia Buxton (2011) notes a historical continuity in the lack of consolidation of liberal democracy in Venezuela from *Puntofijismo* to Bolivarianism: "Certainly it is the case that if Chávez's Venezuela is to be judged by the procedural benchmarks of liberal democracy, there is a deficit of checks and balances on government, the rule of law is weak, the military is not apolitical and executive power is pronounced. But . . . it has never been the case that liberal democracy has consolidated in Venezuela. During the Punto Fijo period, the country had a model of illiberal democracy that delimited participation, restricted access to power, privileged a minority, and politicized all state institutions. The rule of law was historically weak, and corruption and human rights abuses were pronounced. To present the Bolivarian process as some form of democratic regression or authoritarian aberration in this historical context is misleading. It denies the structural legacies of Puntofijismo and negates the progress that has been made in extending social and political inclusion in a historical context characterized by disaffection with political parties, politicians, and institutions" (xv).

4. In addition, many of the missions either directly or indirectly targeted popular-sector women, given their positioning in relations of social reproduction. The missions' designs, objectives, and effects on gender relations are discussed in detail in chapters 3, 4, and 5.

5. Chapters 3 and 4 on Madres del Barrio Mission discuss one of the institutional mechanisms through which the Bolivarian government aimed to incorporate popular-sector women into this new production model.

6. In 2007 and 2008, breakaways and expulsions of deputies from the *Chavista* alliance occurred, but this still left *Chavismo* with more than 90 percent of the National Assembly seats.

7. Ellner (2011) explains that some *Chavistas* envisioned that, in the absence of a liberal democratic separation of powers, the party would serve to counterbalance the state: strong rank-and-file participation and decision-making in the PSUV would serve as an effective check on the government.

8. This refers to a "minimum agenda" for advancing women's rights that women's rights activists aligned and not aligned with *Chavismo* and both within and outside

the state agreed upon: regulation and application of a violence against women law; decriminalization of voluntary abortion; gender parity and alternation in electoral lists; compliance with laws that prohibit gender stereotyping in advertising; and enactment of legislation enabling homemakers' incorporation into the social security system (Espina 2007). These demands were incorporated into MinMujer's "Second Plan for Women's Equality" (2010).

9. However, some legislation did advance lesbian, gay, bisexual, transgender, transsexual, and intersex (LGBTTI) rights that had been demanded by the women's and sexual-gender diversity movements.

10. In the September 2010 National Assembly elections, *Chavismo* did not win the majority of votes, yet it won the majority of legislative seats, because of the design of Venezuela's mixed electoral system (Lalander 2012). With these results, however, *Chavismo* did not enjoy a qualified majority in the National Assembly. A qualified majority was needed to grant the president enabling powers to enact laws by decree and to pass organic laws, foundational laws that organize the public powers, develop constitutional rights, or serve as a normative framework for other laws (Constitución de la República Bolivariana de Venezuela 1999). Thus, during the lame duck period in December 2010—after the September 2010 elections and before the new National Assembly began its term in January 2011—the outgoing National Assembly granted President Chávez enabling powers to last eighteen months (López Maya 2011).

11. In December 2010, the outgoing National Assembly passed twenty-three laws, eight of which were organic laws (Asamblea Nacional de la República Bolivariana de Venezuela). Many of these laws formed a package of socialist bills that the executive presented to the assembly (Interview with Margarita López Maya) and the assembly passed with scarce debate and without popular consultation (López Maya 2011). For example, on both December 21 and December 28, the assembly passed five laws in one day (Asamblea Nacional de la República Bolivariana de Venezuela).

12. Class-based interest mediation between workers' unions, employers, and the state.

13. The granting of enabling powers to the president was not unique to the Bolivarian government; rather, it constitutes a historical Venezuelan political practice that preceded Chávez, was utilized under *Puntofijismo*, was enshrined in the subsequent 1999 Constitution, and has continued past Chávez's tenure.

14. The 1999 enabling law granted Chávez authority to legislate by decree over six months; the 2000–2001 enabling law granted him this authority over one year; the 2007–2008 and 2010–2012 enabling laws separately granted him this authority over eighteen months (Procuraduría General de la República).

15. For example, in 2011 Chávez sanctioned fifteen laws and the National Assembly sanctioned sixteen laws (Lalander 2012).

16. For example, Valencia (2015) shows that Bolivarian state authorities tended to prioritize the revolution's broader goals over the Afro-Venezuelan movement's particular demands.

17. This is not to assert that this phenomenon of sidelining women's specific demands for rights during election campaigns was unique to *Chavismo*. Indeed, León Torrealba (2012) documents both a National Assembly deputy from the PSUV and

one from an opposition party stating that 2012 (a presidential election year) was not the political moment to bring up the issue of abortion. Further, García and Valdivieso (2009) note the absence of gender issues in the 2008 regional election campaigns of women candidates from all political sides.

18. Pérez Marcano states that the National Assembly's Integrated Social Development Commission created a nonpermanent subcommission on gender equity and equality after women's issues were eliminated from the Permanent Commission on Family (Third Interview with Marelis Pérez Marcano).

19. In 2007, the National Assembly did pass two pieces of CPFMJ-proposed legislation that aimed to promote positive discrimination of women—the Law for the Protection of Families, Maternity, and Paternity; and the Law for the Promotion and Protection of Maternal Breastfeeding. Both these laws promote women's maternal roles. As Espina (2009a, 255–257) points out, the ways these laws were written do not challenge "dominant patriarchal culture" because they do not obligate employers and communities to enable parental and state coresponsibility in the care of infants, nor do they protect women's right to work outside the home when rearing young children.

20. The lines between party, government, and state were blurred within Bolivarian Venezuela under Chávez's presidency, and state resources were often directed toward party political ends.

21. Chapter 6 covers this process.

22. The Araña Feminista and its organizing work for advancing women's labor rights are described in chapter 6.

23. See Fernandes 2007 and Motta 2012 for case studies of popular women organizing around social reproduction in Caracas *barrios* and challenging gender relations in their communities in the process.

24. For example: Encounter Points, BanMujer User Networks, Madres del Barrio Committees, and Women's Fronts. By 2008, INaMujer estimated that it had organized around a quarter million women in Encounter Points (Ministerio del Poder Popular para Relaciones Exteriores 2011, 11); and in 2010—the year it was created—the Bicentenary Women's Front counted 30,000 members and organizational presence in all Venezuelan states (Ministerio del Poder Popular para la Mujer y la Igualdad de Género 2011, 7).

25. Chapter 6 empirically illustrates this point in the case of organizing around women's labor rights during the 2012 presidential election year.

26. Adicea Castillo notes, however, that the development of BanMujer under Bolivarianism had begun to change this; this state institution trained popular women in economics as small producers (First Interview with Adicea Castillo).

27. The development of Madres del Barrio Mission and its relationship to the law and Article 88 are discussed in detail in chapter 3.

28. The first decree targeted elderly people seventy and older in a "state of need" and elderly people sixty and older with "total disability" (Chávez Frías, 25 April 2007). The second decree targeted women sixty-five and older in a "vulnerable state" (Chávez Frías, 30 May 2007). I do not possess information on why the beneficiaries of these decrees were targeted or how they were selected. However, Rakowski and Espina (2011) note that researchers attempted to verify the enrollment of the decreed 50,000 poor women in social security and could not find any evidence that such women had been enrolled.

29. Outlawing discrimination based on gender and sexual orientation (Art. 21) and gender parity on electoral lists (Art. 67).

30. Bills undergo at least two rounds of discussion in the National Assembly. The first round of discussion pertains to whether the plenary decides in principle if a bill should be developed. Approval of a bill in first discussion signifies an agreement by the assembly that the bill should be further developed before it returns to the plenary for a second discussion and vote on its passage into law.

31. Chapter 5 discusses popular women's waiting for the Amor Mayor pensions to reach them and their dependents in 2012, and thus raises questions as to the mission's actual capacity.

Chapter 3: State Imaginations of Popular Motherhood within the Revolution

1. Chapter 4 shows how the government empirically resignified the role of popular motherhood and women's unpaid labor within the revolution through an examination of the mission's discourses and practices and popular interpretations of them.

2. Assistentialism, or *assistencialismo*, broadly refers to noncontributory state social assistance to the poor, in contrast to state welfare to which citizens contribute.

3. Molyneux (2006) notes that the notion of coresponsibility draws from earlier social hygiene movements and state-led modernization and civilization projects that targeted the poor in the region in order to facilitate their integration into capitalist society.

4. Mexico's CCT program—Oportunidades—requires children's school enrollment, family members' regular health checkups, mothers' attendance at health and nutrition information sessions, and mothers' performance of community work (usually cleaning work) in exchange for cash transfers to female heads of participating households, food supplements, and health and education subsidies (Escobar Latapí and González de la Rocha 2009; Molyneux 2006).

5. Argentina's CCT program—Plan Familias—requires children's school attendance and health checkups in exchange for cash transfers directly to mothers (Tabbush 2009).

6. Nicaragua's CCT program—Red de Protección Social—requires children's progression through primary schooling, improvements in their nutrition, healthy development of preschool-age children and mothers' attendance at health, hygiene, and childcare information sessions in exchange for temporary cash transfers directly to mothers for children's education, family food security, and payments to private health-care providers (Bradshaw 2008; Bradshaw and Quirós Víquez 2008).

7. Poverty and extreme poverty rates in Venezuela nearly trebled between the beginning of the 1980s and the end of the 1990s. The post-*Caracazo* targeted, compensatory social programs that the Pérez and Caldera governments instituted were unable to mitigate these poverty rates (Gómez Calcaño 1998). The introduction of user fees for state welfare services under neoliberalism (Wilpert 2007) also compounded welfare shortfalls among the popular sectors.

8. During the first stage of the *Chavista* government, Chávez continued some of the Caldera-initiated compensatory social programs, while introducing new targeted emergency social programs carried out by a civil-military alliance (Fernandes 2008). Together, this mix of targeted social programs appears to have contributed

to slightly decreasing poverty rates, but these gains were sharply reversed with the economic crisis triggered by the 2002 coup and the 2002–2003 employer lockout (Weisbrot 2008).

9. D'Elia (2006) notes that during the Chávez government's first years, the president and other high-ranking *Chavista* authorities possessed weak control over the state apparatus. Therefore, the executive "concluded that the political timing of the Venezuelan conflict made it impossible to wait for administrative reforms to improve management capacity in the face of new and urgent demands" (Lander and Navarrete 2007, 24).

10. The exact numbers of people reached by these missions are uncertain because of lack of access to reliable statistics. However, D'Elia and Cabezas (2008) cite Datanálisis surveys indicating that in 2004 Barrio Adentro reached 30 percent of the population and Mercal reached 38.2 percent of the population. They also cite both government authorities and Datanálisis surveys indicating that approximately 2.7 million people had benefited from the educational missions by 2007. The government asserted that Vuelvan Caras had trained 300,000 people by 2005 (D'Elia 2006). Habitat Mission appears not to have had the same massive reach as the other missions—it had constructed only 10,000 houses by June 2005—thus making a small dent in addressing the national housing deficit of approximately 1,800,000 houses (D'Elia 2006).

11. Hawkins, Rosas, and Johnson (2010) note that the missions did not quantitatively mark an increased proportion of the national budget dedicated to social spending (while noting that absolute social expenditure increased as state revenue increased), but they rather marked a qualitative restructuring of the government's social spending in terms of whom social policy reached and how it reached them.

12. This is in contrast to the extant welfare state apparatus created and monitored through liberal democratic means (under both *Puntofijismo* and Bolivarianism), which was subject to legislative approval and oversight.

13. Article 93 of the LSS "prohibits national administration organs and bodies from granting economic benefits of a similar nature" to those outlined in the LSS. The LSS prohibits duplication of social policy, thus developing the 1999 Constitution's mandate and the 2002 Organic Social Security System Law mandate to create a unitary, integrated social security system. The drafters of these mandates created them because the Venezuelan social security system was extremely fragmented— with somewhere between 800 and 1,000 public retirement and pension regimes around the time these mandates were drafted (Interview with Absalón Méndez). The missions also had perpetuated and compounded the fragmentation of social policy because they were instituted in parallel to the extant welfare state apparatus. According to Ana Salcedo, who served on the LSS drafting team, the intention behind the LSS mandate was to eliminate the extra costs that come with state provision of parallel social services in a uncoordinated manner and therefore to streamline public social expenditure (Interview with Ana M. Salcedo González).

The National Assembly passed the LSS when *Chavista* forces held a razor-thin majority in the legislature. The lack of regulation of, observance of, and adherence to the LSS then is not necessarily due to the power dynamic between *Chavismo* and the opposition. Rather, Absalón Méndez—a longtime social security advisor to the National Assembly—argues that, under *Chavismo*, the legislative and executive branches acted uncoordinated from each other on social policy issues, with each branch individually approaching the reconfiguration of the social security from different angles, ultimately impeding the systematization and consolidation of social security in Venezuela (Méndez 2006). According to Méndez, the executive's contravention of the LSS with its establishment of Madres del Barrio Mission is a reflection of the disarticulation between the executive and legislative branches of government at the time (Interview with Absalón Méndez).

14. As this description of Madres del Barrio's development indicates, the presidential commission designed the mission during the time period in which the IVSS was mandated to draft a plan to roll out the 2005 LSS. As chapter 2 explains, the LSS provides a juridical framework for poor and elderly homemakers to receive state economic assistance. If the LSS had been enforced, then based on the claim that the intention of Madres del Barrio was to begin to implement Article 88, the mission would not be necessary. I do not know whether, during this time period, the presidential commission already knew that the IVSS would not draft such a plan and the LSS would therefore become dead on arrival. However, an alternative interpretation could be that the executive's fundamental objective in establishing Madres del Barrio was not about implementing Article 88. Several influential women's movement activists' opinions in favor of this interpretation are detailed in the next section of this chapter.

15. When I asked Mota, she did not reflect an awareness of the design of other Latin American CCT programs. However, she was only one of the mission's designers. It could be possible that other Latin American CCT designs influenced the other Madres del Barrio designers. Yet I do not have access to any information that shows what kind of influence, if any, other Latin American CCTs had on the Madres del Barrio design.

16. These loans were interest-free and supposed to be paid back within five years (Misión Madres del Barrio "Josefa Joaquina Sánchez," n.d.).

17. De facto organizations of two or more people administering a common economic project (Misión Madres del Barrio "Josefa Joaquina Sánchez" 2007, 2).

18. These productive areas were "agriculture, cattle, poultry and fishing; industrial; textile; artisanal; food; tourism; and services" (Misión Madres del Barrio "Josefa Joaquina Sánchez" 2007, 56).

19. "Community councils, land committees, health committees, technical water tables, network of BanMujer users, INaMujer encounter points, social protection committees, and Madres del Barrio committees, amongst others."

20. I am thankful to Alba Carosio for this insight.

21. At first glance, Mota's explanation of the mission's juridical basis appears to be a contradiction. Yet, it may not necessarily be a contradiction, if the executive knew that it would not or might not be able to extend the mission benefit to all poor homemakers throughout Venezuela. Whereas the enforcement of the LSS connotes that poor homemakers would have *rights* to benefits stipulated in the law that the state would have the duty to fulfill, the establishment of a mission did not entail a corresponding right to benefit from it as a Venezuelan citizen. I cannot confirm this interpretation of Mota's explanation, but it may be one of the reasons why the presidential commission designing Madres del Barrio used the LSS without formally citing it.

22. Hawkins, Rosas, and Johnson (2010) note a similar phenomenon in their article on the missions in general.

23. I do not know if information about the mission was publicly accessible before the mission was moved to MinMujer's administration in 2008. Yet, as early as 2008, D'Elia and Cabezas (2008) were noting extreme difficulties in accessing statistical information about the missions.

24. MinMujer also closed the Bolivarian Gender Observatory during Nancy Pérez's tenure as minister.

25. Erin Fletcher (2012)—also a North American academic researcher—details her foiled attempts in 2012 to access statistics on women's issues—in her case, domestic violence statistics—from INaMujer, MinMujer, the National Defender of Women's Rights, and the national police.

26. These authorities never provided me any written response to my research proposal, further illustrating transparency issues with the state gender institutions.

27. Similarly, Petras and Veltmeyer (2009) note a general paternalistic orientation toward the popular sectors by middle-class *Chavista* leaders. Writing about the third and fourth phases of Chávez's government, Fernandes (2010) also notes increasing "manipulat[ion]" of the popular sectors by *Chavista* middle leadership. Motta, too, observes a "logic of governability and power dominates their actions" toward the popular sectors (cited in Spronk and Webber 2011, 244).

28. This picture is detailed in chapter 4.

Chapter 4: Regulating Motherhood in Madres del Barrio

1. I located the former *madres* after state gender institution authorities rebuffed my repeated efforts to get into the mission to conduct my research, as discussed in chapter 3.

2. This process consisted of an original in-depth interview and a postinterview participant validation. I also used this validation process as an opportunity to conduct short follow-up interviews with two of them.

3. This included in-depth interviews with two former municipal mission coordinators in different Venezuelan regions, as well as interviews with other municipal, regional, and national state gender institution workers, in order to gain a top-down perspective of Madres del Barrio.

4. The term "sector" refers to a smaller territorial unit within a *barrio*.

5. Mi Casa Bien Equipada Mission offered discounted prices and low-interest credit through state-owned banks for Chinese-produced household appliances, such as refrigerators, stoves and ovens, air conditioners, televisions, and DVD players.

6. Ribas Mission was an educational mission that offered free continuing high school studies to adults within their own communities.

7. I am grateful to Juana Delgado for making this initial observation.

8. President Chávez issued two limited-duration decrees—one in 2006 and one in 2010—that granted workers who had not completed their mandatory public pension contributions the opportunity to complete them so that they could receive a monthly old-age pension equivalent to the minimum-wage salary.

9. Barrio Adentro was a free community-based public health mission that often relied on Cuban medical personnel to deliver health services in the *barrios*.

10. When Chávez announced Madres del Barrio's launch in the beginning of 2006, he stated that 100,000 women would originally benefit from the mission (Espina 2006). In August 2006, the social security vice minister stated that 150,000 women were already receiving the Madres del Barrio transfer and 40,000 would be added to the beneficiary list by the end of the year (Tejero Puntes 2006). As chapter 3 details, state institutions gave vastly different total numbers of Madres del Barrio. However, various documents from MinMujer indicate that over time the numbers of women incorporated into the mission stayed around 100,000. For example, MinMujer's Bolivarian Gender Observatory stated that 99,633 women were incorporated in the mission in 2008 (Aguirre, Bethencourt, and Testa 2009, 93), and in its 2010 annual report, MinMujer stated that 98,373 women received the mission's transfer that year (Ministerio del Poder Popular Para la Mujer y la Igualdad de Género 2010, 205). Yet, I could not verify this approximate figure.

11. I heard of Carolina's conception of the worst implications of community popular power selection mechanisms for state assistance playing out in a rural town in Falcón. At a meeting organized by state gender institutions with women in this community, one woman who was divorcing her abusive husband told us of her struggle to obtain public housing for herself and her children. She had sought assistance from her communal council's leader, a man well connected with regional party and state authorities. The community women present at this meeting described him as performing his leadership role in an authoritarian way. According to this particular woman, the communal council leader told her he would assist her in obtaining housing if she had sexual relations with him.

12. This report of patronage with selection mechanisms is not unique to Madres del Barrio Mission. Hawkins, Rosas, and Johnson (2011) note that Robinson Mission experienced problems with patronage and cronyism in scholarship distribution during its first year of existence.

13. Such terminology also connotes a perception that the participants in the mission were lazy and unproductive—a popular understanding that reproduced the nonrecognition of the unpaid labor that mission beneficiaries performed.

14. Bolivarian state expectations of popular women to arrive early and sign attendance registers at state-led political events extended beyond Madres del Barrio Mission. At multiple political events that Falcón state gender institutions held with popular women's organizations, including Madres del Barrio, I observed state authorities informing popular women to arrive early and having them sign attendance registers. Even though the state authorities expected popular women to arrive early, the state-led events I observed almost always started late—sometimes hours late, even when they were held outside under the heat of the Caribbean midday sun. Thus, the state's expectations for state-led popular women's political participation included that they wait for the state.

15. I also heard a rumor from a state gender institution worker who was not *Chavista* that there was an "under-the-table decree" that stipulated that no *madre* should be stripped of her mission benefit in 2012 because it was a "political year," and "when you take away what you have given her for six years, she is going to switch sides . . . and surely you are going to have one less political activist" (Interview with Carla). Her remarks illustrate that, in the absence of clear and transparent guidelines about the duration and conditions of the mission benefit, it could be understood to be used politically by state authorities in a multiplicity of ways.

16. This *madre*, referred to me by one of the former *madres* featured in this chapter, gave informed consent to participate in an interview, and I interviewed her. Later, she rescinded her consent to participate in my study, and I therefore destroyed the data from her interview.

17. A popular discourse also existed that the Madres del Barrio cash transfer was a "scholarship" upon which women became dependent. This discourse was also disarticulated from a rights-based conception of social assistance.

18. This is consistent with Hawkins's (2010b) findings more generally regarding popular participation in other Bolivarian missions.

19. I owe the concept of "uncertain clients" to Elisabeth Jay Friedman.

20. This finding is not necessarily made to disprove Miriam's claim; it is possible that no obligations were imposed on her and other Madres del Barrio, especially since it appears that guidelines and procedures for executing and monitoring the mission did not become standardized across time and spaces. But it is also possible that Miriam was providing me with the "public transcript" (Scott 1990) of the mission because of the power and context effects that shaped our interaction. As an outsider and a US American academic researcher at that, I sought to know and document her experience of a Bolivarian government mission that had come into question within Venezuela—a program of a government to which my government had been historically and overtly hostile. Miriam was not immune from the larger geopolitical confrontations between her government and mine—I was told that Miriam initially suspected me of being a spy. Her answers to my questions therefore could potentially be inflected with such suspicions.

21. The Bolivarian government conducted no progressive non-oil-tax reform during Chávez's presidency, yet it did increase non-oil-tax revenue by improving its income tax collection from businesses and individuals (Weisbrot 2011). Venezuela's reported public social spending increased from 18.6 to 21.4 percent of GDP from 2004 to 2011 (Sistema Integrado de Indicadores Sociales de Venezuela, n.d.). Yet its public social spending to GDP ratio for 2011 fell below the ratio of Costa Rica and far below that of Cuba (ECLAC 2013). As Webber (2010) points out, Bolivarian poverty-reduction measures and new social policies during Chávez's presidency were financed not through increasing wealth redistribution to the poor from the elite and the expanding private sector but through the regional primary commodity boom.

22. The state's lack of provision of care services when popular-sector women were participating in state activities was not unique to Madres del Barrio. One telling example is the cinema forum on violence against women that Falcón state gender institutions held one night in 2011 for women in a popular-sector community. The institutions aimed to bring their services directly to the community by holding the event there at a community member's house, but they made no provision for the care of the women community members' children when they attended the forum. Because the topic of the forum was not appropriate for young children, the state workers told the young children to leave, and in turn their caregivers—the women whom the event was aimed to reach—also had to leave.

23. Mota said that the mission was "heading in that direction" of addressing alternative care services because feminism began to "enter the mission" and the mission was engaging in a reflexive analysis of its policies and functioning under her leadership (First Interview with Gioconda Mota). Yet accounts indicate that Mota,

who had since become a leader in national feminist organizations, was forced to resign from her position (Mendez 2008).

24. And in some cases a triple shift if they continued with their community and/ or political work, as both Miriam and Aida were doing after they left the mission.

25. In the same month in 2012, Madres del Barrio Mission stated on its website that since 2006 the *madres* had formed 4,000 socio-productive projects (Misión Madres del Barrio "Josefa Joaquina Sánchez," 13 June 2012) and that they had formed 5,000 socio-productive projects (27 June 2012).

26. To the best of my knowledge, Carosio never worked directly with the Madres del Barrio. She did, however, serve as an advisor to the National Assembly on the Social Protection for Homemakers Bill, which did aim to legislate Madres del Barrio Mission.

27. Aida's comment speaks to how class and spatial divides between the mission participants and mission staff were intersecting.

28. The minister is said to have made this claim, even though, according to Yolimar—a national gender institution worker—the ministry's greatest programmatic focus under Pérez's leadership was Madres del Barrio Mission.

29. This includes not only unpaid household and community work but also political work. For example, when I went with Aida to the political rally mentioned above at which Chávez was expected to speak, after waiting a while with the *madres*, we were informed that the event was postponed to the following afternoon. The *madres* were also expected to attend the next day. If a *madre* was trying to launch a small business in addition to carrying out her housework, how could she afford to lose two afternoons in a row of paid work time at short notice?

30. The former *madres* whom I interviewed told me that the mission staff did not instruct them on how to use their mission transfer, but the two former municipal coordinators' responses indicate some degree of regulatory and disciplinary control by mission staff of the *madres'* use of their benefits. For example, Paula stated that the cash transfer "was for the food, health and care of your children" (Interview with Paula). And Adriana noted that when a *madre* "diverted the money" or did not spend it where it was intended to be spent—such as on alcohol—the mission staff would "educate" the *madre* to follow the mission guidelines (First Interview with Adriana).

31. Soraya had achieved income security in large part because she was now receiving a contributory public pension and her children were now all independent adults.

Chapter 5: In the Shadows of the Magical Revolutionary State

1. Such studies also tend to focus on popular communities and movements in and around Caracas, Venezuela's capital and largest city, leaving a gap in knowledge about popular organization and state–society relations in the rest of Venezuela.

2. Coro is the capital of Falcón state, and lies approximately 280 miles to the west of Caracas.

3. Nine of the women lived in the *barrio* where the interviews were conducted; one lived in a neighboring *barrio*.

4. My research assistant, who was a resident of this *barrio*, used personal con-

tacts and snowball sampling to identify and contact participants who potentially met the criteria for incorporation into Madres del Barrio Mission.

5. Colloquial term for work outside of the house.

6. It should be noted that these lines to purchase food from the mission were outside in the open air. In Coro, where average daily temperatures ranged between 30°C and 42°C and levels of humidity were often quite high, standing in line outside for hours was exhausting and potentially hazardous.

7. While I was in Coro, several violent outbreaks at Mercals had occurred in the city. Also during this time, in a different Falcón municipality, where the Falcón state gender institutions were hosting a community event, assailants used firearms to attack the Mercal that the institutions had arranged for the community.

8. Gran Misión en Amor Mayor Venezuela established a regime for the allocation of a pension equivalent to the minimum-wage salary to all elderly adults who lived in households with incomes less than the minimum-wage salary. Women fifty-five and older and men sixty and older were eligible for the Amor Mayor pension, whether or not they had contributed to the social security system. The mission was supposed to grant priority to the most elderly adults and elderly adults who suffered from disabilities or illnesses that prevented them from being able to take care of themselves (Presidencia de la República, 13 December 2011).

9. Gran Misión Hijos de Venezuela was a conditional cash transfer program decreed as an "extraordinary measure" to tackle "extreme poverty" in Venezuela. It established a regime of "universal" family allowances for households that had incomes less than the minimum-wage salary and children under eighteen years old. An allowance was distributed for each child and for up to three children in such a household. Pregnant teenagers, pregnant women, children under eighteen years old, and all children with disabilities were eligible to receive mission benefits. To receive the family allowance, pregnant teenage mothers had to remain in school, while adult parents were supposed to join Gran Misión Saber y Trabajo to receive productive occupational training if they were unemployed, and ensure that their children stayed in school and passed their classes. Children with disabilities under fifteen who received the allowance had to attend special education programs, and all children with disabilities had to regularly visit therapy centers (Presidencia de la República, 12 December 2011).

10. The quartets were composed of a (1) social activist, whose role was political; (2) a registrar, whose role was technical; (3) a medical student, whose role was to assess households' health conditions and needs; and (4) a popular power spokesperson, who could be a Madre del Barrio or a local community organizer and whose role was to guide the other members of the quartet through their respective community (Segunda Vicepresidencia para el Area Social, March 2012). Thus, these new Bolivarian social programs also drew on the extended reproductive labor of the Madres del Barrio.

11. Potential elderly and child recipients could first be signed up for these great missions through registration tables temporarily placed in communities throughout the country. After signing up, the quartets were supposed to visit them at home to verify their living conditions and determine if they met the missions' eligibility criteria (Segunda Vicepresidencia para el Area Social, March 2012).

12. According to the presidential decree enacting Amor Mayor, "elderly per-

sons who suffer from some disability or illness that impedes them from managing on their own will be prioritized" (Presidencia de la República, 13 December 2011). Given the state of Veronica's elderly mother's illness, her incorporation into the mission therefore could have been considered a priority.

13. Just as Veronica's mother, Joana's elderly mother could be considered a priority for incorporation into the mission according to the presidential decree, because she was blind and could not care for herself.

14. Similarly, Valencia (2015) documents a case in which the Bolivarian state approved a Caracas *barrio*'s communal council's housing project proposal, but it made the council wait in suspension for the funding to arrive. He notes that such experiences were "not uncommon . . . in . . . dealings with some state institutions" (117).

15. These women's description of appearance on the mission beneficiary list was particularly apt, given that the mechanism for beneficiary notification was not unlike the lottery. After submitting their information in the mission's registration and screening process, potential beneficiaries waited for their numbers to be called—in this case, for their national identity numbers to be published on beneficiary lists in state media.

16. Article 86 of the 1999 Constitution states that "every person has the right to social security."

17. BanMujer granted microcredit to women organized collectively in productive activities and also provided them with nonfinancial services, such as political education.

18. Inés did wait further, and her waiting eventually paid off. Around three months after she registered for the bank, the fieldworker informed me that the bank had approved her application, but she would have to wait further for the funds to arrive from Caracas. The year after I left Venezuela, I received news from my research assistant that Inés had received the BanMujer credit.

19. For example, the Organic Law of Communal Councils does include community work toward gender equality as one of the communal councils' potential work ambits through councils' "family and gender equality committees" (Asamblea Nacional de la República Bolivariana de Venezuela 2009). According to the Falcón Collective Authority for Women's Issues and Gender Equality, the proposal for including gender equality committees in the Organic Law of Communal Councils actually came from Falcón.

20. This is not to assert that the Frente de Mujeres Josefa Camejo or the Puntos de Encuentro were necessarily vehicles for women to make demands of the state (especially because they were not autonomous of the state). But they were vehicles to organize women territorially in Falcón and two of the few women's political organizations in Falcón of which I am aware.

21. According to Organic Law of Communal Councils—passed in 2006 and then reformed in 2009—communal councils "are instances of participation, articulation and integration between citizens and the diverse community, social movement and popular organizations, that allow organized people to exercise communal government and the direct administration of public policies and projects oriented to responding to the needs, potentialities and aspirations of the community, in the construction of the new model of socialist society of equality, equity and social justice." To start a communal council, at least 10 percent of the adults in the commu-

nity must attend a citizens' assembly. To make any decision, a communal council must have a quorum of 30 percent in a first meeting, and if that is not met, a quorum of 20 percent in a second meeting. Part of the cycle of communal council decision-making and public administration consists of conducting a community-needs assessment and designing a plan and formulating a budget to implement projects to meet those needs. The law stipulates that state institutions must prioritize the satisfaction of the community needs that community councils identify through public policies and public resource allocation (Asamblea Nacional de la República Bolivariana de Venezuela 2009).

22. The *juntas de vecinos* or *asociaciones de vecinos* (neighborhood associations) were territorially based organizations that represented the interests of local communities and their residents. They emerged in the 1960s and spread throughout Venezuela by the 1990s after municipal governments were mandated to foster their growth (Friedman 2000b).

23. My own calculation derived from numbers of homicides provided in these two national state reports. I was unable to access homicide statistics for Coro and its *barrios*, or statistics on various other forms of violence, including gender violence, in the area. Yet, experiential accounts do speak to high homicide rates in Coro and its *barrios*. In the just under one year I spent doing research in Coro, two of my friends there each lost a friend to gun violence, including my research assistant's friend, who was killed in this same *barrio*.

Chapter 6: Mobilized yet Contained within *Chavista* Populism

1. To do this, I conducted document analysis (popular organizational materials, communications, and proposals from 2010 to 2012) and media analysis of the organic labor law drafting process and women's rights organizing around the law; participant observation of women's organizing events during the drafting process; and interviews with key feminist activists advocating for women's gender interests in the labor law.

2. Enabling powers are constitutionally enshrined powers to legislate by decree that the legislature grants to the executive for it to take urgent actions in specific areas within a fixed period of time.

3. The presidential commission was composed of three national ministers, the attorney general, two Supreme Court magistrates, four National Assembly members, three legal experts, the Bolivarian Socialist Workers Central president, and a pro-*Chavista* industrial federation president.

4. Programa Feminista El Entrompe de Falopio; Género con Clase; Mujer tenía que ser; CEM at UCV; Colectivo Insumisas; Movimiento de Mujeres "Josefa Joaquina Sánchez"; Mujeres por la Vida; Notifalopio Cooperativa Guarura; Divas de Venezuela; MUSA Aragua; Cooperativa Lactarte; Colectivo pormaspostnatal; Movimiento de mujeres campesinas María Lionza; Mujeres de Jira Jara; FALDAS R; Colectivo Cimarrón; MOMUMAS Movimiento Manuelita Sáenz; Círculos Femeninos Populares; Colectivo Crianza en Tribu; Colectivo Contra Natura; Twiteros y twiteras socialistas; Colectivos Fs y Ms por ahora; Cumbé de mujeres afrovenezolanas; Plafam; Movimiento de Mujeres Clara Zetkin; Mujeres revolucionarias

del Zulia; Movimiento de Mujeres de Mérida; Colectivo Apacuanas; Colectivo Los Sinverguenzas; Colectivo Las Deseantes; Andando el Sur; En Jaque Colectiva.

5. Movimiento Socialista por la Calidad de Vida y Salud; Movimiento de Mujeres Ana Soto; Frente Nacional de Mujeres Bicentenario 200; Sindicato de Trabajadoras de Clínicas Privadas; UNETE; Movimiento de abogadas y abogados revolucionarios y revolucionarias al socialismo; Movimiento de Educación para la Emancipacion; Red de Mujeres con Discapacidad; Centro de Investigación y Formación Flanklin Giménez; Unión de Trabajadoras y Trabajadores al Socialismo; Movimiento por la Educación del estado Zulia; Movimiento Gayones; Confederación de Amas de Casa; Alianza sexo-género diversa revolucionaria; Corriente Revolucionaria Bolívar y Zamora; Frente Socialista de Trabajadores por la Salud; Frente De Artesanos Indígenas de Venezuela; Frente Universitario Revolucionario Socialista; Escuela de Formación Proletaria Primero de Mayo; Movimiento de Pobladoras y Pobladores.

6. Independence, in this sense, signifies workers who do not have employers, or own-account workers. In the context of Venezuela, many independent workers labored in the informal sector.

7. This includes the management of the Falcón regional offices of the national Ministry of Women's Popular Power and Gender Equality, the Regional Woman's Institute, and the Secretariat for Development and Gender Equality. All of these regional institutions fell under the management of the Falcón Collective Authority for Women's Issues and Gender Equality in Coro.

8. As chapter 4 discusses, "Chávez's women" (*mujeres de Chávez*) was a common term employed by emcees and authorities at Bolivarian state events to hail popular women in crowds. In functioning as a call-and-response between the state and popular women, it served to interpellate popular women's political identity as not just tied to Chávez but also belonging to him.

Conclusion

1. In relation to the Cuban revolution.

2. Randelis (2015, 159–160), one of the women participants in Valencia's ethnographic study of popular-sector *Chavista* participation in the revolution, also noted that women led grassroots actions because they possessed a collective consciousness that men did not.

3. I owe this insight to comments made by various discussants and reviewers of *Seeking Rights from the Left: Gender, Sexuality, and the Latin American Pink Tide*, ed. E. J. Friedman (2018).

4. Fraser (2009, 111–112) points out that, as a strategy to "[combat] women's poverty and gender subjection, . . . microcredit . . . burgeoned just as states . . . abandoned macrostructural efforts to fight poverty, efforts that small-scale lending cannot not possibly replace."

5. Although the Bolivarian government significantly increased public early-childhood education and day care services for children three to five years old, public childcare services for children up to three years old remained insufficient. Households remained the primary childcare provider for infants (Llavaneras Blanco 2012).

6. From 1998 to 2012, the household poverty rate decreased from 43.9 to 21.2 percent and the household extreme poverty rate decreased from 17.1 to 6 percent (Instituto Nacional de Estadística 2014a).

7. For example, in 2007, 27.8 percent of female-headed households experienced poverty, compared to a 22.8 percent poverty rate for male-headed households (Paredes 2011, 2).

References

Abbott, J. (2011). "Constitution-Making and Democratic Development: The South African and Venezuelan States in Comparative Perspective." Paper given at Temple University, Philadelphia.

Aguirre, V. (2010). *Plan de Igualdad para las Mujeres Juana Ramírez "La Avanzadora" 2009–2013*. Caracas: Ministerio del Poder Popular para la Mujer y la Igualdad de Género.

Aguirre, V., Bethencourt, L., and Testa, P. (2009). *Políticas Públicas Dirigidas Hacia las Mujeres, Resultados 1999–2009*. Caracas: Ministerio del Poder Popular para la Mujer y la Igualdad de Género.

Aguirre, V., and Testa, P. (2010). *Cargos políticos de mujeres por elección del voto popular*. Caracas: Observatorio Bolivariano de Género.

Althusser, L. (1971). *Lenin and Philosophy, and Other Essays*. New York: Monthly Review Press.

Alvarez, S. E. (1994). The (Trans)formation of Feminism(s) and Gender Politics in Democratizing Brazil. In J. S. Jacquette (Ed.), *The Women's Movement in Latin America: Participation and Democracy*, 2nd ed., 13–63. Boulder, CO: Westview.

Alvarez, S. E., Friedman, E. J., Beckman, E., Blackwell, M., Chinchilla, N. S., Lebon, N., Ríos Tobar, M. (2003). Encountering Latin American and Caribbean Feminisms. *Signs: Journal of Women in Culture And Society* 28(2): 537–579.

Angeleri, S. (2012). La Araña Feminista: Estableciendo los parámetros para el estudio de una experiencia de articulación feminista y socialista. Paper presented at the Centro de Estudios de las Mujeres Encuentro de Investigación en Feminismos, Universidad Central de Venezuela, Caracas, Venezuela.

Antrobus, P. (1993). Structural Adjustment: Cure or Curse? Implications for Caribbean Development. In B. Evers (Ed.), *Women and Economic Policy*. Oxford: Oxfam.

Aretuo, S. (16 April 2012). PCV pide difusión de propuestas para nueva LOT. *Últimas Noticias*. http://www.ultimasnoticias.com.ve/noticias/actualidad/politica/pcv-pide-difusion-de-propuestas-para-nueva-lot.aspx.

Armstrong, P., and Armstrong, H. (1983). Beyond Sexless Class and Classless Sex: Towards Feminist Marxism. *Studies in Political Economy* 10:7–43.

Asamblea Nacional Constituyente. (1999a). *Acta de Sesión del día Miércoles 5 de Agosto de 1999*.

————. (1999b). *Acta de Sesión Ordinaria del día Sábado 30 de Octubre de 1999*. Caracas.

————. (1999c). *Acta de Sesión Ordinaria del día Viernes 22 de Octubre de 1999*. Caracas.

————. (1999d). *Acta de Sesión Permanente del día Sábado 7 de Agosto de 1999*. Caracas.

Asamblea Nacional Constituyente, Comisión Constitucional. (1999). *Acta de Reunión del Día Miercoles 29 de Septiembre de 1999*.

Asamblea Nacional Constituyente, Subcomisión Familia, Mujer, Infancia, Juventud y Anciano. (1999a). Transcripción de Sesión de Fecha: 10 de Septiembre de 1999. Tema: Mujer. Caracas.

————. (1999b). Transcripción de Sesión de Fecha: 15 de Septiembre 1999. Propuestas de Mujeres de Diversas Organizaciones y Consejo Nacional de la Mujer. Caracas.

Asamblea Nacional de la República Bolivariana de Venezuela. (2005). *Ley de Servicios Sociales*. Caracas.

————. (2009). *Ley Orgánica de los Consejos Comunales*.

————. Leyes Sancionadas (2010). http://www.asambleanacional.gob.ve/ley?id=5 -Contenido.

Auyero, J. (2012). *Patients of the State: The Politics of Waiting in Argentina*. Durham, NC: Duke University Press.

Auyero, J., and Swistun, D. A. (2009). *Flammable: Environmental Suffering in an Argentine Shantytown*. New York: Oxford University Press.

Azzellini, D. (2010). Constituent Power in Motion: Ten Years of Transformation in Venezuela. *Socialism and Democracy* 24(2): 8–31.

Banco Central de Venezuela. (1983). *División del trabajo, distribución personal del tiempo diario y valor económico del trabajo realizado en los hogares Venezolanos*. Caracas.

Barrientos, A., Gideon, J., and Molyneux, M. (2008). New Developments in Latin America's Social Policy. *Development and Change* 39(5): 759–774.

Barrig, M. (1994). The Difficult Equilibrium between Bread and Roses: Women's Organizations and Democracy in Peru. In J. S. Jacquette (Ed.), *The Women's Movement in Latin America: Participation and Democracy*, 2nd ed., 151–175. Boulder, CO: Westview.

Beasley-Murray, J., Cameron, M. A., and Hershberg, E. (2009). Latin America's Multiple Left Turns: An introduction. *Third World Quarterly* 30(2): 319–330.

Bennholdt-Thomsen, V., and Mies, M. (1999). *The Subsistence Perspective: Beyond the Globalized Economy*. London: Zed Books.

Bezanson, K. (2006). The Neo-liberal State and Social Reproduction: Gender and Household Insecurity in the Late 1990s. In K. Bezanson and M. Luxton (Eds.), *Social Reproduction: Feminist Political Economy Challenges Neo-Liberalism*, 173–214. Montreal: McGill-Queen's University Press.

Blofield, M., Ewig, C., and Piscopo, J. M. (2017). The Reactive Left: Gender Equality and the Latin American Pink Tide. *Social Politics: International Studies in Gender, State and Society* 24(4): 345–369.

Boothroyd, R. (13 November 2011). Chávez Responds to Workers' Protests, Promises Historic New Labour Law. *Venezuela Analysis*. http://venezuelanalysis.com /news/6629.

Bradshaw, S. (2008). From Structural Adjustment to Social Adjustment: A Gendered Analysis of Conditional Cash Transfer Programmes in Mexico and Nicaragua. *Global Social Policy* 8(2): 188–207.

Bradshaw, S., and Quirós Víquez, A. (2008). Women Beneficiaries or Women Bearing the Cost? A Gendered Analysis of the *Red de Protección Social* in Nicaragua. *Development and Change* 39(5): 823–844.

Brand, U., and Sekler, N. (2009). Struggling between Autonomy and Institutional Transformations: Social Movements in Latin America and the Move toward Post-Neoliberalism. In L. Macdonald and A. Ruckert (Eds.), *Post-Neoliberalism in the Americas*, 54–70. Basingstoke: Palgrave Macmillan.

Bruce, I. (2008). *The Real Venezuela: Making Socialism in the Twenty-first Century.* London: Pluto.

Burawoy, M. (1998). The Extended Case Method. *Sociological Theory* 16(1): 4–33.

Buxton, J. (2009). Venezuela: The Political Evolution of Bolivarianism. In G. Lievesley and S. Ludlam (Eds.), *Reclaiming Latin America: Experiments in Radical Social Democracy*, 57–74. London: Zed Books.

———. (2011). Foreword: Venezuela's Bolivarian Democracy. In D. Smilde and D. Hellinger (Eds.), *Venezuela's Bolivarian Democracy: Participation, Politics, and Culture under Chávez*, ix–xxii. Durham, NC: Duke University Press.

Caldera, R. (15 February 1981). Anuncia Mercedes Pulido: Acciones en Favor de las Trabajadoras Hará el Ministerio de la Mujer. *El Nacional.*

———. (21 September 1986). "7° DIA." *El Nacional.*

Cameron, B. (2006). Social Reproduction and Canadian Federalism. In K. Bezanson and M. Luxton (Eds.), *Social Reproduction: Feminist Political Economy Challenges Neo-Liberalism*, 45–74. Montreal: McGill-Queen's University Press.

Cameron, M. A. (2009). Latin America's Left Turns: Beyond Good and Bad. *Third World Quarterly* 30(2): 331–348.

Cannon, B. (2009). *Hugo Chávez and the Bolivarian Revolution: Populism and Democracy in a Globalised Age.* Manchester: Manchester University Press.

Carajo, C. A. V. (2010). Movimiento de Mujeres Ana Soto . . . Rumbo a la Conferencia Mundial de Mujeres de Base Caracas 2011. http://colectivoalexisvivecarajo .blogspot.com/2010/08/movimiento-de-mujeres-ana-sotorumbo-la.html.

Carosio, A. (2010). El trabajo de las mujeres: Desigualdad, invisibilidad y explotación. *Revista Venezolana de Estudios De La Mujer* 15(35): 7–13.

Carroll, W. K. (2011). Crisis, Movements, Counter-Hegemony: In Search of the New. In H. Veltmeyer (Ed.), *21st Century Socialism: Reinventing the Project*, 151–174. Halifax: Fernwood.

Castillo, A., and De Salvatierra, I. H. (2000). Las mujeres y el proceso constituyente venezolano de 1999. *Revista Venezolana de Estudios De La Mujer* 5(14): 37–87.

Centro de Estudios de la Mujer de la Universidad Central de Venezuela. (2011). *Informe de la Situación de Género en Venezuela.* Caracas.

Chávez Frías, H. (5 August 1999). Ideas Fundamentales para la Constitución Bolivariana de la V República. Caracas.

———. (November 2004). El Nuevo Mapa Estratégico. Caracas.

———. (24 March 2006). *Decreto No. 4.342. Gaceta Oficial de la República Bolivariana de Venezuela. No. 38.405.*

———. (25 October 2006). *Reforma Parcial del Decreto No. 4.342. Gaceta Oficial No. 38.549.*

———. (25 April 2007). *Decreto No 5.316 Gaceta Oficial No. 38.673.* Caracas.

———. (30 May 2007). *Decreto No 5.370 Gaceta Oficial No. 38.694.* Caracas.

———. (15 August 2007). Ahora la Batalla es por el Sí. Discurso de presentación del Proyecto de Reforma Constitucional ante la Asamblea Nacional. Caracas: Ministerio del Poder Popular para la Comunicación y la Información.

———. (30 April 2012). *Decreto No. 8.938. Ley Orgánica del Trabajo, los Trabajadores y las Trabajadoras*. Caracas.

Ciccariello-Maher, G. (2013a). Constituent Moments, Constitutional Processes, Social Movements and the New Latin American Left. *Latin American Perspectives* 20(10): 1–20.

———. (2013b). *We Created Chávez: A People's History of the Venezuelan Revolution*. Durham, NC: Duke University Press.

Círculos Femeninos Populares. (1986). Manifiesto de las Madres. *Mujeres en Lucha, Periódico Cuatrimestral de los Círculos Femeninos*, 14.

Combellas, R. (2005). El Proceso Constituyente y la Constitución de 1999. In E. Plaza and R. Combellas (Eds.), *Procesos Constituyentes y Reformas Constitucionales en La Historia de Venezuela: 1811–1999*, 765–808. Caracas: Universidad Central de Venezuela, Facultad de Ciencias Jurídicas y Políticas.

Comisión Permanente de Familia, Mujer, y Juventud de la Asamblea Nacional. (15 July 2008). *Proyecto de Ley de Protección a las Amas de Casa*. Caracas.

Comité "Juntas por Venezuela Camino a Beijing." (1995). Diez y ocho propuestas con motivo de la Cumbre de Desarrollo Social. Caracas.

Conell, R. W. (2001). Gender and the State. In K. Nash and A. Scott (Eds.), *The Blackwell Companion to Political Sociology*, 117–126. Malden, MA: Blackwell.

CONG de Mujeres. (16 July 1986). Carta a Ciudadano Presidente y Demás Miembros de la Comisión Delegada del Congreso Nacional. Caracas.

Constitución de la República Bolivariana de Venezuela. (1999).

Coronil, F. (1997). *The Magical State: Nature, Money, and Modernity in Venezuela*. Chicago: University of Chicago Press.

———. (2001). Smelling Like a Market. *The American Historical Review* 106(1): 119–129.

———. (n.d.). *Magical History: What's Left of Chávez?* http://lanic.utexas.edu/project/etext/llilas/vrp/coronil.pdf.

Coronil, F., and Skurski, J. (2006). Dismembering and Remembering the Nation: The Semantics of Political Violence in Venezuela. In F. Coronil and J. Skurski (Eds.), *States of Violence*, 83–143. Ann Arbor: University of Michigan Press.

Craske, N. (1999). *Women and Politics in Latin America*. Cambridge: Polity.

———. (2003). Gender, Poverty and Social Movements. In S. Chant (Ed.), *Gender in Latin America*, 46–70. New Brunswick, NJ: Rutgers University Press.

Cubitt, T., and Greenslade, H. (1997). Public and Private Spheres: The End of Dichotomy. In E. Dore (Ed.), *Gender Politics in Latin America: Debates in Theory and Practice*, 52–64. New York: Monthly Review Press.

Dagnino, E. (2007). Citizenship: A Perverse Confluence. *Development in Practice* 17(4–5): 549–556.

D'Elia, Y. (Ed.) (2006). *Las Misiones Sociales en Venezuela: Una aproximación a su comprensión y análisis*. Caracas: Instituto Latinoamericano de Investigaciones Sociales.

D'Elia, Y., and Cabezas, L. F. (2008). *Las Misiones Sociales en Venezuela*. Caracas: Instituto Latinoamericano de Investigaciones Sociales.

del Mar Álvarez, M., and Castañeda, N. (May 1999). Propuestas para la Constitución de la República de Venezuela desde la Mirada de las Mujeres.

Dirección de Investigación y Asesoría Económica y Financiera, Dirección General de Investigación y Desarrollo Legislativo. (July 2008). Informe de Impacto Presupuestario del Proyecto de Ley de Protección Social a las Amas de Casa. Caracas: Asamblea Nacional de la República Bolivariana de Venezuela.

———. (September 2009). Informe de Impacto Económico y Presupuestario del Proyecto de Ley de Protección Social de las Amas de Casa. Caracas: Asamblea Nacional de la República Bolivariana de Venezuela.

Dobrowolsky, A. (2003). Women, Constitutionalism and Contestation: Some Tentative Conclusions. In A. Z. Dobrowolsky and V. Hart (Eds.), *Women Making Constitutions: New Politics and Comparative Perspectives*, 236–249. Basingstoke: Palgrave Macmillan.

Dobrowolsky, A., and Hart, V. (2003). Introduction: Women, New Politics and Constitutional Change. In A. Dobrowolsky and V. Hart (Eds.), *Women Making Constitutions: New Politics and Comparative Perspectives*, 1–19. Basingstoke: Palgrave Macmillan.

Duran, M. (19 February 1999). Angela Zago: Chávez tiene capacidad para interpretar lo que el pueblo quiere. *El Nacional*.

ECLAC. (2013). *Social Panorama of Latin America 2012*. Santiago, Chile: United Nations.

El Comité de Mujeres Ucevistas "Cipriana Velásquez." (1985). El Comité de Mujeres "Cipriana Velásquez" en campaña por las 20 mil firmas de apoyo a la Reforma de la Ley del Trabajo. Caracas.

Ellner, S. (2003). Introduction: The Search for Explanations. In S. Ellner and D. Hellinger (Eds.), *Venezuelan Politics in the Chávez Era: Class, Polarization, and Conflict*, 7–26. Boulder, CO: Lynne Rienner.

———. (2005). Revolutionary and Non-Revolutionary Paths of Radical Populism: Directions of the *Chavista* Movement in Venezuela. *Science and Society* 69(2): 160–190.

———. (2008). *Rethinking Venezuelan Politics: Class, Conflict, and the Chávez Phenomenon*. Boulder, CO: Lynne Rienner.

———. (2011). Venezuela's Social-Based Democratic Model: Innovations and Limitations. *Journal of Latin American Studies* 43(3): 421–449.

Escobar Latapí, A., and González de la Rocha, M. (2009). Girls, Mothers and Poverty Reduction in Mexico: Evaluating Progresa-Oportunidades. In S. Razavi (Ed.), *The Gendered Impacts of Liberalization: Towards "Embedded Liberalism"?*, 267–289. New York: Routledge.

Espina, G. (November 1998). Las mujeres en la próxima Constitución. Caracas.

———. (10 January 2006a). Asignaciones económicas para las amas de casa en estado de necesidad. Caracas.

———. (16 June 2006b). Las Mujeres del presidente y la pensión al ama de casa que no llega. Fundamul. Caracas.

———. (2007). Beyond Polarization: Organized Venezuelan Women Promote Their "Minimum Agenda." *NACLA Report on the Americas* 40(2): 20–24.

———. (2009a). El inconsciente saboteador y las políticas públicas: Venezuela. In A. Girón (Ed.), *Género y globalización*, 253–271. Buenos Aires: CLASCO.

———. (2009b). Feminist Activism in a Changing Political Context: Venezuela. In J. S. Jacquette (Ed.), *Feminist Agendas and Democracy in Latin America*, 65–80. Durham, NC: Duke University Press.

Espina, G., and Rakowski, C. (2002). ¿Movimiento de mujeres o mujeres en movimiento? El caso Venezuela. *Cuadernos del Cendes* 49.

Espina, G., and Rakowski, C. A. (2010). Waking Women Up? Hugo Chávez, Populism and Venezuela's "Popular" Women. In K. Kampwirth (Ed.), *Gender and Populism in Latin America: Passionate Politics*, 180–201. University Park: Pennsylvania State University Press.

Esping-Andersen, G. (1990). *The Three Worlds of Welfare Capitalism.* Cambridge: Polity.

Feldman, S. (1992). Crises, Poverty, and Gender Inequality: Current Themes and Issues. In L. Benería and S. Feldman (Eds.), *Unequal Burden: Economic Crises, Persistent Poverty, and Women's Work*, 1–25. Boulder, CO: Westview.

Ferguson, S. (1999). Building on the Strengths of the Socialist Feminist Tradition. *Critical Sociology* 25(1): 1–15.

Fernandes, S. (2007). Barrio Women and Popular Politics in Chávez's Venezuela. *Latin American Politics and Society* 49(3): 97–127.

———. (2008). Social Policy in Chávez's Venezuela: A Radical Alternative or More of the Same? *ReVista: Harvard Review of Latin America*, Fall, 40–42.

———. (2010). *Who Can Stop the Drums? Urban Social Movements in Venezuela.* Durham, NC: Duke University Press.

Ferrara, V. (1989). Solo para Mujeres. Paper presented at the IV Encuentro de Grupos Feministas Venezolanos, Poso de Rosas, Venezuela.

First Interview with Adicea Castillo. (22 July 2011). Caracas.

First Interview with Adriana. (20 April 2012). Falcón state, Venezuela.

First Interview with Gioconda Espina. (21 July 2011). Caracas.

First Interview with Gioconda Mota. (3 October 2011). Caracas.

First Interview with Marelis Pérez Marcano. (23 August 2011). Caracas.

Fletcher, E. (2012). No manejamos ese tipo de información. *Caracas Chronicles.* http://caracaschronicles.com/2012/09/10/no-manejamos-ese-tipo-de-informacion/.

Fourth Interview with Marelis Pérez Marcano. (6 September 2012). Caracas.

Fox, J. (1997). The Difficult Transition from Clientelism to Citizenship: Lessons from Mexico. In D. A. Chalmers, C. M. Vilas, K. Hite, S. B. Martin, K. Piester, and M. Segarra (Eds.), *The New Politics of Inequality in Latin America*, 391–420. Oxford: Oxford University Press.

Fraser, N. (1997). *Justice Interruptus: Critical Reflections on the "Postsocialist" Condition.* New York: Routledge.

———. (2009). Feminism, Capitalism and the Cunning of History. *New Left Review* 56:97–117.

Friedman, E. J. (2000a). State-Based Advocacy for Gender Equality in the Developing World: Assessing the Venezuelan National Women's Agency. *Women and Politics* 21(2): 47–80.

———. (2000b). *Unfinished Transitions: Women and the Gendered Development of Democracy in Venezuela, 1936–1996.* University Park: Pennsylvania State University Press.

———. (2009). Gender, Sexuality and the Latin American Left: Testing the Transformation. *Third World Quarterly* 30(2): 415–433.

Friedman, E. J., and Tabbush, C. (2018). Contesting the Pink Tide. In E. J. Friedman (Ed.), *Seeking Rights from the Left: Gender, Sexuality, and the Latin American Pink Tide*, 1–47. Durham, NC: Duke University Press.

Gaceta Oficial No. 36.364. (1999).

Gaceta Oficial No. 36.669. (25 March 1999).

García, C. T., and Valdivieso, M. (2009). Las mujeres venezolanas y el proceso Bolivariano: Avances y contradicciones. *Revista Venezolana de Economía y Ciencias Sociales* 15(1): 133–153.

García Maldonado, A. L., Vera, E., Castillo, A., Deutsch, H., Ruiz Tirado, T., Espina, G., Barreto, M., et al. (28 January 1999). Letter to President-Elect Chávez.

García-Guadilla, M. P. (2003). Civil Society: Institutionalization, Fragmentation, Autonomy. In S. Ellner and D. Hellinger (Eds.), *Venezuelan Politics in the Chávez Era: Class, Polarization, and Conflict*, 179–196. Boulder, CO: Lynne Rienner.

García-Guadilla, M. P., and Hurtado, M. (2000). *Participation and Constitution Making in Colombia and Venezuela: Enlarging the Scope of Democracy?* Paper presented at the Latin American Studies Association, Miami.

García-Guadilla, M. P., and Mallén, A. L. (2012). El momento fundacional de la Venezuela bolivariana: El problema de la legitimidad en la Asamblea Nacional Constituyente venezolana de 1999. *Revista Politeia* 35(49): 65–98.

Gay, R. (2006). The Even More Difficult Transition from Clientelism to Citizenship: Lessons from Brazil. In P. Fernández-Kelly and J. Shefner (Eds.), *Out of the Shadows: Political Action and the Informal Economy in Latin America*. University Park: Pennsylvania State University Press.

Goldfrank, B. (2011). The Left and Participatory Democracy: Brazil, Uruguay, and Venezuela. In S. Levitsky and K. Roberts (Eds.), *The Resurgence of the Latin American Left*, 162–183. Baltimore: Johns Hopkins University Press.

Gómez Calcaño, L. (1998). Redefining the State's Social Policies: The Case of Venezuela. In M. Vellinga (Ed.), *The Changing Role of the State in Latin America*, 213–237. Boulder, CO: Westview.

Gran Misión Hijos de Venezuela. (2012). Grandes Misiones del Área Social Sistema de Acompañamiento.

Grindle, M. S. (2000). *Audacious Reforms: Institutional Invention and Democracy in Latin America*. Baltimore: Johns Hopkins University Press.

Grupo Ese. (2007). ¿Qué es lo que quiere el grupo ese? Caracas.

Gupta, A. (1995). Blurred Boundaries: The Discourse of Corruption, the Culture of Politics, and the Imagined State. *American Ethnologist* 22(2): 375–402.

———. (2005). Narratives of Corruption: Anthropological and Fictional Accounts of the Indian State. *Ethnography* 6(1): 5–34.

Hassim, S. (2006). Gender Equality and Developmental Social Welfare in South Africa. In S. Razavi and S. Hassim (Eds.), *Gender and Social Policy in a Global Context: Uncovering the Gendered Structure of "the Social,"* 109–129. Basingstoke and New York: Palgrave Macmillan and United Nations Research Institute for Social Development.

Hassim, S., and Razavi, S. (2006). Gender and Social Policy in a Global Context: Uncovering the Gendered Structure of "the Social." In S. Razavi and S. Hassim (Eds.), *Gender and Social Policy in a Global Context: Uncovering the Gendered Structure of "the Social,"* 1–39. Basingstoke and New York: Palgrave Macmillan and United Nations Research Institute for Social Development.

Hawkins, K. A. (2003). Populism in Venezuela: The Rise of Chavismo. *Third World Quarterly* 24(6): 1137–1160.

———. (2010a). *Venezuela's Chavismo and Populism in Comparative Perspective.* Cambridge: Cambridge University Press.

———. (2010b). Who Mobilizes? Participatory Democracy in Chávez's Bolivarian Revolution. *Latin American Politics and Society* 52(3): 31–66.

Hawkins, K. A., Rosas, G., and Johnson, M. E. (2010). Populist Policy: The Missions of the Chávez Government. In K. A. Hawkins (Ed.), *Venezuela's Chavismo and Populism in Comparative Perspective*, 195–230. Cambridge: Cambridge University Press.

———. (2011). The Misiones of the Chávez Government. In D. Smilde and D. Hellinger (Eds.), *Venezuela's Bolivarian Democracy: Participation, Politics, and Culture under Chávez*, 186–218. Durham, NC: Duke University Press.

Hellinger, D. (2003). Political Overview: The Breakdown of *Puntofijismo* and the Rise of *Chavismo*. In S. Ellner and D. Hellinger (Eds.), *Venezuelan Politics in the Chávez Era: Class, Polarization, and Conflict*, 27–53. Boulder, CO: Lynne Rienner.

Hernández Toledo, Y. (24 April 2012). Chávez espera firmar LOT esta semana. *Ciudad CCS.* http://www.ciudadccs.info/?p=284611.

Hershberg, E., and Rosen, F. (2006). Turning the Tide? In E. Hershberg and F. Rosen (Eds.), *Latin America After Neoliberalism: Turning the Tide in the 21st Century?*, 1–25. New York and London: The New Press and North American Congress on Latin America.

Hochstetler, K. (2000). Democratizing Pressures from Below? Social Movements in the New Brazilian Democracy. In P. R. Kingstone and T. J. Power (Eds.), *Democratic Brazil: Actors, Institutions, and Processes*, 162–182. Pittsburgh: University of Pittsburgh Press.

Htun, M. (2002). Puzzles of Women's Rights in Brazil. *Social Research* 69(3): 733–751.

Instituto Nacional de Estadística. (2007). Perfil de la pobreza, según concepto, II semestre 2007. http://www.ine.gov.ve/pobreza/menupobreza.asp.

———. (2014a). Pobreza por línea de ingreso, 1er semestre 1997—2do semestre 2013. Caracas: Instituto Nacional de Estadística.

———. (2014b). *XIV Censo Nacional de Población y Vivienda. Resultados Total Nacional de la República Bolivariana de Venezuela.* http://www.ine.gob.ve/documentos/Demografia/CensodePoblacionyVivienda/pdf/nacional.pdf.

———. (n.d.). Población por sexo, según grupo de edad, Censo de 2001. http://www.ine.gov.ve/documentos/Demografia/CensodePoblacionyVivienda/html/PobSexoSegunEdad.html.

Interview with Absalón Méndez. (12 March 2012). Caracas.

Interview with Alba Carosio. (9 March 2012). Caracas.

Interview with Ana M. Salcedo González. (13 March 2012). Caracas.

Interview with Carla. (5 June 2012). Falcón state, Venezuela.

Interview with Carolina. (28 January 2012).

Interview with Claudia. (29 May 2012). Falcón state, Venezuela.

Interview with Inocencia Orellana. (8 September 2011). Caracas.

Interview with Laura. (10 July 2012).

Interview with Master's Student in Women's Studies. (10 August 2012).

Interview with Margarita López Maya. (28 September 2012). Caracas.

Interview with María Auxiliadora Torrealba. (28 September 2011). Caracas.

Interview with Morelba Jiménez. (14 July 2011). Caracas.

Interview with Nora Castañeda. (2 August 2011). Caracas.

Interview with Paula. (6 September 2012). Caracas.

Interview with Red Todas Juntas Cofounder. (19 July 2012).

Interview with Sandra Angeleri. (6 August 2012). Caracas.

Interview with Virginia Aguirre. (6 September 2012). Caracas.

Interview with Yolimar. (24 July 2012).

Jacquette, J. S. (1994). Conclusion: Women's Political Participation and the Prospects for Democracy. In J. S. Jacquette (Ed.), *The Women's Movement in Latin America: Participation and Democracy*, 2nd ed., 223–237. Boulder, CO: Westview.

Jayaweera, S. (1994). Structural Adjustment Policies, Industrial Development and Women in Sri Lanka. In P. Sparr (Ed.), *Mortgaging Women's Lives: Feminist Critiques of Structural Adjustment*, 96–115. London: Zed Books.

Jelin, E. (1990a). Citizenship and Identity: Final Reflections. In E. Jelin (Ed.), *Women and Social Change in Latin America*, 184–207. London: Zed Books.

———. (1990b). Introduction. In E. Jelin (Ed.), *Women and Social Change in Latin America*, 1–11. London: Zed Books.

———. (1996). Women, Gender, and Human Rights. In E. Jelin and E. Hershberg (Eds.), *Constructing Democracy: Human Rights, Citizenship and Society in Latin America*, 177–196. Boulder, CO: Westview.

Jiménez, M. (2000). Las mujeres en el proceso constituyente. In M. Jiménez (Ed.), *Mujeres protagonistas y proceso constituyente en Venezuela*, 17–29. Caracas: Embajada Británica, Unifem, Programa de las Naciones Unidas para el Desarrollo, and Editorial Nueva Sociedad.

Kabeer, N. (2007). *Marriage, Motherhood and Masculinity in the Global Economy: Reconfigurations of Personal and Economic Life*. Brighton: Institute of Development Studies.

Kampwirth, K. (2010). Introduction. In K. Kampwirth (Ed.), *Gender and Populism in Latin America: Passionate Politics*, 1–24. University Park: Pennsylvania State University Press.

Kwengwere, P. (2007). *The State, Privatisation and the Public Sector in Malawi*. Harare, Lilongwe, and Cape Town: Southern African Peoples' Solidarity Network, Malawi Economic Justice Network, and Alternative Information and Development Centre.

La Araña Feminista. (2010). Ley Orgánica del Trabajo Revolucionaria. http://ley deltrabajo.blogspot.com/.

———. (2012). Araña Feminista . . . y socialista. http://encuentrofeminista.weebly .com/nuestra-red.html.

La Araña Feminista y otros colectivos. (8 March 2011). Comunicado 8 de Marzo de 2011, Día de la Mujer Trabajadora.

Laclau, E. (1977). *Politics and Ideology in Marxist Theory*. London: NLB.

———. (2005). *On Populist Reason*. London: Verso.

La Coordinadora de ONG de Mujeres. (24 October 1990). Carta de la Coordinadora de Mujeres a Todas las ONG convocadas al taller organizado por la COPRE. Caracas.

La Red Nacional de Apoyo de Organizaciones Populares de Mujeres "Todas Juntas." (1986). Críticas y Proposiciones sobre la Regulación del Trabajo de la Mujer en el Ante-Proyecto de la Ley del Trabajo para la Consideración de la Comisión Bicameral del Congreso de la República para el Estudio de la Ley del Trabajo. Caracas.

Lalander, R. (2012). Venezuela 2010–2011: Polarización y Radicalización del Proyecto Socialista. Revista de Ciencia Política 32(1): 293–313.

Lander, E. (2005). Venezuelan Social Conflict in a Global Context. Latin American Perspectives 32(2): 20–38.

Lander, E., and Navarrete, P. (2007). The Economic Policy of the Latin American Left in Government: Venezuela. Amsterdam: Havens Center, Rosa Luxemburg Stiftung, and Transnational Institute.

Las Organizaciones No Gubernamentales. (18 February 1986). Memorandum de las Organizaciones No Gubernamentales Para la Comisión Bicameral que Estudia el Proyecto de Ley del Trabajo. Caracas.

Leiva, F. I. (2008). Latin American Neostructuralism: The Contradictions of Post-Neoliberal Development. Minneapolis: University of Minnesota Press.

León, M. (2000). El movimiento de mujeres debe ser un movimiento de grandes mayorías. In M. Jiménez (Ed.), Mujeres protagonistas y proceso constituyente en Venezuela, 89–100. Caracas: Embajada Británica, Unifem, Programa de las Naciones Unidas para el Desarrollo, and Editorial Nueva Sociedad.

León, M., and Tremont, A. (15 February 1999). Reducción de la Jornada de Trabajo a Treinta y Seis Horas Semanales. Paper presented at the II Congreso Constituyente de Angostura, Ciudad Bolivar, Venezuela.

León Torrealba, M. (2012). Temas centrales en el debate sobre el aborto en Venezuela y argumentos teóricos para su despenalización. (Maestría en Estudios de la Mujer). Universidad Central de Venezuela, Caracas.

Levine, D. H. (2006). Civil Society and Political Decay in Venezuela. In R. Feinberg, C. H. Waisman, and L. Zamosc (Eds.), Civil Society and Democracy in Latin America, 169–192. New York: Palgrave Macmillan.

Levitsky, S., and Roberts, K. (2011a). Conclusion: Democracy, Development, and the Left. In S. Levitsky and K. Roberts (Eds.), The Resurgence of the Latin American Left, 399–427. Baltimore: Johns Hopkins University Press.

———. (2011b). Introduction: Latin America's "Left Turn": A Framework for Analysis. In S. Levitsky and K. Roberts (Eds.), The Resurgence of the Latin American Left, 1–28. Baltimore: Johns Hopkins University Press.

Lind, A. (2005). Gendered Paradoxes: Women's Movements, State Restructuring, and Global Development in Ecuador. University Park: The Pennsylvania State University Press.

———. (2012a). Contradictions That Endure: Family Norms, Social Reproduction, and Rafael Correa's Citizen Revolution in Ecuador. Politics and Gender 8(2): 254–261.

———. (2012b). "Revolution with a Woman's Face"? Family Norms, Constitutional Reform, and the Politics of Redistribution in Post-Neoliberal Ecuador. Rethinking Marxism: A Journal of Economics, Culture and Society 24(4): 536–555.

Lister, R. (2001). Citizenship and Gender. In K. Nash and A. Scott (Eds.), *The Blackwell Companion to Political Sociology*, 323–332. Malden, MA: Blackwell.

Llavaneras Blanco, M. (2012). Análisis de la demanda de cuidados de los hogares con niñas y niños de 0 a 6 años en Venezuela desde una perspectiva de género: principales características y mecanismos públicos y de mercado a los que se accede para su satisfacción. Maestría en Estudios de la Mujer, Universidad Central de Venezuela, Caracas.

———. (2017). The Travels of an Exotic Bird: The Transnational Trajectories of Venezuela's Constitutional Recognition of the Value of Unpaid Work. *Global Social Policy* 17(3): 328–346.

López Maya, M. (2003). Hugo Chávez Frías: His Movement and His Presidency. In S. Ellner and D. Hellinger (Eds.), *Venezuelan Politics in the Chávez Era: Class, Polarization, and Conflict*, 73–91. Boulder, CO: Lynne Rienner.

———. (2011). Venezuela entre incertidumbres y sorpresas. *Nueva Sociedad*, 235, 4–16.

López Maya, M., Lander, L. E., and Ungar, M. (2002). Economics, Violence and Protest in Venezuela: A Preview of the Global Future? In K. Worcester, S. A. Bermanzohn, and M. Ungar (Eds.), *Violence and Politics: Globalization's Paradox*, 184–208. New York: Routledge.

Luccisano, L., and Wall, G. (2009). The Shaping of Motherhood through Social Investment in Children. In L. Macdonald and A. Ruckert (Eds.), *Post-Neoliberalism in the Americas*, 199–214. Basingstoke: Palgrave Macmillan.

Luxton, M. (2006). Feminist Political Economy in Canada and the Politics of Social Reproduction. In M. Luxton and K. Bezanson (Eds.), *Social Reproduction: Feminist Political Economy Challenges Neo-liberalism*, 11–44. Montreal: McGill-Queen's University Press.

Macdonald, L., and Ruckert, A. (2009). Post-Neoliberalism in the Americas: An Introduction. In L. Macdonald and A. Ruckert (Eds.), *Post-Neoliberalism in the Americas*, 1–18. Basingstoke: Palgrave Macmillan.

Mahon, R., and Macdonald, L. (2009). Poverty Policy and Politics in Canada and Mexico. In L. Macdonald and A. Ruckert (Eds.), *Post-Neoliberalism in the Americas*, 184–198. Basingstoke: Palgrave Macmillan.

Maingon, T., Pérez Baralt, C., and Sonntag, Y. H. R. (2000). La batalla por una nueva constitución para Venezuela. *Revista Mexicana de Sociología* 62(4): 91–124.

Marea Socialista Press. (27 March 2012). Interview: Stalin Perez Borges: "A Referendum Is Necessary so the Working People Can Approve the New Labour Law." *Venezuela Analysis*. http://venezuelanalysis.com/analysis/6895.

Martínez, Á. (2010). Determinantes de la participación laboral femenina en Venezuela: Aplicación de un modelo probit para el año 2005. *Revista Venezolana de Estudios De La Mujer* 15(35): 17–44.

Martinez, C., Fox, M., and Farrell, J. (2010). Introduction. In C. Martinez, M. Fox, and J. Farrell (Eds.), *Venezuela Speaks! Voices from the Grassroots*, 1–9. Oakland, CA: PM Press.

Martínez, M. (22 March 2012). Reforma de la LOT entra en la fase final. *Últimas Noticias*. http://www.ultimasnoticias.com.ve/noticias/actualidad/economia/reforma-de-la-lot-entra-en-la-fase-final.aspx.

Martínez Rodríguez, M. (17 March 2012). Operativo para recibir propuestas de la

LOT. *Últimas Noticias*. http://www.ultimasnoticias.com.ve/noticias/actualidad/politica/operativo-para-recibir-propuestas-de-la-lot.aspx.

Mblinyi, M. (1993). Struggles over Patriarchal Structural Adjustment in Tanzania. In B. Evers (Ed.), *Women and Economic Policy*. Oxford: Oxfam.

Meltzer, J. (2009). Hugo Chávez and the Search for Post-Neoliberal Policy Alternatives in Venezuela. In L. Macdonald and A. Ruckert (Eds.), *Post-Neoliberalism in the Americas*, 89–104. Basingstoke: Palgrave Macmillan.

Mendez, Adriana. (22 April 2008). Sale inexplicablemente Presidenta de la Misión Madres del Barrio. *Aporrea*. http://www.aporrea.org/misiones/a55578.html.

Méndez, Absalón. (2006). Tres momentos en el proceso de reforma de la Seguridad Social en Venezuela. In A. M. Salcedo González (Ed.), *Consideraciónes sobre la Reforma de la Seguridad Social en Venezuela*, 11–43. Caracas: Comisión de Estudios de Postgrado, Facultad de Ciencias Ecónomicas y Sociales, Universidad Central de Venezuela.

Mies, M. (1986). *Patriarchy and Accumulation on a World Scale: Women in the International Division of Labour*. London: Zed Books.

———. (1988). Social Origins of the Sexual Division of Labour. In M. Mies, V. Bennholdt-Thomsen, and C. von Werlhof (Eds.), *Women: The Last Colony*, 67–95. London: Zed Books.

Ministerio del Poder Popular Para la Mujer y la Igualdad de Género. (2010). Memoria y Cuenta 2010. Caracas: Ministerio del Poder Popular Para la Mujer y la Igualdad de Género.

———. (2011). Memoria y Cuenta 2010. Caracas: Ministerio del Poder Popular Para la Mujer y la Igualdad de Género.

Ministerio del Poder Popular para la Salud. (2014). *Anuario de Mortalidad 2011*. Caracas: Gobierno Bolivariano de Venezuela.

Ministerio del Poder Popular para Relaciones Exteriores. (2011). Informe Nacional Cairo +15. Evaluación de los Avances en la Implementación del Programa de Acción de la Conferencia Internacional Sobre Población y Desarrollo a 15 Años de su Firma. Caracas: Gobierno Bolivariano de Venezuela.

Ministerio de Salud y Desarrollo Social. (2000). *Anuario de Mortalidad 1999*. Caracas: Gobierno Bolivariano de Venezuela.

Misión Madres del Barrio "Josefa Joaquina Sánchez." (2007). Informe General de Resultados Año 2007. Caracas: Gobierno Bolivariano de Venezuela, Ministerio del Poder Popular para la Participación y Protección Social.

———. (October 2007a). Manual del Enuestador(a). Caracas: Gobierno Bolivariano de Venezuela, Ministerio del Poder Popular para la Participación y Protección Social.

———. (October 2007b). Métodos y Estilos de Trabajo Comunitario. Guía de Apoyo para las Voceras de los Comités de Madres del Barrio. Caracas: Gobierno Bolivariano de Venezuela, Ministerio del Poder Popular para la Participación y Protección Social.

———. (August 2007c). Fondo Especial Solidario de la Misión Madres del Barrio "Josefa Joaquina Sánchez". Guía para la Presentación de Proyectos. Caracas: Gobierno Bolivariano de Venezuela, Ministerio del Poder Popular para la Participación y Protección Social.

———. (13 June 2012). Vilma Melo: Misión Madres del Barrio despertó mi conciencia social. http://www.minmujer.gob.ve/madresdelbarrio/index.php?option=com _contentandview=articleandid=105:vilma-melo-mision-madres-del-barrio -desperto-mi-conciencia-socialandcatid=1:noticiasandItemid=4.

———. (27 June 2012). Madres del Barrio y Revolución. http://www.minmujer.gob .ve/madresdelbarrio/index.php?option=com_contentandview=articleandid=109 :madres-del-barrio-y-revolucionandcatid=1:noticiasandItemid=4.

———. (n.d.). Lineamientos Conceptuales del Fondo Especial Solidario de la Misión Madres del Barrio "Josefa Joaquina Sánchez." Caracas: Gobierno Bolivariano de Venezuela, Ministerio del Poder Popular para la Participación y Protección Social.

Molina, J. E., and Pérez, C. (2004). Radical Change at the Ballot Box: Causes and Consequences of Electoral Behavior in Venezuela's 2000 Elections. *Latin American Politics and Society* 46(1): 103–134.

Molyneux, M. (1985). Mobilization without Emancipation? Women's Interests, the State, and Revolution in Nicaragua. *Feminist Studies* 11(2): 227–254.

———. (2001). *Women's Movements in International Perspective: Latin America and Beyond.* Houndmills: Palgrave.

———. (2006). Mothers at the Service of the New Poverty Agenda: The PROGRESA/Oportunidades Programme in Mexico. In S. Razavi and S. Hassim (Eds.), *Gender and Social Policy in a Global Context: Uncovering the Gendered Structure of "the Social,"* 43–67. Basingstoke and New York: Palgrave Macmillan and United Nations Research Institute for Social Development.

———. (2008a). Conditional Cash Transfers: A "Pathway to Women's Empowerment"? *Pathways Working Paper, 5.* http://www.pathwaysofempowerment.org /PathwaysWP5-website.pdf.

———. (2008b). The "Neoliberal Turn" and the New Social Policy in Latin America: How Neoliberal, How New? *Development and Change* 39(5): 775–797.

Momsen, J. H. (1991). *Women and Development in the Third World.* London: Routledge.

Moser, C. O. (1993). Adjustment from Below: Low-income Women, Time and the Triple Role in Guayaquil, Ecuador. In S. A. Radcliffe and S. Westwood (Eds.), *"Viva": Women and Popular Protest in Latin America,* 173–196. London: Routledge.

Mota Gutiérrez, G. (2 March 2012). LA ARANA FEMINISTA/ Trabajadoras somos todas. *Ciudad CCS.*

Motta, S. C. (2009). Venezuela: Reinventing Radical Social Democracy from Below? In G. Lievesley and S. Ludlam (Eds.), *Reclaiming Latin America: Experiments in Radical Social Democracy,* 75–90. London: Zed Books.

———. (2010). Populism's Achilles' Heel: Popular Democracy beyond the Liberal State and the Market Economy. *Latin American Perspectives* 38(1): 28–46.

———. (2012). Reinventing Revolutionary Subjects in Venezuela. *La manzana de la discordia* 7(1): 49–59.

Mujeres Revolucionarias. (8 March 2012). Propuesta de las Mujeres Revolucionarias para una Nueva Ley de Trabajo con Equidad de Género.

"Mujer Hazte Presente." Conclusiones y Resoluciones. Primer Seminario para la Evaluación de la Condición de la Mujer en Venezuela. (1968). Caracas.

Oakley, A. (1984). *Taking It Like a Woman*. London: Cape.

OAS Hemispheric Security Observatory. (n.d.). OAS Observatory on Citizen Security-Data Repository. Countries-Details. Venezuela. http://www.oas.org /dsp/Observatorio/database/countriesdetails.aspx?lang=enandcountry=VEN.

O'Connor, J. S. (1993). Gender, Class and Citizenship in the Comparative Analysis of Welfare State Regimes: Theoretical and Methodological Issues. *The British Journal of Sociology* 44(3): 501–518.

Olcott, J. (2010). The Politics of Opportunity: Mexican Populism under Lázaro Cárdenas and Luis Echeverría. In K. Kampwirth (Ed.), *Gender and Populism in Latin America*, 25–46. University Park: Pennsylvania State University Press.

Orloff, A. S. (1993). Gender and the Social Rights of Citizenship: The Comparative Analysis of Gender Relations and Welfare States. *American Sociological Review* 58(3): 303–328.

Paredes, R. (2011). Los ámbitos de las políticas dirigidas a las mujeres y la pobreza femenina: Desafíos para el Desarrollo Humano. *Revista Latinoamericana de Desarrollo Humano 73*.

Pascall, G., and Lewis, J. (2004). Emerging Gender Regimes and Policies for Gender Equality in a Wider Europe. *Journal of Social Policy* 33(3): 373–394.

Pearson, R. (1997). Renegotiating the Reproductive Bargain: Gender Analysis of Economic Transition in Cuba in the 1990s. *Development and Change* 28:671–705.

Petras, J., and Veltmeyer, H. (2009). *What's Left in Latin America? Regime Change in New Times*. Abingdon: Ashgate.

Picchio, A. (1992). *Social Reproduction: The Political Economy of the Labour Market*. Cambridge: Cambridge University Press.

Poleo de Baez, Y. (11 November 1975). Sentencia dictada el día 11 de Noviembre de 1975, por el Juzgado Superior Primero del Transito de la Circunscripción Judicial del Distrito Federal y Estado Miranda, a cargo de la Doctora Yolanda Poleo de Baez.

———. (12 July 1977). La Participación de la Mujer en el Desarrollo del País. Paper presented at the XXXIII Asamblea Anual de FEDECAMERAS, Maracay, Venezuela.

Polo Patriótico. (15 August 1999). Propuesta.

Polo Patriótico de Mujeres. (1999). Aportes a la Asamblea Nacional Constituyente.

Portocarrero, B. (2000). Soy una tejedora de cambios, de la visión que la gente tenga del mundo y sobre todo de la mujer. In M. Jiménez (Ed.), *Mujeres protagonistas y proceso constituyente en Venezuela*, 151–165. Caracas: Embajada Británica, Unifem, Programa de las Naciones Unidas para el Desarrollo, Editorial Nueva Sociedad.

Postero, N. G. (2007). *Now We Are Citizens: Indigenous Politics in Multicultural Bolivia*. Stanford, CA: Stanford University Press.

Power, M. (2004). Social Provisioning as a Starting Point for Feminist Economics. *Feminist Economics* 10(3): 3–19.

Prensa Presidencial. (3 December 2007). Otro "por ahora": Palabras del Presidente Hugo Chávez tras los resultados del referendo. http://www.aporrea.org /actualidad/n105763.html.

Presidencia de la República. (12 December 2011). *Decreto No. 8.625*. Caracas.

———. (13 December 2011). *Decreto No. 8.694*. Caracas: Gaceta Oficial de la República Bolivariana de Venezuela.

Presidencia de la República Bolivariana de Venezuela. (2006). *Proyecto Nacional Simón Bolívar Primer Plan Socialista Desarrollo Económico y Social de la Nación 2007–2013*. Caracas.

Primero Congreso Extraordinario del PSUV. (2010). Declaración de Principios. Caracas.

Procuraduría General de la República. *Leyes Habilitantes*. Gobierno Bolivariano de Venezuela. http://www.pgr.gob.ve/index.php?option=com_contentandview =articleandid=2911.

PSUV. (2011). Líneas Estratégicas de Acción Política. Caracas.

Raby, D. L. (2006). *Democracy and Revolution: Latin America and Socialism Today*. Ann Arbor, MI: Pluto.

Radcliffe, S. A., and Westwood, S. (1993). Gender, Racism and the Politics of Identities in Latin America. In S. A. Radcliffe and S. Westwood (Eds.), *"Viva": Women and Popular Protest in Latin America*, 1–29. London: Routledge.

Rakowski, C. (2003). Women's Coalitions as a Strategy at the Intersection of Economic and Political Change in Venezuela. *International Journal of Politics, Culture and Society* 16(3): 387–405.

Rakowski, C., and Espina, G. (2010). Women's Struggles for Rights in Venezuela: Opportunities and Challenges. In E. Maier and N. Lebon (Eds.), *Women's Activism in Latin America and the Caribbean: Engendering Social Justice, Democratizing Citizenship*, 255–272. New Brunswick, NJ, and Tijuana: Rutgers University Press and El Colegio de la Frontera Norte A.C.

———. (2011). Advancing Women's Rights from Inside and Outside the Bolivarian Revolution, 1998–2010. In T. Ponniah and J. Eastwood (Eds.), *The Revolution in Venezuela: Social and Political Change under Chávez*, 155–192. Cambridge, MA: Harvard University Press.

Razavi, S. (2009). The Gendered Impacts of Liberalization: Towards "Embedded Liberalism"? In S. Razavi (Ed.), *The Gendered Impacts of Liberalization: Towards "Embedded Liberalism"?*, 1–34. New York: Routledge.

Red Popular de los Altos Mirandinos. (4 February 2006). Comunicado de las mujeres amas de casa trabajadoras del hogar a presidente Chávez. Estado Miranda, Venezuela.

Richter, J. (2007). Segmentadas y segregadas: Las mujeres en la fuerza de trabajo en Venezuela. *Revista Politeia* 39(30): 151–185.

Roberts, K. (2003). Social Polarization and the Populist Resurgence in Venezuela. In S. Ellner and D. Hellinger (Eds.), *Venezuelan Politics in the Chávez Era: Class, Polarization, and Conflict*, 55–72. Boulder, CO: Lynne Rienner.

Robinson, W. I. (2004). Global Crisis and Latin America. *Bulletin of Latin American Research* 23(2): 135–153.

Rodríguez, R. (10 November 2011). Chávez anuncia nueva Ley del Trabajo para el 1 de mayo de 2012. *El Universal*. http://www.eluniversal.com/economia/111110 /chavez-anuncia-nueva-ley-del-trabajo-para-el-1-de-mayo-de-2012.

Safa, H. I. (1990). Women's Social Movements in Latin America. *Gender and Society* 4(3): 354–369.

Sanjuán, A. M. (2002). Democracy, Citizenship, and Violence in Venezuela. In S. Rotker (Ed.), *Citizens of Fear: Urban Violence in Latin America*, 87–101. New Brunswick, NJ: Rutgers University Press.

Schiller, N. (2011). Catia Sees You: Community Television, Clientelism, and the State in the Chávez Era. In D. Smilde and D. Hellinger (Eds.), *Venezuela's Bolivarian Democracy: Participation, Politics, and Culture under Chávez*, 104–130. Durham, NC: Duke University Press.

Scott, J. C. (1990). *Domination and the Arts of Resistance: Hidden Transcripts*. New Haven, CT: Yale University Press.

Sección de Edición, División de Servicio y Atención Legislativa. (15 July 2008). Transcripción de Primera Discusión del Proyecto de Ley de Protección Social a las Amas de Casa. Caracas: Asamblea Nacional de la República Bolivariana de Venezuela.

Second Interview with Adicea Castillo. (5 October 2011). Caracas.

Second Interview with Adriana. (23 April 2012). Falcón state, Venezuela.

Second Interview with Gioconda Espina. (29 September 2011). Caracas.

Second Interview with Gioconda Mota. (14 March 2012). Caracas.

Second Interview with Luisa. (17 October 2012). Coro, Venezuela.

Second Interview with Marelis Pérez Marcano. (14 September 2011). Caracas.

Secor, A. J. (2007). Between Longing and Despair: State, Space, and Subjectivity in Turkey. *Environment and Planning D: Society and Space* 25:33–52.

Segunda Vicepresidencia para el Area Social, Consejo de Ministros del Gobierno Bolivariano. (March 2012). Taller Metodológico para la Activación del Plan de Acompañamiento para la superación de la pobreza enmarcado en la Gran Misión Hijos de Venezuela y en la Gran Misión en Amor Mayor. San Antonio de los Altos, Venezuela: Gobierno Bolivariano de Venezuela.

Segura, R., and Bejarano, A. M. (2013). The Difference a Constituent Assembly Makes: Explaining Divergent Constitutional Outcomes in Colombia and Venezuela. Paper presented at the Latin American Studies Association, Washington, DC.

Sistema Integrado de Indicadores Sociales de Venezuela. (n.d.). Total/Inversión pública social como porcentaje del PIB. *Indicadores*. http://sisov.mppp.gob.ve /indicadores/GA010080000000/.

Smith, D. E. (1987). *The Everyday World as Problematic: A Feminist Sociology*. Boston: Northeastern University Press.

———. (1999). From Women's Standpoint to a Sociology for People. In J. L. Abu-Lughod (Ed.), *Sociology for the Twenty-First Century: Continuities and Cutting Edges*, 65–82. Chicago: University of Chicago Press.

Smith, L. M., and Padula, A. (1996). *Sex and Revolution: Women in Socialist Cuba*. Oxford: Oxford University Press.

Spronk, S., and Webber, J. R. (2011). The Bolivarian Process in Venezuela: A Left Forum. *Historical Materialism* 19(1): 233–270.

Stephen, L. (1997). *Women and Social Movements in Latin America: Power from Below*. Austin: University of Texas Press.

Subcomisión de Derechos de la Mujer, Comisión Permanente Familia, Mujer y Juventud. (29 August 2001). Transcripción de Reunión Extraordinaria. Caracas: Asamblea Nacional, República Bolivariana de Venezuela.

Subcomisión de Familia, Niños, Niñas y Adolescentes de la Comisión Permanente de Familia, Mujer y Juventud. (2007). Transcripción de Reunión Ordinaria, 29 de Mayo de 2007. Caracas: Asamblea Nacional.

Tabbush, C. (2009). Gender, Citizenship and New Approaches to Poverty Relief.

In S. Razavi (Ed.), *The Gendered Impacts of Liberalization: Towards "Embedded Liberalism"?*, 290–326. New York: Routledge.

Taylor, L. (2004). Client-ship and Citizenship in Latin America. *Bulletin of Latin American Research* 23(2): 213–227.

Taylor, M. (2009). The Contradictions and Transformations of Neoliberalism in Latin America: From Structural Adjustment to "Empowering the Poor." In L. Macdonald and A. Ruckert (Eds.), *Post-Neoliberalism in the Americas*, 21–36. Basingstoke: Palgrave Macmillan.

Tejero Puntes, S. (4 August 2006). Destinados Bs 191 millardos a Misión Madres del Barrio. *El Universal.* http://www.eluniversal.com/2006/08/04/eco_art_04204A .shtml.

Third Interview with Marelis Pérez Marcano. (5 September 2012). Caracas.

Últimas Noticias. (12 April 2012). UNT exigió al gobierno presentar la nueva LOT. *Últimas Noticias.* http://www.ultimasnoticias.com.ve/noticias/actualidad/politica /unt-exigio-al-gobierno-presentar-la-nueva-lot.aspx.

UNIFEM, MAM, and CEM (UCV). (2006). Agenda de las Mujeres para el Trabajo Parlamentario y Legislativo 2006–2011. Caracas.

United Nations Office on Drugs and Crime. (2013). Homicide Counts and Rates, Time Series 2000–2012. *UNODC Homicide Statistics 2013.* http://www.unodc .org/gsh/en/data.html.

Valencia, C. (2015). *We Are the State! Barrio Activism in Venezuela's Bolivarian Revolution.* Tucson: University of Arizona Press.

Vargas Arenas, I. (2007). *Historia, mujer, mujeres: Origen y desarrollo histórico de la exclusión social en Venezuela. El caso de los colectivos femeninos.* Caracas: Fundación Editorial el perro y la rana.

Velasco, A. (2015). *Barrio Rising: Urban Popular Politics and the Making of Modern Venezuela.* Berkeley: University of California Press.

Verucci, F. (1991). Women and the New Brazilian Constitution. *Feminist Studies* 17(3): 557–568.

"Visita a la redacción de *El Mundo*: Participación proporcional a la del hombre pedirá Consejo de la Mujer en la Constituyente." (24 May 1999). *El Mundo.*

Viterna, J., and Fallon, K. (2008). Democratization, Women's Movements, and Gender-Equitable States: A Framework for Comparison. *American Sociological Review* 73:668–689.

von Werlhof, C. (1988). On the Concept of Nature and Society in Capitalism. In M. Mies, V. Bennholdt-Thomsen, and C. von Werlhof (Eds.), *Women: The Last Colony*, 96–112. London: Zed Books.

Vosko, L. (2006). Crisis Tendencies in Social Reproduction: The Case of Ontario's Early Years Plan. In K. Bezanson and M. Luxton (Eds.), *Social Reproduction: Feminist Political Economy Challenges Neo-Liberalism*, 145–172. Montreal: McGill-Queen's University Press.

Waylen, G. (2006). Constitutional Engineering: What Opportunities for the Enhancement of Gender Rights? *Third World Quarterly* 27(7): 1209–1221.

Webber, J. R. (2010). Venezuela under Chávez: The Prospects and Limitations of Twenty-First Century Socialism, 1999–2009. *Socialist Studies* 6(1): 11–44.

Weisbrot, M. (2008). Poverty Reduction in Venezuela: A Reality-Based View. *Revista: Harvard Review of Latin America*, Fall, 36–39.

————. (2011). Venezuela in the Chávez Years: Its Economy and Influence on the Region. In T. Ponniah and J. Eastwood (Eds.), *The Revolution in Venezuela: Social and Political Change under Chávez*, 193–223. Cambridge, MA: Harvard University Press.

Weyland, K. (2001). Clarifying a Contested Concept: Populism in the Study of Latin American Politics. *Comparative Politics* 34(1): 1–22.

Wilpert, G. (2007). *Changing Venezuela by Taking Power: The History and Policies of the Chávez Government*. London: Verso.

Zapata, M. H. (14 April 1999). CONG de Mujeres tiene precandidatas a la Asamblea Constituyente. *El Impulso*.

Index